INTERNATIONALER DESIGNPREIS
BADEN-WÜRTTEMBERG
UND MIA SEEGER PREIS 2024

BADEN-WÜRTTEMBERG
INTERNATIONAL DESIGN AWARD
AND MIA SEEGER PRIZE 2024

DESIGN CENTER
BADEN-WÜRTTEMBERG

avedition

FOCUS OPEN 2024

INHALT

VORWORTE 4–11

Mehr als nur Ästhetik
→ Dr. Patrick Rapp MdL 4

Benchmarks für das Neue
→ Susanne Bay und Christiane Nicolaus 6

Design für die Zukunft 12
→ Armin Scharf

DIE JURY
Prof. Tulga Beyerle 44
Andreas Brunkhorst 72
Henning Rieseler 96
Mirjam Rombach 126
Alexander Schlag 144
Carolin Schmitt 182

AUSGEZEICHNETE PRODUKTE 18–181
1 Investitionsgüter, Werkzeuge 18
2 Healthcare 34
4 Küche, Haushalt, Tischkultur 68
5 Interior 74
7 Licht 86
9 Freizeit, Sport, Spielen 106
10 Gebäudetechnik 116
11 Public Design, Urban Design 134
12 Mobility 154
14 Kommunikationsdesign 168
15 Materials & Surfaces 178

INTERVIEWS
Thomas Diepold und
 Sebastian Ahlberg, Magnosco GmbH 40
René Stern, Starmed GmbH 50, 58
Jean-Marc da Costa,
 Serien Raumleuchten GmbH 92
Sebastian Rieger,
 UP Designstudio Gmbh & Co. KG 122
Laureen und Luis Seider, Visuell GmbH 140
Frank Schuster, Tricon AG 160

MIA SEEGER PREIS 2024 184–201

APPENDIX A–Z
Adressen 202
Namensregister 206
Das Design Center
 → Vom Musterlager
  zum Design-Booster 208
 → Let's Thank 212
 → Alle Formate und Services 214
Impressum 216

CONTENTS

FOREWORDS 4–11

More than just aesthetics
→ Dr Patrick Rapp MdL 5

Benchmarking new ideas
→ Susanne Bay and Christiane Nicolaus 9

Design for the Future 14
→ Armin Scharf

THE JURY
Prof. Tulga Beyerle 44
Andreas Brunkhorst 72
Henning Rieseler 96
Mirjam Rombach 126
Alexander Schlag 144
Carolin Schmitt 182

THE AWARD-WINNING PRODUCTS 18–181
1 Capital goods, tools 18
2 Healthcare 34
4 Kitchen, household, table 68
5 Interiors 74
7 Lighting 86
9 Leisure, sports, play 106
10 Building technology 116
11 Public design, urban design 134
12 Mobility 154
14 Communication design 168
15 Materials & surfaces 178

INTERVIEWS
Thomas Diepold and
 Sebastian Ahlberg, Magnosco GmbH 40
René Stern, Starmed GmbH 50, 58
Jean-Marc da Costa,
 Serien Raumleuchten GmbH 92
Sebastian Rieger,
 UP Designstudio Gmbh & Co. KG 122
Laureen and Luis Seider, Visuell GmbH 140
Frank Schuster, Tricon AG 160

MIA SEEGER PREIS 2024 184–201

APPENDIX A–Z
Addresses 202
Index of names 206
The Design Center
 → From sample store
  to hub for innovative design 208
 → Let's Thank 212
 → All formats and services 214
Publishing details 216

MEHR ALS NUR ÄSTHETIK
DR. PATRICK RAPP MDL

Sehr geehrte Damen und Herren,
liebe Preisträgerinnen und Preisträger,

es ist mir eine große Freude, Ihnen das Jahrbuch des Designpreises des Landes Baden-Württemberg 2024 vorzustellen. In diesem Jahr feiern wir nicht nur herausragende kreative Leistungen, sondern auch die Innovationskraft und den unermüdlichen Einsatz unserer Designerinnen und Designer, die mit ihren Ideen und Konzepten die Welt um uns herum gestalten.

Der Landesregierung Baden-Württembergs ist die Designwirtschaft ein besonderes Anliegen. Der seit 1991 jährlich vom Design Center Baden-Württemberg ausgelobte Internationale Designpreis des Landes unterstreicht, dass große wie kleine Unternehmen großartige Designlösungen auf den Markt bringen.

Zu einem guten Design gehören verschiedene Faktoren wie Ästhetik, Funktionalität, Benutzerfreundlichkeit und Konsistenz. Gutes Design muss ansprechend sein, die Bedürfnisse der Nutzerinnen und Nutzer erfüllen und eine klare Botschaft vermitteln. Immer wichtiger wird dabei das Thema der Nachhaltigkeit, das daher auch beim diesjährigen Focus Open im Mittelpunkt steht.

Design ist also mehr als nur Ästhetik – es ist Ausdruck von Kultur, Identität und Fortschritt. Die eingereichten Arbeiten zeigen eindrucksvoll, wie Design als treibende Kraft für nachhaltige Entwicklung und soziale Verantwortung dienen kann. In einer Zeit, in der wir vor großen Herausforderungen stehen, eröffnen Kreativität und Einfallsreichtum von Designerinnen und Designern neue Perspektiven.

Gutes Design ist damit gerade auch in Zeiten von wirtschaftlichem Wandel wichtiger Wertschöpfungsfaktor und Impulsgeber für unsere Wirtschaft. Baden-Württemberg hat hier viel zu bieten. Das zeigen auch die aktuellen Zahlen: Die Designwirtschaft konnte im Jahr 2023 in fast allen Segmenten vom Industrie-, Produkt- und Modedesign über das Grafikdesign bis hin zu Schmuckherstellung zulegen und wuchs im Vergleich zum Vorjahr um sieben Prozent.

Mit dem Internationalen Designpreis Baden-Württemberg, dem FOCUS OPEN, möchte das Land innovative Design-Ideen weiter unterstützen und den herausragenden Stellenwert von Designleistungen gerade in Zeiten wirtschaftlicher und nachhaltigkeitsorientierter Transformation unterstützen.

Das aktuelle Jahrbuch liefert seinen Leserinnen und Lesern wichtige Hintergrundinformationen zum Entstehungsprozess vieler großartiger Projekte und gibt Einblicke in die Arbeit von Designerinnen und Designern.

Mein Dank gilt allen Interviewpartnerinnen und -partnern, die dem Design Center diese Einblicke gewährt haben, sowie allen, die sich in diesem Jahr dem internationalen Wettbewerb im Rahmen der FOCUS OPEN gestellt haben. Danke auch an das Design Center Baden-Württemberg und die Jury, ohne deren Arbeit dieser Preis nicht möglich wäre.

Im Namen der Landesregierung von Baden-Württemberg wünsche ich Ihnen allen weiterhin viel Erfolg und noch viele weitere gute Designlösungen!

DR. PATRICK RAPP MDL
Staatssekretär für Wirtschaft,
Arbeit und Tourismus des
Landes Baden-Württemberg

MORE THAN JUST AESTHETICS

DR PATRICK RAPP MDL

Dear Readers,
Dear Prize Winners,

It gives me great pleasure to present the Baden-Württemberg International Design Award 2024 yearbook. This year, we are celebrating not only some outstanding creative achievements but also the innovative prowess and tireless efforts of our designers, whose ideas and concepts shape the world around us.

The state government of Baden-Württemberg regards the design industry as a vital part of its economic and cultural landscape. The state's International Design Award, which has been presented annually by the Design Centre Baden-Württemberg since 1991, showcases the innovative power of both large and small companies.

Good design includes various factors such as aesthetics, functionality, user-friendliness and consistency. It must also be attractive, meet the needs of users and convey a clear message. Given the growing importance of sustainability, eco-conscious design features strongly in this year's Focus Open.

Design transcends aesthetics, serving as a powerful expression of culture, identity, and progress. The entries demonstrate the potential of design to create a more sustainable and socially responsible future. As we negotiate these challenging times, the creative vision of designers can offer new approaches and solutions.

As a cornerstone of the value chain, good design drives economic prosperity, particularly during economic uncertainty. Baden-Württemberg has much to contribute here, as is shown by the latest figures. In 2023, our design industry experienced robust growth, with a seven percent year-on-year surge across sectors spanning industrial, product, fashion, graphic design and jewellery.

The Baden-Württemberg International Design Award, Focus Open, underscores the state's commitment to innovative design and highlights the importance of design achievements, particularly in times of economic and sustainability-driven change.

The current edition of the yearbook provides readers with important background information on the processes involved in these projects and offers insights into the work of the designers who contributed to them.

I would like to thank all the interview partners who have taken the time to provide the Design Center with these insights as well as everyone who has contributed to this year's international Focus Open competition. Thanks also to the Design Centre Baden-Württemberg and the jury, without whose work these awards would not be possible.

On behalf of the state government of Baden-Württemberg, I wish you all every success. May your design talents continue to flourish in the future.

DR PATRICK RAPP MDL
State Secretary of Economic Affairs,
Labour and Tourism
Baden-Württemberg

FOCUS OPEN 2024

BENCHMARKS FÜR DAS NEUE

Spricht man über die Wirtschaft in Baden-Württemberg, dann steht die Autoindustrie samt ihrer vielen Zulieferer meist an erster Stelle. Das ist richtig, keine Frage, aber letztlich etwas zu kurz gedacht. Denn dabei übersieht man eine eher stillere, aber enorm innovative und vielfältige Sparte: die Medizintechnik. Ihre Relevanz ist, vor dem Hintergrund der demografischen Entwicklung oder dem Mangel an medizinischen Fachkräften, enorm.

Mehr als 600 Unternehmen zählt die Medizintechnik allein in Baden-Württemberg – die Bandbreite reicht vom höchst spezialisierten Kleinunternehmen über den klassischen, eigentümergeführten Mittelständler bis hin zu Ablegern multinationaler Konzerne. Rund 25 Prozent des bundesweiten Umsatzes der Branche wird hier im Südwesten generiert, die Exportquote steigt kontinuierlich. Noch erstaunlicher ist, dass mehr als die Hälfte des Umsatzes auf Produkte und Services zurückgeht, die noch keine drei Jahre im Markt sind. Diese enorm hohe Innovationsdynamik resultiert aus der Vernetzung von Unternehmen, Hochschulen und anderen Forschungseinrichtungen. Neueste Erkenntnisse können also rasch ihren Weg in die Anwendung finden, Nischen inklusive. Nicht zuletzt dank dieser medizinischen Innovationen ist die Lebenserwartung enorm gestiegen. Wurden 1871 die Frauen in Deutschland durchschnittlich nur 38,5 Jahre alt (Männer 35,6 Jahre), so dürfen sich die Menschen 2020 über ein mehr als doppelt so langes Leben freuen. Frauen leben heute rund 83,4 Jahre, Männer 78,5 Jahre.

MEDIZINTECHNIK BRAUCHT DESIGN

Der FOCUS OPEN 2024 prämiert gleich mehrere, ausgesprochen zukunftsweisende Produkte dieses Bereiches. Wie man Nischen erfolgreich bespielt, zeigt ein kleines Unternehmen aus Stetten am Bodensee. Es hat sich auf Transportlösungen im klinischen Bereich spezialisiert und wurde gleich zwei Mal mit Gold ausgezeichnet – für Produkte, die exakt auf die spezifischen Anforderungen der Notfallmedizin zugeschnitten sind. Dass es dafür ein tiefes Wissen und auch Erfahrung braucht, muss wohl nicht besonders erwähnt werden. Das gilt in ähnlicher Weise für den ebenfalls ausgezeichneten CityCaddy, ein hybrides Produkt, das zugleich Gehhilfe wie auch Einkaufshelfer ist. Weil die Designerin für sich selbst kein adäquates Produkt fand, entwickelte und gestaltete sie es kurzerhand selbst. Auch das ist eine Erfolgsgeschichte, die begeistert, Mut macht und als beispielhaft gelten kann. Schließlich zeigt der CityCaddy, was ein medizinisches Produkt Endverbraucherinnen und Endverbrauchern bieten muss: hohe Funktionalität, selbsterklärende Handhabung und vor allem eine nicht stigmatisierende Ästhetik.

Keine Frage: Medizintechnik ist ein zentrales Designthema – auf mehreren Ebenen. Design kann entlasten, beispielsweise medizinisches, tendenziell überlastetes Personal unterstützen – durch bessere Ergonomie, durch selbsterklärende und fehlerresistente Bedienabläufe oder durch so profan erscheinende Aspekte wie die optimierte Reinigungsfähigkeit. Das verlangt von den Gestaltenden die Fähigkeit, sich in die komplexen Realitäten der Kliniken, Praxen und Therapieeinrichtungen einzudenken. Als wären diese Anforderungen nicht schon groß, kommt noch die emotionale Komponente hinzu – gerade bei Geräten, die direkt mit den Patientinnen und Patienten in Kontakt kommen. Nahbares Design kann Vorbehalte, Ängste und Hemmungen zumindest relativieren und zu einer empathischen Atmosphäre beitragen. Das gilt übrigens auch für den wachsenden Bereich der Selbsttherapie, für die ein ebenfalls ausgezeichneter Neurostimulator geradezu exemplarisch steht. Erst das durchdachte Design macht dieses innovative Therapieprinzip überhaupt nutzbar.

Die soziale Relevanz von Medical Design ist groß, Designerinnen und Designer übernehmen daher eine hohe Verantwortung – ihren produzierenden Kunden gegenüber genauso wie den Patientinnen und Patienten. Mitunter wird Medical Design als Kür innerhalb der Gestaltung bezeichnet, was durchaus zutrifft, die anderen Designsparten in ihrer Bedeutung aber nicht schmälert. Denn auch dort spielt das Design alles andere als eine Nebenrolle – was spätestens klar wird, wenn man die ganze Bandbreite der Auszeichnungen des FOCUS OPEN 2024 auf sich wirken lässt.

DER FOCUS OPEN WEIST NACH VORNE

37 Auszeichnungen – das ist die Bilanz des FOCUS OPEN 2024. Verglichen mit manchen Vorjahren oder gar anderen Designawards ist das eine überschaubare Zahl, zugegeben. Dieses Ergebnis erlaubt aber keinesfalls Rückschlüsse auf die Qualität

SUSANNE BAY
Regierungspräsidentin
Regierungsbezirk Stuttgart

der Einreichungen. Im Gegenteil: Es lässt sich weiterhin beobachten, dass Design in all seinen Facetten und Kontexten erstens immer selbstverständlicher wird und zweitens sein qualitatives Niveau kontinuierlich steigt. Auf den ersten Blick scheint dies im Widerspruch zur Zahl 37 zu stehen, suggeriert zumindest der erste Blick. Richtig ist allerdings, dass die Benchmarks für gutes Design immer wieder neu kalibriert sein wollen – nur so lässt sich das selektieren, was über das Heute hinaus beispielhaft ausstrahlt. Diese Nachjustierung der Bewertungskriterien übernimmt die alljährlich neu bestellte Jury selbstständig. Sechs Praktikerinnen und Praktiker aus verschiedenen Designsparten kommen zwei Tage zusammen, um zu sichten, zu diskutieren und um all das auszuzeichnen, was als Benchmark gelten kann. Tatsächlich agiert die Jury frei von Vorgaben – was zählt, ist die Qualität, die Innovation, die Stimmigkeit der Lösungen, ihre Zukunftstauglichkeit und letztlich auch die Sinnhaftigkeit. Gerade in dieser Hinsicht sorgen die Ergebnisse des FOCUS OPEN gern für Aha-Effekte, weil hier auch Produkte, Services oder Konzeptionen eine Chance haben, die Nischen bedienen oder auf neuen Denkansätzen basieren.

DESIGN ERÖFFNET NEUE ERFAHRUNGEN

Ein gutes Beispiel dafür ist der Spielzeugtraktor, den Designer neu entwickelten. Der Traktor wartet nicht mehr fertig in seiner Packung, sondern in Einzelteilen, will also zunächst zusammengebaut werden. Das ist didaktisch wertvoll und erleichtert zusätzlich die Reparatur, sollten Teile beim Spiel kaputtgehen. Die beiden Parameter Reparatur und Wartung begleiteten auch die Designerinnen und Designer beim Entwurf der nächsten Generation der Stuttgarter Stadtbahn. Beschädigungen, mutwillig hervorgerufen oder einfach durch intensiven Gebrauch entstehend, beseitigt der Betreiber umgehend – das Design des Interiors muss diese betriebliche Routine ermöglichen und erleichtern.

Neben der Kooperation zwischen Design und Engineering bewährt sich immer häufiger auch die Zusammenarbeit zwischen Architektur und Design. Ein gutes Beispiel hierfür ist ein prämiertes, modulares Holzgebäude, mit dem sich Waldkindergärten einfacher etablieren lassen. Ausstellungskonzepte wiederum überzeugen, wenn das Thema mit den Erwartungen der Besuchenden und dem architektonischen Rahmen in Resonanz kommt. Wie das eine das andere beeinflusst, lässt sich gut am Firmenmuseum Stihl ablesen. Oder am goldprämierten Museum in Glems, das sich in einem denkmalgeschützten Gebäude der Streuobstkultur widmet, auf sinnliche Erfahrungen setzt und die Potenziale des ehrenamtlichen Trägervereins berücksichtigt. Dieses kulturelle Kleinod am Fuße der Schwäbischen Alb ist mehr als nur einen Abstecher von Metzingen aus wert.

Interessant sind auch all jene Produkte, die weniger in Erscheinung treten, weil sie bestimmten Nutzergruppen vorbehalten sind – zum Beispiel all das, was in der Kategorie der Investitionsgüter angesiedelt ist. Dazu gehören in diesem Jahr ein Schutzhelm, der speziell für den Einsatz bei Waldbränden optimiert ist – oder jener elektrische Schraubendreher, der nicht nur Vielschrauber unterstützt. Design spielt auch auf der Ebene von Vorprodukten eine wichtige Rolle, etwa dann, wenn neu entwickelte, nachhaltige Materialien ihr Potenzial klar präsentieren sollen – auch das wurde von der Jury als auszeichnungswert erachtet.

DRANBLEIBEN!

Die Aufgabe der Jury ist die Selektion – nur so wird der Blick frei auf das Neue, auf das, was Benchmarks für das Morgen setzt. Das bedeutet im Umkehrschluss, dass viele Einreichungen den Sprung in die Auszeichnungsliste nicht geschafft haben. Unser Dank gilt daher nicht nur den Preisträgerinnen und Preisträgern, sondern auch all jenen Unternehmen, Agenturen, Freelancern, die keine Auszeichnung erhalten haben. Bleiben Sie dran, wir freuen uns, wenn Sie in den nächsten Jahren wieder dabei sind!

Und wenn Sie bislang die Teilnahme nicht erwogen haben, denken Sie nochmals darüber nach. Es lohnt sich auf jeden Fall, gerade für KMUs oder Start-ups mit ihren frischen Ideen und Geschäftsmodellen, dabei zu sein. Denn es ist die Vielzahl an Impulsen, die Diversität, die uns voranbringt. Nur wer offen bleibt, kann die Zukunft positiv gestalten.

CHRISTIANE NICOLAUS
Direktorin
Design Center Baden-Württemberg

KATEGORIEN

1 INVESTITIONSGÜTER, WERKZEUGE
2 HEALTHCARE
4 KÜCHE, HAUSHALT, TISCHKULTUR
5 INTERIOR
7 LICHT
9 FREIZEIT, SPORT, SPIELEN
10 GEBÄUDETECHNIK
11 PUBLIC DESIGN, URBAN DESIGN
12 MOBILITY
14 KOMMUNIKATIONSDESIGN
15 MATERIALS & SURFACES

KRITERIEN

- ✓ GESTALTUNGSQUALITÄT
- ✓ FUNKTIONALITÄT
- ✓ INNOVATIONSHÖHE
- ✓ ERGONOMIE
- ✓ INTERFACE DESIGN/ CONNECTIVITY
- ✓ USABILITY
- ✓ NACHHALTIGKEIT
- ✓ ÄSTHETIK
- ✓ BRANDING
- ✓ ENTWICKLUNGSVORSPRUNG
- ✓ USER JOURNEY
- ✓ DIGITALE INTELLIGENZ

FOCUS OPEN 2024

37 AUSZEICHNUNGEN
7 GOLD-AWARDS
9 SILVER-AWARDS
21 SPECIAL MENTION AWARDS

DIE JURY

- ✓ PROF. TULGA BEYERLE
- ✓ ANDREAS BRUNKHORST
- ✓ HENNING RIESELER
- ✓ MIRJAM ROMBACH
- ✓ ALEXANDER SCHLAG
- ✓ CAROLIN SCHMITT

While discussions about Baden-Württemberg's economy usually revolve around the automotive industry and its many component suppliers, it's important to recognise that, although the auto industry is an important part of the economy, it's by no means all of it. Though less prominent, another tremendously innovative sector also makes a valuable contribution to the region's economic landscape: medical technology. Its importance is especially significant given demographic trends and the shortage of medical professionals.

There are more than 600 medical technology companies in Baden-Württemberg alone, ranging from highly specialised small companies to well-established, owner-managed SMEs and offshoots of multinational corporations. The South West accounts for approximately 25% of the sector's national turnover, and its export performance is steadily increasing. What is even more astonishing is that more than half of this turnover is generated by products and services that have been on the market for less than three years. This tremendous innovation dynamic is fuelled by the networking of companies, universities and other research institutions, which accelerates the implementation of cutting-edge knowledge into practical applications, even in niche areas. These medical breakthroughs have been instrumental in the huge rise in life expectancy. Compared to 1871, when women in Germany lived to an average age of just 38.5 years (men 35.6 years), life expectancy in 2020 was more than double. Today, women can expect to live 83.4 years, men 78.5 years.

MEDICAL TECHNOLOGY RELIES ON DESIGN

FOCUS OPEN 2024 honours several highly innovative products in this field. A small company from Stetten on Lake Constance has shown how to carve out a successful market niche. It specialises in transport solutions for the clinical sector and has won two gold awards for products carefully tailored to the specific needs of emergency medicine. Success in this field requires extensive expertise and experience. This also applies to the CityCaddy, a hybrid product that functions as a shopping aid as well as a walking aid. Inspired by her own needs, the designer took matters into her own hands and developed a product that was missing from the market. This is another success story that is inspiring and encouraging – and sets a great example. Indeed, the CityCaddy delivers exactly what users want from a medical product: exceptional functionality, intuitive operation, and a stigma-free design.

There is no question that innovative design has become a key consideration in medical technology – on several levels. For example, design can alleviate the burden on overworked medical staff through thoughtful ergonomics, user-friendly and error-resistant interfaces and easy-to-clean surfaces. Creating these features requires designers to become familiar with the complex realities of clinics, surgeries and therapy facilities. As if this were not enough, they also need to factor in the emotional component, especially when dealing with devices that come into direct contact with patients. Approachable design can mitigate reservations, fears and inhibitions, and foster empathy. Incidentally, this also extends to the burgeoning field of self-therapy, as demonstrated by the award-winning neurostimulator, whose carefully considered design is responsible for making this innovative therapy so user-friendly.

The social impact of medical design is substantial and this places a high degree of responsibility on designers to serve the needs of both manufacturers and patients. Medical design is often referred to as the "freestyle" design discipline. While this is certainly true, it is essential to recognise the importance of other fields of design, which also play a crucial role in their business sectors. It will become clear just how crucial this role is when you explore the full scope of the FOCUS OPEN 2024 awards.

FOCUS OPEN: A VISION OF THE FUTURE

37 – the total number of FOCUS OPEN 2024 award winners. While the number of entries may be modest compared to some previous years and other design awards, this does not diminish the exceptional calibre of the submissions. On the contrary, it's clear that design is becoming increasingly evident in all aspects of life and its quality is steadily improving. At first glance, this seems to contradict the figure of 37. What is true, however, is that we need to constantly reassess our standards for exceptional design to ensure we select the truly outstanding work that will stand the test of time. The assessment criteria are independently reviewed and

SUSANNE BAY
President,
Stuttgart District Government

CHRISTIANE NICOLAUS
Director,
Design Center Baden-Württemberg

adjusted annually by the newly appointed jury. Over two days, six design professionals from various disciplines discuss and sift through the submissions and then select the ones they deem to be benchmarks of excellence. The jury evaluates submissions based solely on their quality, innovation, coherence, future viability and intrinsic value, without any predetermined criteria. The FOCUS OPEN results are a breath of fresh air because they also highlight the potential of niche products, services and concepts based on novel ideas.

DESIGN ENABLES NEW EXPERIENCES
A good example of this is the toy tractor re-imagined by its designers. The tractor no longer sits waiting in its box. It comes in individual parts and needs to be assembled first. The toy is therefore not only educational but also easy to repair, ensuring it can be enjoyed for a long time. The two parameters of repair and maintenance also guided the designers working on the next generation of Stuttgart's Stadtbahn or light rail system. The operators can quickly repair any damage to the vehicles, whether caused wilfully or simply through intensive use, because the design of the interior has been optimised to enable and facilitate this.

Besides collaborations between designers and engineers, collaboration between designers and architects is increasingly proving its worth. A good example of this is an award-winning, modular timber building that facilitates the setting up of forest kindergartens. Exhibition concepts are successful when the theme aligns with the expectations of the visitors and the architectural context. The Stihl company museum is a good example of how one influences the other. Another award-winning museum is located in a listed building in Glems, a historic orchard museum that focuses on creating sensory experiences and leverages the potential of its volunteer-run sponsoring association. The short journey from Metzingen to this cultural gem at the base of the Swabian Alb is definitely worth the effort.

Another interesting product category is capital goods, although these are sometimes overlooked because they have been designed for specialist user groups. This year, they include a safety helmet specially optimised for use in forest fires and an electric screwdriver aimed at both occasional and frequent screwdriver users. The jury also acknowledged the value of design in highlighting the potential of newly developed, sustainable materials, especially in the initial stages of product development.

STICK WITH IT!
The jury's choice of outstanding entries gives us an insight into new ideas that are likely to shape the future. Unfortunately, this selection process means that many submissions have not made it onto the final award list. Our thanks therefore go not only to the award winners but also to all of the companies, agencies and freelance designers who missed out this year. Do stick with it, and we hope to see you again in the coming years!

And if you haven't yet considered taking part, maybe you should. It's definitely worthwhile, especially for SMEs and start-ups with fresh ideas and business models. After all, the diversity of your ideas is what keeps us moving forward. And all our futures depend on those who remain open to new ideas.

CATEGORIES

1 CAPITAL GOODS, TOOLS
2 HEALTHCARE
4 KITCHEN, HOUSEHOLD, TABLE
5 INTERIORS
7 LIGHTING
9 LEISURE, SPORTS, PLAY
10 BUILDING TECHNOLOGY
11 PUBLIC DESIGN, URBAN DESIGN
12 MOBILITY
14 COMMUNICATION DESIGN
15 MATERIALS & SURFACES

CRITERIA

- ✓ DESIGN QUALITY
- ✓ FUNCTIONALITY
- ✓ INNOVATIVENESS
- ✓ ERGONOMICS
- ✓ INTERFACE DESIGN/ CONNECTIVITY
- ✓ USABILITY
- ✓ SUSTAINABILITY
- ✓ AESTHETICS
- ✓ BRANDING
- ✓ STEP CHANGE IN DEVELOPMENT
- ✓ USER JOURNEY
- ✓ DIGITAL INTELLIGENCE

FOCUS OPEN 2024

37 PRIZE WINNERS
7 GOLD AWARDS
9 SILVER AWARDS
21 SPECIAL MENTION AWARDS

THE JURY

- ✓ PROF. TULGA BEYERLE
- ✓ ANDREAS BRUNKHORST
- ✓ HENNING RIESELER
- ✓ MIRJAM ROMBACH
- ✓ ALEXANDER SCHLAG
- ✓ CAROLIN SCHMITT

FOCUS OPEN
2024

DESIGN FÜR DIE ZUKUNFT

Es ist schwierig. Und kompliziert, um nicht zu sagen: komplex. Doch wann, bitteschön, war es je einfach? Allenfalls in der beschönigenden Rückschau, nostalgisch gefärbt, wenn es um die guten, alten Zeiten geht. Damals, wann immer das auch gewesen sein soll, war alles klar, simpler, logischer. So das verbreitete, aber ziemlich realitätsferne Denken weiter gesellschaftlicher Kreise, die genau das als „Normalität" reklamieren. Zugegeben, die Probleme von heute sind vielschichtig, sie scheinen überall zu sein, sind miteinander verwoben und überfordern uns tendenziell, weil es keine einfachen Lösungen gibt.

DAS PRIMAT DER ÄSTHETIK HAT AUSGEDIENT

Auch im Design ist diese Komplexität längst angekommen, gutes Design ist mehrdimensional, nicht nur im räumlichen Sinne, sondern auch, was die Anforderungen betrifft. Genügte es einst, ein funktional durchdachtes und dazu noch gut aussehendes Produkt zu kreieren, geht es heute – und mehr noch morgen – um viel mehr. Ganz oben steht Sustainability, also Nachhaltigkeit, ein Begriff mit Buzzword-Potenzial, der inzwischen leider bei jeder noch so sinnfreien Gelegenheit vorgebracht wird. Dabei ist Nachhaltigkeit eine Notwendigkeit, ein Muss, um überhaupt all die Herausforderungen von heute und morgen zu meistern.

Design for Future bedeutet, Lösungen zu finden, die unsere heutigen Bedürfnisse erfüllen, die aber künftigen Generationen nichts verbauen. Es geht also um nichts Geringeres, als die Folgen des eigenen Schaffens aus der Zukunft zu betrachten. Diskurse über Radien, Oberflächen oder Anmutungen mögen mitunter erbaulich sein, aber sie wirken abgehoben angesichts der heutigen, substanziellen Fragen.

Design, auch als Querschnittsdisziplin bezeichnet, steht an einer Schlüsselposition für mehr Nachhaltigkeit. Design vermittelt zwischen Produzierenden und „Verbrauchenden", beeinflusst also die Qualität der Erzeugnisse, mehr denn je auch in ökologischer Hinsicht. Design kann Komplexitäten hinterfragen und dort, wo es möglich ist, auch ein Stück weit auflösen. Es geht darum, kluge Produktkonzepte zu lancieren, die auf lange Sicht brauchbar sind, die auf klimafreundlichen Werkstoffen basieren, die in den Kreislauf rückführbar sind, die ressourcensparsam gedacht sind und auch übermorgen noch Bestand haben. Also in etwa genau das Gegenteil von Fast Fashion, Fast Furniture oder Fast Electronics.

FAST DESIGN?

An Wissen mangelt es nicht, eher am Umsetzungswillen. Dann heißt es: Der Kunde möchte das nicht, also können wir als Gestaltende auch nichts machen. Das mag so sein, aber muss es das? Design hat sich über die Jahre leider tendenziell expansiven Marketingideen untergeordnet, der Schritt zum Fast Design ist da nicht mehr weit. Das klingt verkürzt und ungerecht dargestellt, denn es gibt sie ja, die Designerinnen und Designer, die nicht in der bequemen Abwehr verharren, sondern nach vorne schauen und eine neue Agenda verfolgen. Oder solche, die im persönlichen Gespräch ihre Bauchschmerzen, ihre Zweifel äußern ob dessen, was sie so gestalten. Das stimmt optimistisch. Gleiches gilt auf der Seite der Unternehmen, die sich schon mitten in der Transformation befinden oder nur noch Impulse brauchen. Impulse, die auch vom Design kommen müssen.

Wie gesagt, das Wissen um das, was geht, ist da. Wenn nicht, lässt es sich rasch aneignen, theoretisch und praktisch. Es geht darum, anzufangen, ein Zeichen zu setzen. Man denke nur an den – vergleichsweise banalen – Verzicht auf Plastiktüten beim Einkauf, der lange als nicht machbar galt. Ein Händler fing an, plötzlich zogen andere nach. Oft hilft dabei, die Dinge von der anderen Seite her zu denken, also vom Ende des Life Cycles beispielsweise. Die Perspektiven zu wechseln ist eine der zentralen Fähigkeiten des Designs. Also los geht es, worauf warten wir?

IN DESIGN IST VIEL ZUKUNFT DRIN – EIGENTLICH

Wir brauchen keine aktivistisch kurz aufblühenden Designers for Future, sondern Design for Future! Ein Design, das hinterfragt, verständlich ist, aktiv Alternativen aufzeigt, sich als Teil der Lösung unserer komplexen Krisen versteht und etwas ändern will. Dazu braucht es Wissen, Mut und Selbstbewusstsein, keine Worthülsen, sondern greifbare Konzepte mit Vorbildcharakter und Anschlussfähigkeit. Und ja, es darf auch mal über Ethik und Design diskutiert werden. Oder, um aus dem Buch „Zukunft" von Florence Gaub zu zitieren: „Der Motor, der die Zukunft zu mehr als einer Wiederholung der Vergangenheit macht, ist immer die Kreativität".

ARMIN SCHARF
Freier Design- und Technikjournalist

FOCUS OPEN
2024

DESIGN FOR THE FUTURE

It is difficult. And complicated, not to say complex. But when has the world ever been simple? The notion of "simplicity" often underpins our longing for a bygone era. We romanticise times when problems seemed more straightforward, solutions simpler and more obvious. Although unrealistic, this is a widely shared perspective. Yet today's challenges are undeniably complex, interwoven; they seem to be everywhere, overwhelming us and demanding multifaceted solutions.

AESTHETICS NO LONGER REIGNS SUPREME
This complexity has extended into design; good design now demands a multidimensional approach that extends beyond the purely functional and visual. While it was once enough to create a functionally well thought-out and good-looking product, today it is about much more – and tomorrow even more so. Sustainability has emerged as a paramount concern, often invoked superficially but still essential for addressing the challenges of our time.

Design for the future entails creating solutions that meet our current needs without compromising the ability of future generations to do the same. It requires a deep understanding of the long-term consequences of our choices. While discussions about radii, surface finishes and aesthetic appeal can be enlightening, they seem superficial in the face of today's pressing issues.

As a cross-sectional discipline, design occupies a pivotal position in promoting sustainability. It mediates between producers and consumers, influencing the quality and ecological footprint of products. By scrutinizing complexities and proposing innovative solutions, design can contribute to a more sustainable future. It's about creating objects that stand the test of time, both functionally and environmentally. Sustainable design using eco-friendly materials delivers products that are durable, resource-efficient and recyclable. It's the antithesis of fast fashion, fast furniture and fast electronics,

FAST DESIGN?

The challenge is often not in a lack of knowledge but in a reluctance to implement. Excuses like "the customer doesn't want it" may be valid, but they shouldn't be limiting. Over time, design has unfortunately been subordinated to marketing strategies, which has led to a focus on speed over substance. However, there are designers who are looking beyond the status quo, seeking to shape a new agenda, and others whose personal doubts and frustrations indicate a desire for change. This is an optimistic sign. The same applies to companies that are already in the midst of transformation and can benefit greatly from design-driven innovation.

The knowledge to create sustainable solutions is readily available. If not, it can be acquired quickly, both theoretically and practically. It's about taking the first step, setting an example. Consider the once-unfeasible decision to eliminate plastic bags. One retailer's initiative led to widespread adoption. Thinking from the perspective of a product's life cycle can drive meaningful change. Designers possess the essential skill of changing perspectives. So let's do it. What are we waiting for?

THE FUTURE OF DESIGN IS BRIGHT

We don't need activists or short-lived movements; we need Design for the Future. This means design that scrutinises, is easily understood, actively proposes alternatives, sees itself as part of the solution to our complex crises and wants to bring about change. Such design requires knowledge, courage, and self-confidence, not empty words but tangible concepts with a role model character and connectivity. And yes, ethics and design can and should be discussed. As Florence Gaub stated in her book *Future:* "The engine that makes the future more than a repetition of the past is always creativity."

ARMIN SCHARF
Freelance journalist for design and technology

HENNING RIESELER
Studio F.A. Porsche,
Berlin
studiofaporsche.com

→ SEITE/PAGE
96

MIRJAM ROMBACH
Hochparterre AG,
Zürich, Schweiz
hochparterre.ch

→ SEITE/PAGE
126

ALEXANDER SCHLAG
yellow design gmbh,
Pforzheim/Tokyo
yellowdesign.com

→ SEITE/PAGE
144

CAROLIN SCHMITT
Phoenix Design GmbH & Co. KG,
Stuttgart
phoenixdesign.com

→ SEITE/PAGE
182

ANDREAS BRUNKHORST
braun-steine GmbH,
Amstetten
braun-steine.de

→ SEITE/PAGE
72

PROF. TULGA BEYERLE
Museum für Kunst und Gewerbe,
Hamburg
mkg-hamburg.de

→ SEITE/PAGE
44

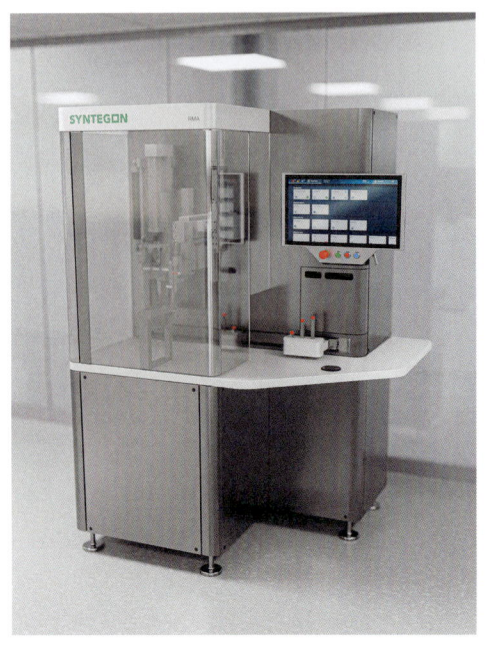

1 → SEITE/PAGE
20, 26

2 → SEITE/PAGE
21, 27

3 → SEITE/PAGE
22, 28

4 → SEITE/PAGE
23, 29

5 → SEITE/PAGE
24, 30

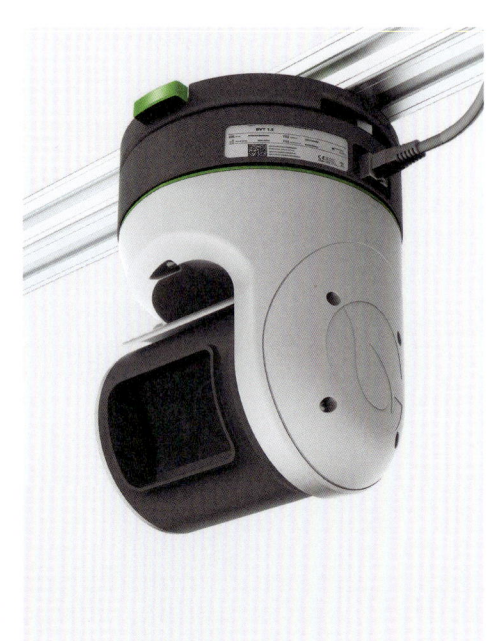

6 → SEITE/PAGE
25, 31

INVESTITIONSGÜTER, WERKZEUGE
CAPITAL GOODS, TOOLS

SILVER:
1 **RMA**
Syntegon Technology GmbH
Waiblingen

SPECIAL MENTION:
2 **HEROS H10**
Rosenbauer International AG
Leonding
Österreich/Austria

3 **SPEED E® POCKETDRIVE**
Wiha Werkzeuge GmbH
Schonach

4 **QRBLUV00I_C1190**
Georg Schlegel® GmbH & Co. KG
Dürmentingen

5 **EAO-4**
Sprimag Spritzmaschinenbau
GmbH & Co. KG
Kirchheim/Teck

6 **GARDIN PLATFORM**
Gardin Ltd.
Abingdon
Großbritannien/United Kingdom

Funktionalität und Design ergänzen sich ideal – das beweisen für den Profibereich konzipierte Maschinen und Tools. Industriedesign strukturiert Bedienabläufe, optimiert die Ergonomie, treibt Innovationen voran und verbessert im Idealfall die ökologische Bilanz. Die Kategorie zeigt sich dabei äußerst vielfältig und eröffnet einen Einblick in sehr spezielle Wirtschaftsbereiche.

Many of the machines and tools used by professionals bear witness to the synergy that exists between functionality and design. Industrial design shapes operating procedures, optimises ergonomics, drives innovation and, at its best, can even improve our ecological footprint. This category is extremely diverse and provides an insight into some very specialised business sectors.

SILVER RMA   BEFÜLLANLAGE
        → SEITE/PAGE FILLING SYSTEM
        26

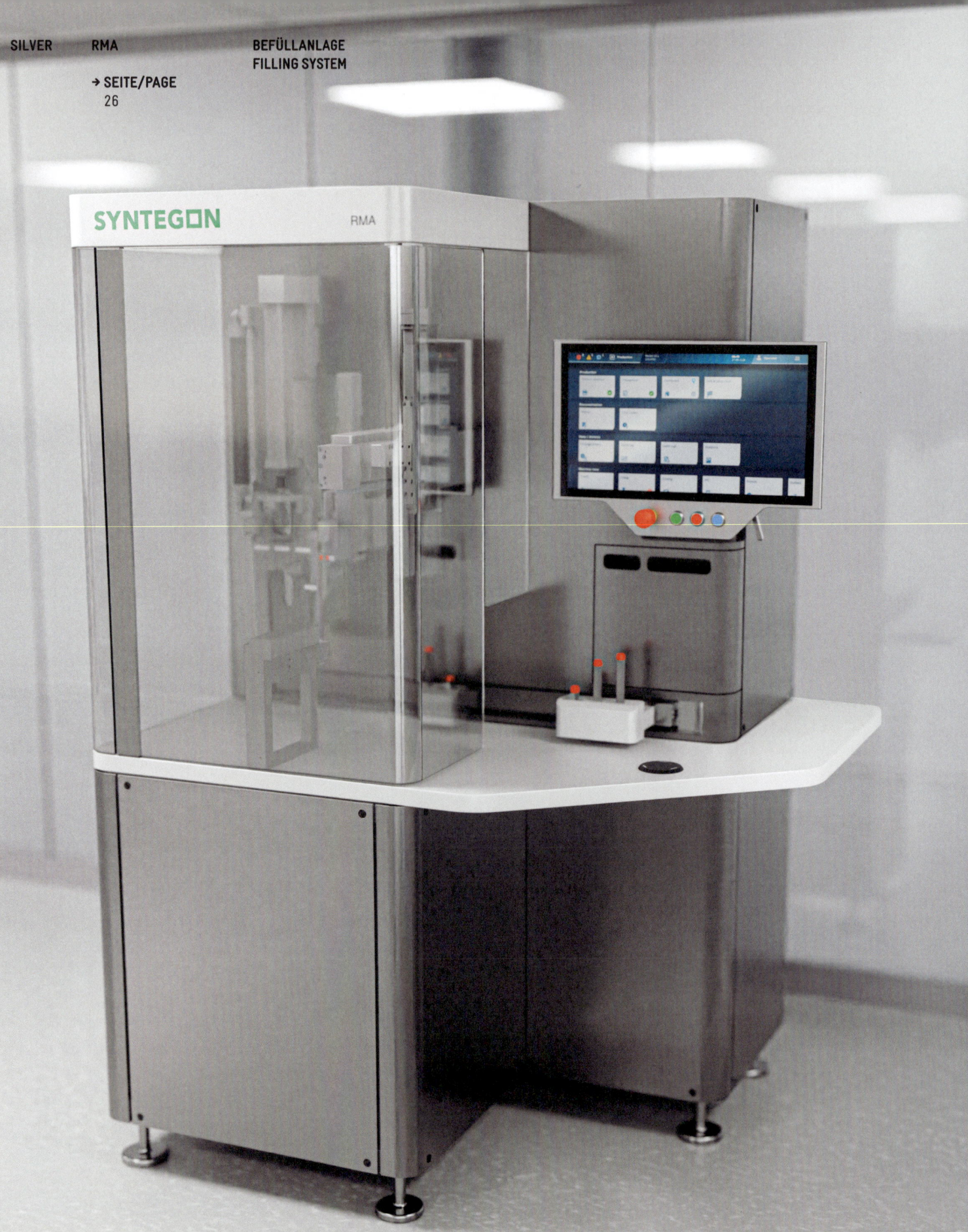

SPECIAL MENTION

SPEED E® POCKETDRIVE
→ SEITE/PAGE
28

ELEKTRISCHER SCHRAUBENDREHER
ELECTRIC SCREWDRIVER

SPECIAL MENTION

EAO-4
→ SEITE/PAGE 30

TUBENGLÜHOFEN
ANNEALING OVEN

SPECIAL MENTION

GARDIN
→ SEITE/PAGE 31

SENSOR
SENSOR

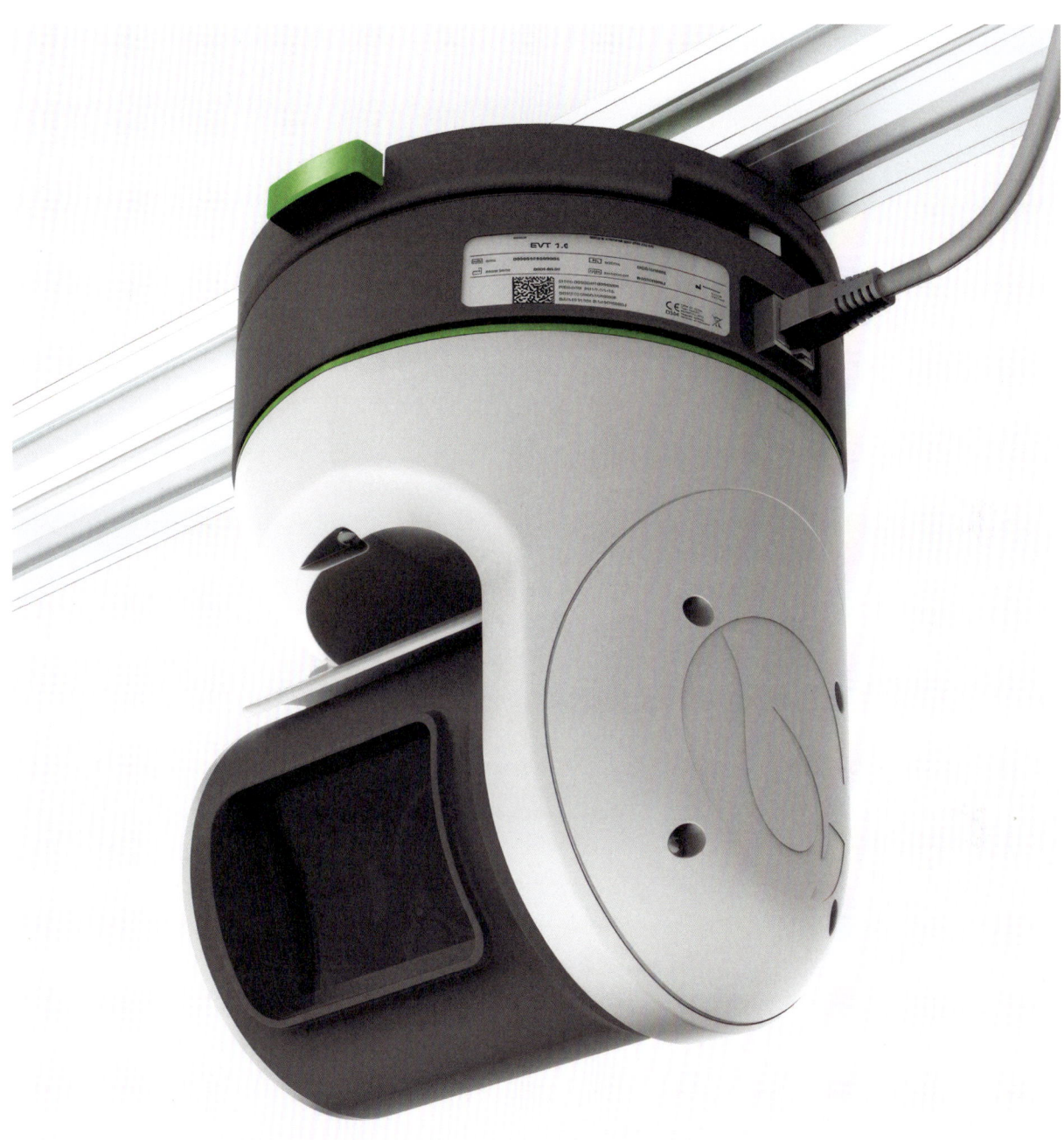

SILVER — RMA — BEFÜLLANLAGE / FILLING SYSTEM

JURY STATEMENT

Obwohl die Anlage weitgehend auf standardisierten Elementen basiert, entsteht ein signifikantes, der Verwendung angemessenes Design. Die Trennung des Arbeits- und Befüllbereichs verbessert die Abläufe und begründet ein eigenständiges Erscheinungsbild.

Despite using mostly standard components, the system boasts a unique and effective design, perfectly suited for its intended purpose. Separating the working and filling areas optimises the filling process and creates a unique aesthetic.

HERSTELLER/MANUFACTURER
Syntegon Technology GmbH
Waiblingen

DESIGN
whiteID GmbH & Co. KG
Schorndorf

Bei bestimmten medizinischen Therapien werden Medikamente ganz genau auf die Patientinnen und Patienten zugeschnitten, produziert und konfektioniert. Letzteres übernimmt die kompakte Anlage – sie befüllt Kleinserien von Auto-Injektionssystemen oder Pens für die personalisierte Medizin oder für klinische Studien.

Das Konzept der Anlage basiert auf der räumlichen Trennung des automatisierten Befüllraums und des manuellen Arbeitsbereichs. Dort werden die Medikationsträger in den Befüllschlitten gegeben, der dann linear in den Prozessraum fährt. Dank der Schutzverglasung lässt sich der Befüllablauf visuell beobachten und kontrollieren.

Bei der Konzeption des Arbeitsbereichs wurde auf leichte Reinigung und fugenfreie Flächen sowie eine ergonomisch geeignete Arbeitshöhe geachtet. Das geschlossene Anlagenvolumen bietet ausreichend Platz für unterschiedliche Prozesstechniken und gute Zugänglichkeit.

Certain medical conditions require personalised medications that have been designed, produced and packaged to meet a patient's specific needs. This compact system takes care of the latter requirement: it dispenses precise doses of medication into auto-injectors or pens used in personalised treatment plans or clinical research.

The system concept is based on the physical separation of the automated filling area and the manual work area. The medication containers are manually placed in the filling carriage, which then moves smoothly into the processing area. The protective glazing makes it possible to observe and monitor the filling process.

The work area boasts easy-to-clean, joint-free surfaces and an ergonomic working height. The enclosed area offers plenty of space for different processes and is also easily accessible.

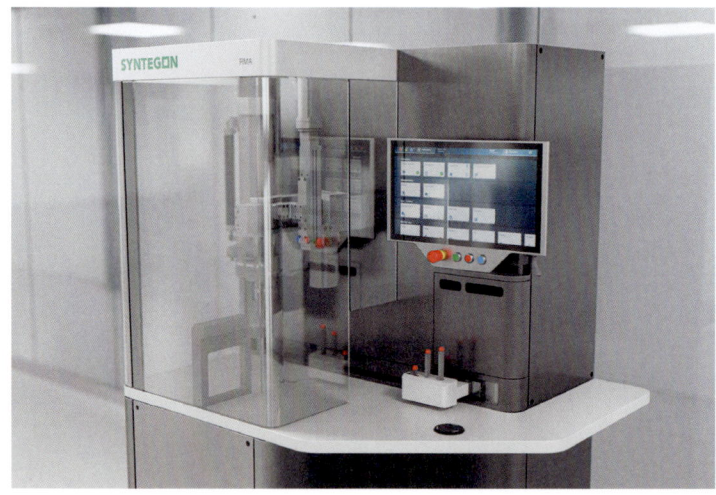

| SPECIAL MENTION | HEROS H10 | WALDBRANDHELM |
| | | FIREFIGHTING HELMET |

JURY STATEMENT

Der Helm orientiert sich an den anderen Modellen des Herstellers und stärkt so die Gesamtmarke. Das Design visualisiert das hohe Schutzniveau und die Zuverlässigkeit in Extremsituationen. Sehr gut gelöst wurde die multifunktionale und modulare Erweiterung des Helms mittels definierter Schnittstellen.

The helmet builds on the heritage of the manufacturer's other successful models and enhances the identity of the brand. The design communicates the high level of protection and reliability in extreme situations. The multi-functional, modular expansion of the helmet via special attachment points is a particularly good solution.

HERSTELLER/MANUFACTURER
Rosenbauer International AG
Leonding
Österreich/Austria

DESIGN
formquadrat GmbH
Linz
Österreich/Austria
Harry Müller
Mario Zeppetzauer

Neben dem primären Einsatzszenario, der Bekämpfung von Wald- und Flächenbränden, lässt sich der Heros H10 auch bei Höhen- und Wasserrettungen, bei technischen Hilfeleistungen sowie im Arbeitskontext nutzen. Die im Spritzgussverfahren produzierte Schale ist mit rund 500 Gramm Gewicht die leichteste dieser Helmklasse. Das bedeutet mehr Tragekomfort und weniger Ermüdung bei langen, körperlich fordernden Einsätzen. Die dreidimensionale, kantenbetonte Formensprache reduziert die Schalendicke und damit das Gewicht – und vermittelt durch ihre Expressivität Robustheit, Leistung und maximale Zuverlässigkeit. Zudem berücksichtigt die Formensprache die thermisch notwendige Be- und Entlüftung, während das Tragesystem im Inneren für die einfache Adaption an unterschiedliche Kopfformen sorgt. Definierte Anbaupunkte ermöglichen die funktionale Erweiterung des Helms, beispielsweise mit Gehörschutz, Visieren oder Scheinwerfern.

While originally designed to excel in fighting forest and wildfires, the Heros H10 also proves its versatility in sea and air rescue, technical rescue and industrial safety applications. The injection-moulded shell weighs approximately 500 grams, making it the lightest helmet in its class. This translates into greater wearing comfort and less fatigue during long, physically demanding deployments. The sharply defined contours of the three-dimensional design reduce the thickness and therefore the weight of the shell whilst also conveying robustness, performance and maximum reliability. The design language also acknowledges the need for ventilation, while the interior support system adapts easily to different head shapes. The helmet features attachment points for customisation, allowing users to add ear defenders, visors, lights and other compatible accessories.

SPECIAL MENTION

SPEED E® POCKETDRIVE
ELEKTRISCHER SCHRAUBENDREHER
ELECTRIC SCREWDRIVER

JURY STATEMENT

Ein intuitiv nutzbares Tool, dessen Funktionen sich sofort erschließen und das ein großes Entlastungspotenzial für handwerkliche Tätigkeiten bietet. Das Design wirkt ausgesprochen aufgeräumt und ist ergonomisch durchdacht.

A user-friendly tool with instantly recognisable functions capable of speeding up maintenance and repair tasks. The design shines with clean lines and thoughtful ergonomics.

HERSTELLER/MANUFACTURER
Wiha Werkzeuge GmbH
Schonach

DESIGN
Inhouse/In-house

Es ist nicht der erste Schraubendreher mit elektrischem Antrieb, den Wiha entwickelt hat. Dieses Modell ist universeller gedacht und dank seiner ergonomischen Griffform weiterhin manuell nutzbar. Der integrierte Motorschutz erlaubt es, Drehmomente bis 12 Nm einzubringen. Im elektrisch betriebenen Modus lässt sich per Taster zwischen maximalen Drehmomenten von 1 Nm für feine Verschraubungen und 5 Nm für größere Schrauben umschalten, LEDs zeigen den gewählten Modus an. Sechs im vorderen Bereich integrierte LEDs leuchten den Arbeitsbereich automatisch aus, geladen wird die integrierte Batterie über eine USB-C Schnittstelle.

Gedacht ist das 329 Gramm schwere Gerät sowohl für Hand- als auch Heimwerker, die schnell und kraftsparend arbeiten möchten.

This is not the first electric screwdriver that Wiha has developed. This model is intended for universal use and features an ergonomic handle that also allows for manual operation. When used manually, the built-in motor protection allows torques of up to 12 Nm to be applied. In electrically powered mode, the torque is adjustable at the touch of a button between 1 Nm for fine screws and 5 Nm for larger screws; LEDs indicate the mode selected. The device is fitted with six LEDs which automatically illuminate the working area. Charging of the integrated battery is via a standard USB-C cable.

At just 329 grams, this lightweight unit enables both professionals and DIYers to work quickly and effortlessly.

SPECIAL MENTION QRBLUV001_C1190 **NOTHALT-TASTER**
EMERGENCY STOP BUTTON

JURY STATEMENT

Ein auf seine sicherheitsrelevante Funktion klar reduziertes Produkt, das die Welt der Notaus-Taster elegant erweitert. Der Status lässt sich sehr einfach und eindeutig auch aus der Distanz erkennen.

This elegantly designed emergency stop button is focused solely on its safety function. The status is easily and clearly seen even from a distance.

HERSTELLER/MANUFACTURER
Georg Schlegel® GmbH & Co. KG
Dürmentingen

DESIGN
Inhouse/In-house

Sie gehören zur sicherheitsrelevanten Grundausstattung von Maschinen und Anlagen aller Art: Nothalt-Taster. Nicht nur bei größeren Anlagen mit mehreren, verteilt positionierten Schaltern ist daher die visuelle Anzeige des Schalterstatus wichtig. Denn so lassen sich Notfälle schnell erkennen und beheben.

Beim hier ausgezeichneten Nothalt-Taster visualisieren im sogenannten Blockierschutzkragen integrierte LEDs dessen Status. Das Lichtsignal ist dabei individuell konfigurierbar, beispielsweise kann sein Leuchten statt eines Notfalls auch seine Funktionsbereitschaft anzeigen. Für zwei Ampere Dauerstrom und 50.000 Schaltgänge ausgelegt, kombiniert die Schaltfunktion zwei Öffner und einen Schließer. Dank seiner Konstruktion entspricht der Schalter den Anforderungen IP65 sowie IP54 und eignet sich damit auch für die Nutzung in raueren Umgebungen.

Emergency stop buttons are essential for safety on all types of machinery. A clear visual indication of the switch status is important, not just on complex systems but also on switches with multiple positions, as it helps personnel to quickly identify and respond to emergencies.

The status of this award-winning emergency stop button is indicated by LEDs integrated in the anti-lock collar. The light can be individually configured to indicate a "ready for operation" state, for example, rather than an emergency state. Designed for two amps continuous current and 50,000 switching operations, the switching function combines one normally open and two normally closed contacts. The switch complies with IP65 and IP54 requirements and is therefore suitable for use in harsh environments.

SPECIAL MENTION   EAO-4   TUBENGLÜHOFEN / ANNEALING OVEN

JURY STATEMENT

Besonders positiv zu bewerten ist hier der enorme Qualitätssprung zwischen dem Vorgängermodell und der aktuellen Konfiguration. Es wird dabei deutlich, welch positive Wirkung kluges Design auf alle Bereiche einer Anlage haben kann – und zudem für die Wiedererkennbarkeit der Marke sorgt.

The dramatic leap in quality between the current and previous model is particularly impressive. It shows the positive effect that clever design can have on all aspects of a system – and how it can make a valuable contribution to brand recognition.

HERSTELLER/MANUFACTURER
Sprimag Spritzmaschinenbau GmbH & Co. KG
Kirchheim/Teck

DESIGN
Braake Design
Stuttgart

Diese Anlage ist ein wichtiges Element in der Produktion von Aluminiumtuben, die später unterschiedlichste Befüllungen aufnehmen werden. Sie übernimmt das Weichglühen der Rohlinge bei Temperaturen um 450°C, kontrolliert und sortiert. Verglichen mit anderen Anlagen dieser Art ist sowohl der Durchsatz mit 200 Tuben pro Minute bemerkenswert als auch die Reduktion des Energiebedarfs um rund 70 Prozent. Dazu trägt die Konzeption des Maschinen-Housings bei – etwa durch die großen Mineralglasfenster, die eine visuelle Kontrolle des Prozesses bei geschlossenen Türen ermöglichen.

Das Designkonzept sorgt für die Wiedererkennung der Marke, für Bediensicherheit und -ergonomie. Letzteres zeigt die explosionsgeschützte Bedieneinheit mit neuem HMI-Design. Glatte Oberflächen im Inneren erleichtern die Reinigung und sorgen damit für ein hohes Maß an Hygiene.

This industrial oven plays a vital role in the production of aluminium tubes that will subsequently be used to hold a variety of products. Its task is to soft anneal blanks at a temperature of around 450°C and then to inspect and sort them. Compared to other similar systems, the throughput of 200 tubes per minute is remarkable – as is the reduction in energy consumption of around 70 per cent. The design of the external housing also contributes to the oven's energy efficiency. For instance, large mineral glass windows allow for visual monitoring of the process with the doors closed.

The design concept contributes to brand recognition, operating safety and ergonomics. The latter is demonstrated, for example, by the explosion-proof operating panel, which features a new HMI design. The smooth interior surfaces aid effortless cleaning and ensure exceptional hygiene.

SPECIAL MENTION — GARDIN PLATFORM — SENSOR SENSOR

JURY STATEMENT

Der autonom arbeitende Lasersensor ist für sein Anwendungsgebiet adäquat gestaltet, seine Funktionsweise lässt sich aus seiner sachlichen Formgebung sofort ableiten. Er vermittelt stellvertretend für das ganze Daten- und Auswertungssystem dahinter hohe Präzision und Zuverlässigkeit.

The laser sensors run autonomously and have been developed specifically for this application. The design reveals its functionality at a glance. It reflects the comprehensive data and evaluation system upon which it is based, conveying high precision and reliability.

HERSTELLER/MANUFACTURER
Gardin Ltd.
Abingdon
Großbritannien/United Kingdom

DESIGN
Thinkable Studio GmbH
Offenburg
Jörg Schlieffers
Paul Scarfe
Nicolai Rauser
Benjamin Gaigé
Steve Remy

Die Agrar-Produktion wird sich künftig vom witterungs- und klimaabhängigen Feldanbau zu einer Form weiterentwickeln, die unter kontrollierbaren Bedingungen stattfindet, also in Gewächshäusern oder Vertikalfarmen. In solchen Umgebungen kann das Wachstum von Pflanzen aktiv unterstützt und optimiert werden. Eine wichtige Rolle spielt dabei das kontinuierliche Monitoring der Pflanzen, um Stress, Nährstoff- oder Wassermangel zu erkennen. Die Gardin-Plattform ist ein solches System, das Sensordaten Cloud-basiert zusammenträgt und auswertbar macht.

Die Rohdaten dafür kommen vom Lasersensor, der die Chlorophyll-Fluoreszenz der Pflanzen ermittelt, aus denen dann deren Zustand abgeleitet wird. Der kompakte Scanner erfasst alle Richtungen und ist für die typischen Umgebungsbedingungen optimiert.

In the future, farming will move away from its current dependence on unpredictable weather and variable climates towards the more precisely controlled environments offered by greenhouses and vertical farms, where cultivation can be actively supported and optimised. Continuous monitoring of crops plays an important role in detecting stress and nutrient or water deficiencies. The Gardin Platform is a cloud-based crop intelligence system that collates sensor data and uses it to generate growth insights.

The condition of the plants is derived from raw data provided by a laser sensor that measures the chlorophyll fluorescence of the plants. The compact sensor unit scans in all directions and is optimised for use in typical operating environments.

1 → SEITE/PAGE 36–43

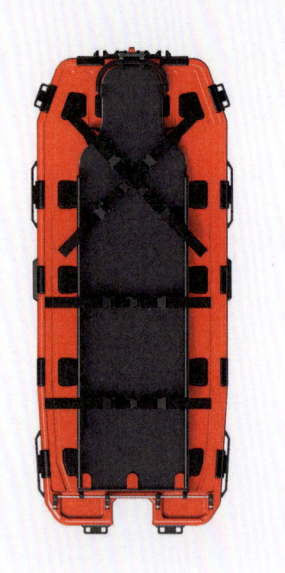

2 → SEITE/PAGE 46–53

3 → SEITE/PAGE 54–61

4 → SEITE/PAGE 62, 64

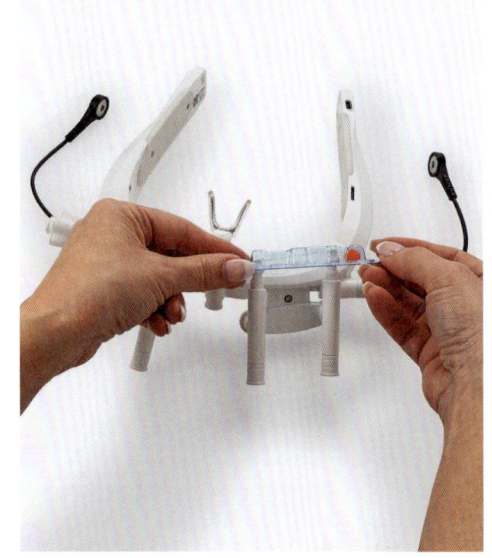

5 → SEITE/PAGE 63, 65

HEALTHCARE
HEALTHCARE

GOLD:
1. **MAGNOS**
   Magnosco GmbH
   Berlin

2. **TRAUMA-COVER ER**
   StarMed GmbH –
   medical rescue systems
   Stetten am Bodensee

3. **HELISTAR-HTS**
   StarMed GmbH –
   medical rescue systems
   Stetten am Bodensee

SPECIAL MENTION:
4. **CITYCADDY**
   CityCaddy
   UG (haftungsbeschränkt)
   Hamburg

5. **OKUSTIM**
   Okuvision GmbH
   Reutlingen

Wer medizinische Geräte gestaltet, bewegt sich in einem besonders sensiblen Bereich und übernimmt große soziale Verantwortung – für Patientinnen und Patienten wie auch für das medizinische Personal. Design hilft hier, Lücken in der medizinischen Versorgung zu schließen, unterstützt die Implementierung neuer Diagnose- und Therapiemethoden oder erhöht die Bediensicherheit.

Designers of medical equipment operate in a particularly sensitive area and have a high level of social responsibility towards both patients and medical staff. Design helps to close gaps in medical care, supports the implementation of new diagnostic and therapeutic techniques and improves user safety.

2

GOLD · MAGNOS · DERMATOSKOP / DERMATOSCOPE

MAGNOS

DERMATOSKO

HEALTHCARE
HEALTHCARE

FOCUS GOLD

P

magnosco

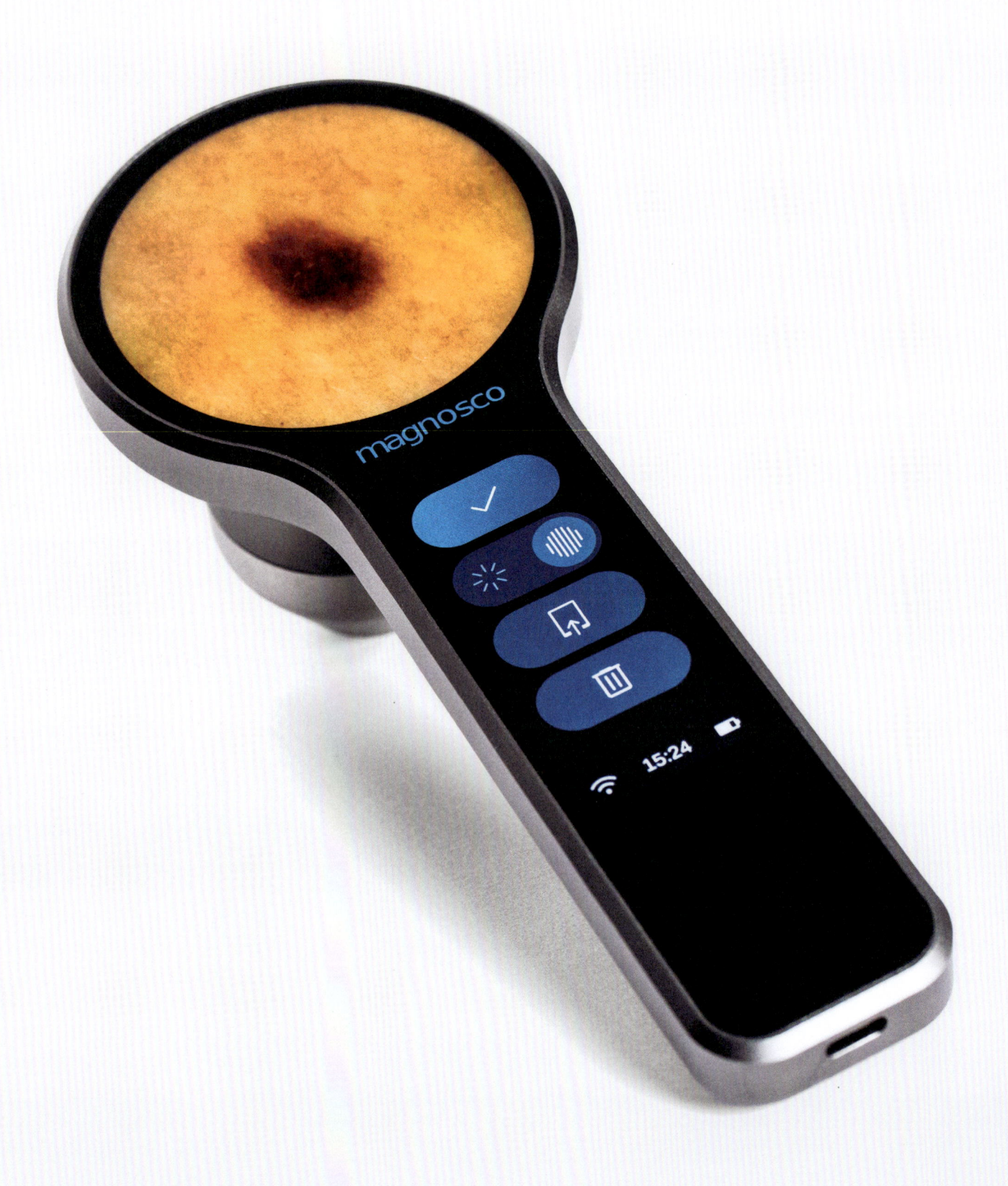

GOLD MAGNOS DERMATOSKOP
DERMATOSCOPE

JURY STATEMENT

Eine sehr perfekte Gestaltung, taktil stimmig, ergonomisch durchdacht sowie hochwertig in seiner Materialität. Die Anmutung erinnert eher an ein Consumerprodukt als an ein medizinisches Gerät. Das wirkt vertrauensbildend, macht es nahbar und bringt einen neuen Ansatz für ein zunehmendes medizinisches Problem.

A meticulously designed device with a comfortable, intuitive grip, crafted from high quality materials. By eschewing the traditional medical device aesthetic in favour of a consumer-friendly design, this device fosters trust and approachability, and offers a fresh perspective on managing a growing medical concern.

HERSTELLER/MANUFACTURER
Magnosco GmbH
Berlin

DESIGN
WILDDESIGN GmbH
Gelsenkirchen
Anna-Lena Gölz
Alexander Fries

Das Berliner Unternehmen entwickelt neue Methoden und Geräte für die effizientere Hautdiagnostik. Bislang erfolgen Diagnosen mit Hilfe analoger Dermatoskope, vereinfacht gesagt, mit speziellen Lupen. Bewertung und Dokumentation obliegen den jeweiligen Medizinerinnen und Medizinern. Das Gerät Magnos, derzeit noch ein Prototyp, arbeitet hingegen voll digital und wurde zusammen mit Dermatologen aus der Praxis entwickelt. Das smarte Dermatoskop speichert und verarbeitet die Bilder mit bis zu 20-facher Vergrößerung über den internen Rechner, die Kalibrierung verbessert dank der farbechten Bilder die Diagnosezuverlässigkeit. Die Formgebung sowie die Bedienung per Touch-Display fördern die intuitive, am Smartphone-Leistungslevel orientierte Nutzung.

This Berlin-based company develops innovative methods and devices for effective skin diagnostics. Until now, screening for skin conditions has generally been carried out in an analogue way, with the help of a magnifying glass and light, with doctors responsible for diagnosis and documentation. In contrast, the Magnos device, currently a prototype, is entirely digital and was developed in collaboration with practising dermatologists. The smart dermatoscope uses an internal computer to process and store images with up to 20x magnification. Diagnostic reliability is greatly improved thanks to its calibration function and the high resolution of its colour images. The sleek design and touch display offer an intuitive smartphone-like user experience.

THOMAS DIEPOLD UND SEBASTIAN AHLBERG GESCHÄFTSFÜHRER, MAGNOSCO GMBH

»Das Magnos kann unabhängig von der Größe der Hand sehr gut bedient und gegriffen werden.«

»Magnos offers excellent grip and operability for all hand sizes.«

THOMAS DIEPOLD AND SEBASTIAN AHLBERG — **MANAGING DIRECTORS, MAGNOSCO GMBH**

Dermatoskope sind nicht neu – was macht das Magnos so innovativ?

Sebastian Ahlberg: Vor über 30 Jahren hat die Revolution in der Dermatologie begonnen. Seitdem haben analoge Dermatoskope die Diagnostik erheblich verbessert. Die Digitalisierung bietet der Dermatologie eine ganze Reihe neuer, aufregender Möglichkeiten, um Herausforderungen wie den demografischen Wandel oder eine unzureichende diagnostische Qualität zu meistern. Ärzte haben aktuell die Wahl zwischen teuren High-End-Produkten oder günstigen Geräten, die aber beide nicht den Ansprüchen genügen. Denn weder die teuren High-End-Produkte noch die kostengünstigen Geräte eignen sich wirklich, um die analogen Dermatoskope abzulösen und den Weg in die Breite zu finden. Mit dem Magnos haben wir nun ein Produkt entwickelt, das die Bedürfnisse der User erfüllt. Es ermöglicht erstklassige dermatoskopische Aufnahmen, ist intuitiv bedienbar und überzeugt durch seine hochwertige Verarbeitung und seinen Preis – ein absoluter Game-Changer für Dermatologinnen und Dermatologen sowie Hausärztinnen und Hausärzte.

Inwieweit integriert das Magnos schon KI-gestützte Diagnosen?

Thomas Diepold: Mit seinen hochauflösenden, dermatoskopischen Aufnahmen liefert es die Grundlage für eine erstklassige Diagnostik. Demnächst stellen wir eine neue App vor, die es unerfahrenen, nach Unterstützung suchenden Ärztinnen und Ärzten ermöglicht, die hochauflösenden Magnos-Bilder auf innovative Weise zu verarbeiten.

Das Gerät ist kein Leichtgewicht, liegt aber dennoch prima in der Hand – wie wichtig waren für Sie ergonomische Gesichtspunkte?

Thomas Diepold: Es ist eigentlich nur etwas schwerer als ein Smartphone. Damit das Magnos gerne und regelmäßig benutzt wird, braucht es natürlich eine ausgeklügelte Ergonomie. Uns war wichtig, dass das Magnos unabhängig von der Größe der Hand sehr gut bedient und gegriffen werden kann. Und das ist uns sehr gut gelungen. Das Gewicht ist ausbalanciert und ergibt sich aus hochwertigen, robusten Materialien. Wir haben beispielsweise bewusst auf Spritzgussteile verzichtet, was sich in der Wertigkeit widerspiegelt.

Dermatoscopes aren't new – what makes the Magnos so innovative?

Sebastian Ahlberg: The revolution in dermatology began over 30 years ago. Since then, analogue dermatoscopes have greatly improved the accuracy of diagnostics. Digitalisation now provides dermatology with a diverse array of innovative solutions to address challenges such as demographic shifts and inadequate diagnostic accuracy. Doctors currently have the choice of expensive high-end products or inexpensive devices, neither of which adequately satisfy their needs. However, neither high-end nor low-cost digital dermatoscopes have achieved broad acceptance as substitutes for traditional analogue devices. Magnos is a groundbreaking product that effectively addresses the needs of users. It produces excellent dermatoscopic images, is user-friendly and built to last – all at a price that is an absolute game changer for dermatologists and GPs.

To what extent does the Magnos already integrate AI-supported diagnoses?

Thomas Diepold: The high-resolution dermatoscopic images produced by Magnos provide the basis for first-class diagnostics. We are about to launch a new app that will enable both novice and experienced doctors to apply innovative techniques for processing high-resolution Magnos images.

Although not a lightweight device, it is surprisingly comfortable to hold. How important were ergonomics in your design process?

Thomas Diepold: It's actually not much heavier than a smartphone. Optimal ergonomics is a key factor in ensuring a positive experience for regular users of the Magnos. An important design consideration was ensuring that the device could accommodate a wide range of hand sizes. We achieved that aim. The device is well-balanced and made from tough, high-quality materials. Our decision to avoid the use of injection-moulded parts has resulted in a higher quality product.

THOMAS DIEPOLD UND SEBASTIAN AHLBERG   **GESCHÄFTSFÜHRER, MAGNOSCO GMBH**

Die Interaktion mit der komplexen Technik ist vergleichsweise einfach – wie gelang Ihnen dies?
Sebastian Ahlberg: Der User muss sich mit Magnos wohlfühlen und es intuitiv bedienen können. Um diese UX zu testen, haben wir potenzielle User, also medizinisches Personal, zu deren Vorlieben und Wünschen interviewt und Ideen immer wieder hinterfragt. Ein aufwendiger Prozess, keine Frage. Das Team war in jeder Phase des Entwicklungsprozesses involviert und hat aktiv Änderungen und Entscheidungen vorangetrieben. Denn nur durch viele, multidisziplinäre Sichtweisen – dazu zählen auch negative Meinungen – kann ein außergewöhnliches Produkt entstehen.

Wie eng arbeiteten Engineering und Design zusammen?
Sebastian Ahlberg: Die Dermatologie vereinigt Wissenschaft, Forschung und Medizin unter einem Dach und ist zudem eine ästhetische Disziplin. Design hat die Aufgabe, Technologie in bestmöglicher Form zu ermöglichen und in Funktionalität zu übersetzen. Ein Beispiel: Die Handhabung muss einfach sein, das Magnos muss dies unterstützen. So gehen Funktion und Form eine untrennbare Verbindung ein. Wir sind ein überschaubar großes Team und können alle Aspekte daher einfach abstimmen. Das ist ein riesiger Vorteil für ein agiles Start-up wie unseres.

Welche Aspekte würden Sie rückblickend als größte Challenge der Entwicklung bezeichnen?
Thomas Diepold: Wir haben uns zum Ziel gesetzt, die analoge Welt und die gewohnte Bedienbarkeit der optischen Dermatoskope in die digitale Welt der Smart Devices zu übertragen. Dafür haben wir uns für eine Kombination aus zwei Multitouch-Displays entschieden, eine technisch anspruchsvolle Lösung. Zugleich ist sie ein echtes Alleinstellungsmerkmal für das Magnos. So haben wir das Ziel der einfachen Bedienung erreicht.

Das Smartphone diente auch Ihnen als Benchmark – in welcher Beziehung?
Ahlberg: Wir müssen uns mit Smart Devices messen, denn Lösungen für das Smartphone existieren bereits und werden verwendet. Auch wenn diese Lösungen nicht alles können, sind Smartphones und Apps generell aus unserem Leben nicht mehr wegzudenken. Das Magnos ist die logische Ergänzung und führt den gewohnten analogen Workflow weitestgehend fort. Für Nutzerinnen und Nutzer fühlt es sich deshalb an, als wäre das Gerät schon immer dagewesen und hätte eine natürliche Evolution durchlaufen.

Magnosco wurde 2014 gegründet und widmet sich als Start-up der Diagnostik von Melanomen und anderen Hauterkrankungen. Gestartet ist das Unternehmen, um ein Forschungsprojekt in ein Medizinprodukt zu überführen. 2017 erhielt diese laserbasierte Methode zur Hautkrebs-Erkennung nach drei Jahren klinischer Tests die Zulassung. Das Magnos ist eine komplette Neuentwicklung mit eigener Technologie. Seit 2022 gehört Magnosco mit Sitz in Berlin-Adlershof zur LBT Holding.

www.magnosco.com

THOMAS DIEPOLD AND SEBASTIAN AHLBERG — MANAGING DIRECTORS, MAGNOSCO GMBH

Interacting with the complex technology is relatively easy. How did you manage this?
Sebastian Ahlberg: Our goal was to provide an intuitive and user-friendly experience for Magnos users. To test the UX, we asked potential users, such as doctors and medical staff, about their preferences and requirements and analysed their ideas. It was a time-consuming process, there's no doubt about that. Our team participated in every stage of the development process, actively shaping changes and decisions. Ultimately, creating an exceptional product requires a wide range of multi-disciplinary perspectives, including constructive criticism.

How closely did your engineers and designers collaborate?
Sebastian Ahlberg: Dermatology is a blend of science, research and medicine but it also has an aesthetic component. Design has the task of transforming technology into meaningful and functional products. We wanted to make the Magnos easy for users to operate, seamlessly merging form and function. Our manageable team size allows for efficient coordination across all areas – a huge advantage for an agile start-up like ours.

Looking back, what was the biggest challenge to the development of your product?
Thomas Diepold: We sought to replicate the familiar functionality of the optical dermatoscope within the digital realm of smart devices. To achieve this, we chose the technically challenging solution of combining two multi-touch displays. Today, this is a genuine unique selling point for the Magnos. It's also how we were able to achieve our goal of intuitive operation.

The smartphone also served as a benchmark for you – in what respect?
Ahlberg: We have to measure ourselves against smart devices because solutions for the smartphone already exist and are in use. Even if these solutions can't do everything, smartphones and apps in general have become an integral part of our lives. Magnos is a logical progression that continues the familiar analogue workflow as far as possible. For the user, the device feels like a familiar friend that has undergone a natural evolution.

Founded in 2014, Magnosco is a start-up dedicated to the diagnosis of melanoma and other skin diseases. The company was launched to transform a research project into a medical product. After three years of clinical testing, its laser-based method of detecting skin cancer received approval In 2017. The Magnos is a completely new development based on proprietary technology. Magnosco is headquartered in Berlin-Adlershofn and has been part of LBT Holding since 2022.

www.magnosco.com

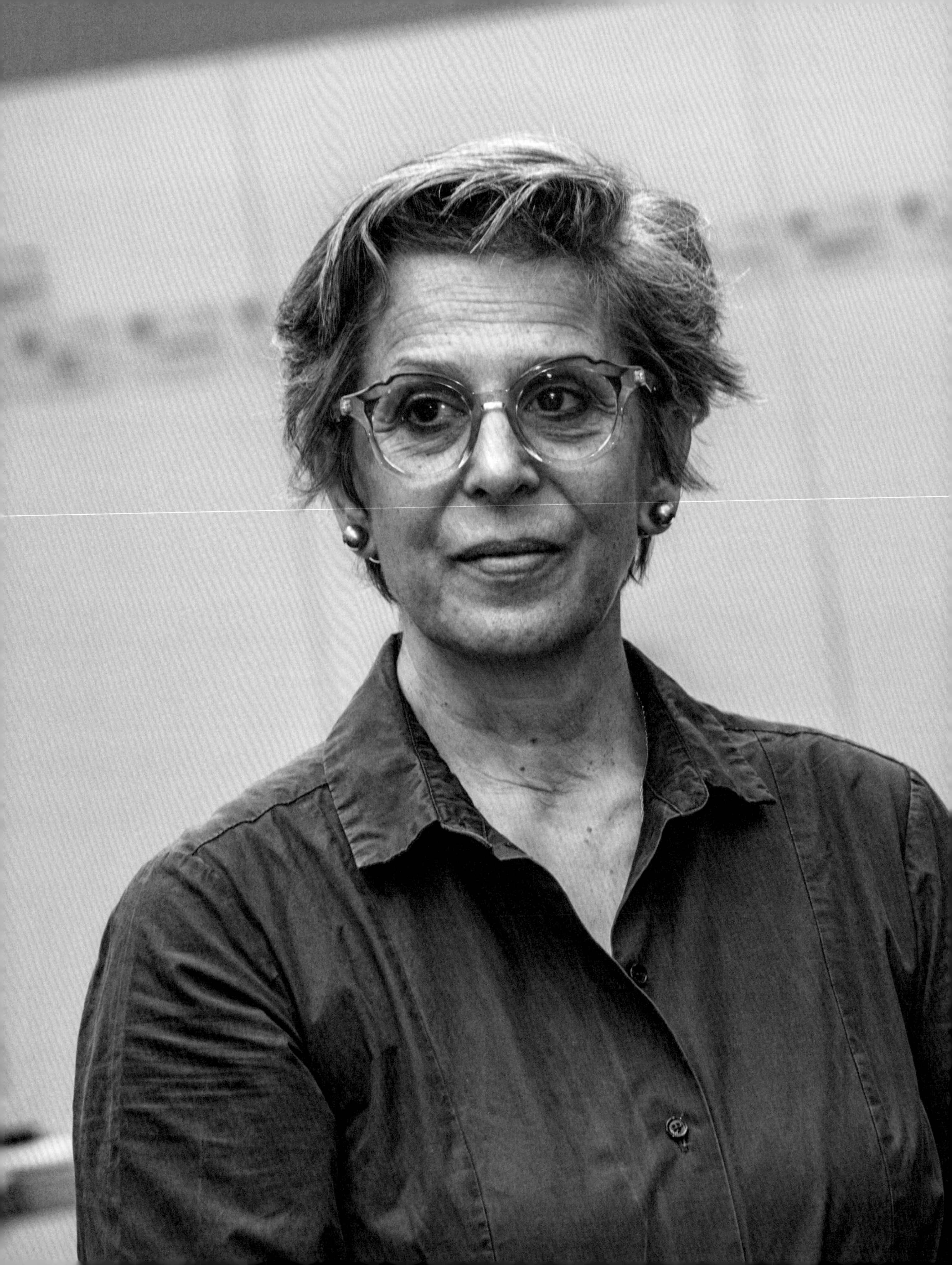

PROF. TULGA BEYERLE **MUSEUM FÜR KUNST UND GEWERBE, HAMBURG**

»Design lediglich als Marketing-Tool zu begreifen, ist ein großer Fehler: Design gestaltet auch Prozesse und definiert unser Miteinander.«

»Seeing design solely as a marketing tool is a big mistake. Design goes beyond that: it shapes processes and defines how we interact.«

Tulga Beyerle ist seit 2018 Direktorin des Hamburger Museums für Kunst und Gewerbe. Beyerle studierte Industriedesign an der Universität für angewandte Kunst in Wien und unterrichtete eben dort. Viele Jahre als selbstständige Kuratorin in ganz Europa aktiv, gründete sie 2006 mit Lilli Hollein sowie Thomas Geisler die Vienna Design Week und war von 2014 bis 2018 Direktorin des Kunstgewerbemuseums in Dresden.

Tulga Beyerle has been the director of the Museum für Kunst und Gewerbe in Hamburg since 2018. After completing her degree in industrial design at the University of Applied Arts in Vienna, she went on to teach there. She worked as a freelance curator for many years all over Europe and co-founded Vienna Design Week with Lilli Hollein and Thomas Geisler in 2006. She was also the director of the Kunstgewerbemuseum in Dresden from 2014 to 2018.

www.mkg-hamburg.de

www.mkg-hamburg.de

GOLD | TRAUMA-COVER ER | MOBILE NOTFALL-PLATTFORM
MOBILE EMERGENCY PLATFORM

TRAUMA—
COVER ER

MOBILE
NOTFALL—
PLATTFORM

HEALTHCARE
HEALTHCARE

FOCUS
GOLD

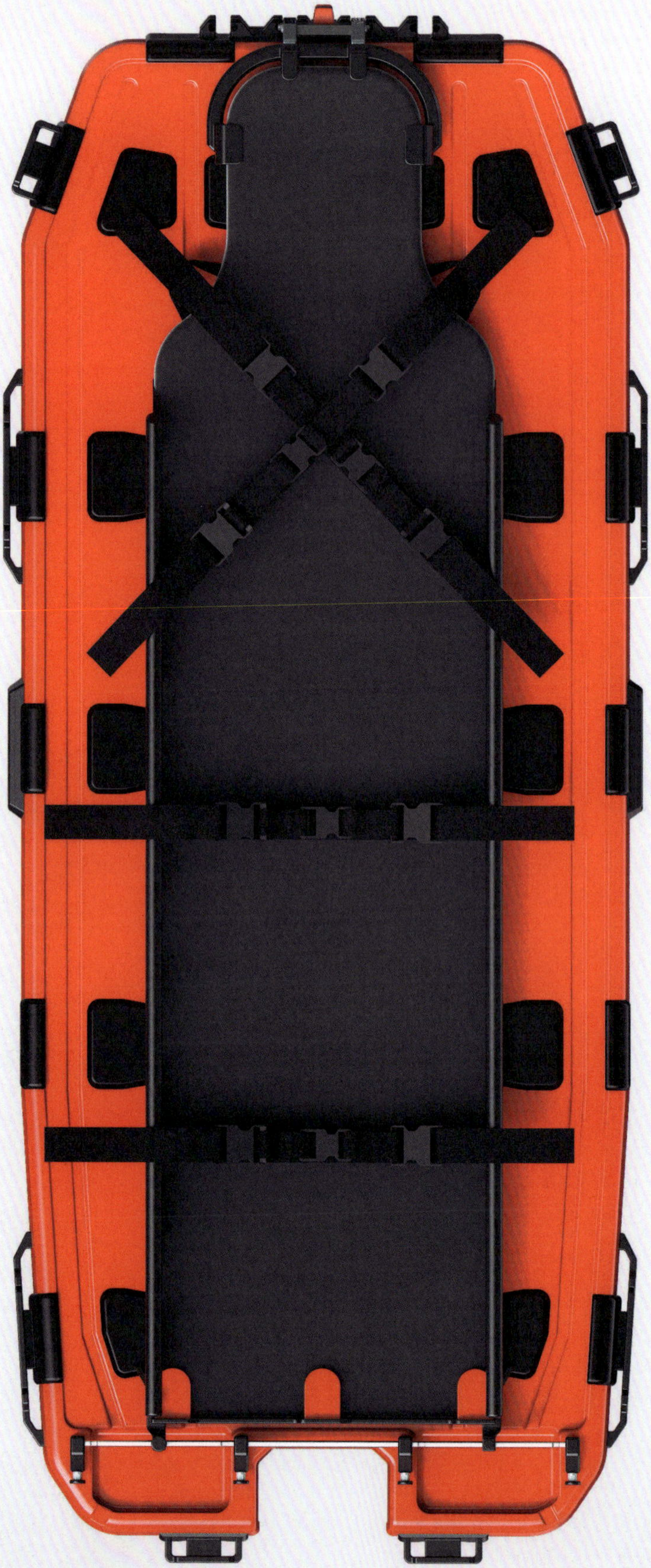

GOLD — TRAUMA-COVER ER

MOBILE NOTFALL-PLATTFORM / MOBILE EMERGENCY PLATFORM

JURY STATEMENT

Dieses Produkt zeigt das breite Potenzial von Design. Statt der Ästhetik steht hier die nutzerzentrierte Funktionalität im Vordergrund, alle Details sind eingehend durchdacht, die Anforderungen maximal umgesetzt. Letztendlich hilft das Design, Leben zu retten.

This product demonstrates the vast potential of innovative design. Every detail has been carefully considered and the requirements have been fully implemented. It is good to know that effective design can help save lives.

HERSTELLER/MANUFACTURER
StarMed GmbH –
medical rescue systems
Stetten am Bodensee

DESIGN
Inhouse/In-house

Polytraumatisierte und lebensbedrohlich Verletzte werden in Schockräumen unter extremem Zeitdruck erstversorgt. In der Regel kommen dabei hygienisch problematische Röntgen- oder Notfallliegen zum Einsatz, die aber zu schmal sind, um etwa die spontane Umpositionierung der Patientinnen und Patienten zu ermöglichen.

Das wannenförmige Trauma-Cover dient als Ebene zwischen dem mobilen Chassis der Liege und der sogenannten Trauma-Matratze. In der Summe entsteht so eine funktionsoptimierte Kombination aus Umlagerungshilfe, Versorgungsplattform sowie schnellem Intensivtransporter. Das Trauma-Cover bietet sowohl Andockpunkte für Geräte wie für die Matratze, besteht aus leichtgewichtigem CFK (carbonfaserverstärkter Kunststoff) und ist mit einem roten, reinigungsfreundlichen Gelcoat beschichtet. Und es ist breit genug, um die Patientinnen und Patienten je nach akutem Bedarf anders zu platzieren.

Severely traumatised patients with life-threatening injuries receive initial treatment in trauma rooms, where medical teams work under extreme time pressure. As a rule, X-ray or emergency tables are used here, which not only pose hygiene challenges but are also too narrow to allow the patient to be repositioned quickly.

The bathtub-shaped trauma cover bridges the gap between the stretcher base and the "trauma mattress". The design combines the functions of a repositioning aid, a care platform and a critical care trolley. The trauma cover has docking points for equipment and for the mattress. It is made of lightweight CFRP (carbon fiber reinforced polymer) and finished in a red, easy-to-clean gel coat. Last but not least, it is wide enough to allow patients to be positioned in different positions depending on their particular needs.

RENÉ STERN GESCHÄFTSFÜHRER,
STARMED GMBH

»Es gibt bisher kein vergleichbares Produkt.«

»There is no comparable product on the market.«

RENÉ STERN — MANAGING DIRECTOR, STARMED GMBH

Das Trauma-Cover ist ein Produkt, das in einem sehr speziellen und kaum sichtbaren Kontext zum Einsatz kommt. Wie haben Sie den Bedarf erkannt?

Der Entwicklung des Trauma-Cover ging die Anfrage eines Kunden voraus, wie man unseren Transporter Heavystar durch eine Auflage noch besser nutzen kann. Der Transporter ist ja für die schnelle und schonende Verlegung innerhalb einer Klinik gedacht. Auf die Anfrage hin haben wir uns dann stark in das Thema eingedacht, insbesondere bezogen auf Schockräume. Man muss wissen, dass Schockräume in Kliniken dazu da sind, akut Schwerstverletzten das Überleben zu ermöglichen. Da kann es – je nach Trauma – mitunter recht blutig zugehen. Uns war schnell klar, dass hier großer Bedarf besteht.

Inwiefern?

Bisher arbeitet man mit unterschiedlichsten Liegen und Tragen, die den Anforderungen im Schockraum eigentlich nicht gerecht werden. Sie sind zu schmal, schwer zu handhaben und zu reinigen, zudem hygienisch problematisch. Spontane Umlagerungen der Verletzten sind schwierig, medizinische Geräte werden auf einem Andockwagen platziert, die Reinigung ist intensiv und blockiert den Raum oft lange. All das bremst die schnelle Traumaversorgung.

Was ändert das Trauma-Cover?

Vieles. Das Produkt ist eine Art Zwischenebene. Es wird auf unserem Heavystar-Transporter platziert, der genügend Kapazität für das Equipment bietet, beispielsweise Beatmungsgerät, Defibrillator, Medikationsgeräte oder Infusionsständer. Der Patient selbst liegt auf einer schmalen Trauma-Matratze, die sich auf dem breiteren Trauma-Cover schnell verschieben lässt. Das ist notwendig, um die Verletzten sofort umlagern zu können, wenn es notwendig ist. Sie müssen nicht mehr anheben, sondern nur noch verschieben. Unser Trauma-Cover erhöht also letztlich die Überlebenschancen.

The Trauma Cover is a product that is used in a very specialised and barely visible context. How did you recognise the need?

We began developing the Trauma Cover in response to a customer's request for a cover that would improve the effectiveness of our Heavystar transporter. The transporter is designed to move patients swiftly and gently between hospital departments. The enquiry prompted us to delve deeply into the topic, particularly with reference to trauma rooms. It's important to realise that the primary function of hospital trauma rooms is to provide life-saving care for severely injured patients. Depending on the trauma, things can sometimes become quite bloody. It immediately became apparent that there was a huge demand for the product.

Why was that?

We had previously been working with a wide variety of beds and stretchers that don't actually meet the requirements of the trauma room. They are too narrow, difficult to handle and clean, as well as being hygienically problematic. It's difficult to quickly adjust the patient's position, medical equipment is placed on a docking trolley, cleaning is intensive and frequently hinders other activities within the room. All of this reduces the speed of trauma care.

What does the Trauma Cover change?

A lot. The product provides an additional, intermediate level. It sits on our Heavystar transporter, which offers plenty of space for equipment such as ventilators, defibrillators, medication devices and infusion stands. The patient lies on a narrow trauma mattress, which can be moved quickly onto the wider Trauma Cover. The injured person can therefore be repositioned quickly if necessary. You no longer have to lift, just move. Our Trauma Cover therefore ultimately increases the chances of survival.

RENÉ STERN — GESCHÄFTSFÜHRER, STARMED GMBH

Das hört sich sehr komplex an.
Die Entwicklung lief extrem schnell, nach eineinhalb Jahren war das Trauma-Cover einsatzbereit. Wir haben natürlich eng mit dem medizinischen Personal zusammengearbeitet und waren gleich sehr nahe am Serienstatus. Wobei wir stets Verbesserungen aufnehmen, wenn wir Potenzial sehen. Aktuell haben wir einen magnetisch fixierbaren, transparenten Vorhang entwickelt, der den Transporter mitsamt der dort untergebrachten Geräte vor Blutspritzern schützt.

Ins Auge fällt einem Nicht-Mediziner natürlich sofort die rote Farbe.
Die Verletzten verlieren im Schockraum mitunter viel Blut, das sich zum größten Teil auf dem Trauma-Cover sammelt. Das sähe ziemlich drastisch aus, wenn das Cover beispielsweise weiß wäre. Rot hingegen schwächt die Wirkung dank des fehlenden Kontrastes ab. Außerdem zeigt die Farbe, dass hier der Mittelpunkt des Schockraumes ist. Wir bedienen uns übrigens einer Gelcoat-Beschichtung, sie erleichtert die Reinigung, lässt das Blut besser ablaufen und schützt das Kohlefaser-Verbundmaterial des Covers.

Warum Kohlefaser?
Ganz einfach: Der Werkstoff ist leicht und extrem belastbar. Das Trauma-Cover wiegt 28 Kilogramm und ist bis 280 Kilogramm belastbar. Das heißt nicht, dass die Verletzten so schwer sind, aber im Notfall kniet dann doch mal ein Arzt auf dem Cover. Da addiert sich manches.

Die Beschichtung kommt aus dem Yachtbau, lässt sich das so einfach im Medizinbereich nutzen?
Wir denken kreativ und suchen nach Lösungen auch außerhalb des medizinischen Bereichs. Wir müssen auch nicht steril sein, denn die Verletzten sind es ja auch nicht. Erst wenn ein Eingriff erfolgt, wird lokal steril gearbeitet.

Mit welchen Stückzahlen rechnen Sie?
Momentan haben wir ein Exemplar im Einsatz, sammeln noch Feedback und machen kleine Verbesserungen – siehe den erwähnten Spritzschutz. Die Vermarktung starten wir noch in diesem Jahr in der Kombination mit dem Heavystar-Transporter. Wie groß die Nachfrage sein wird, können wir noch nicht abschätzen, es gibt bisher kein vergleichbares Produkt, an dem wir uns orientieren könnten. Außerdem begeben wir uns in ein neues Marktsegment, den innerklinischen Bereich. Bis jetzt waren wir eher außerklinisch aktiv, also in der Rettungskette vor dem Schockraum.

Das Trauma-Cover ist bereits mit einem Patent geschützt – warum?
Wir sind ein eher kleines Unternehmen, das in einer wichtigen Nische arbeitet und von Innovationen lebt. Da muss man seine Entwicklungen gut schützen. Wir haben seit unserer Gründung schon reichlich Patente angemeldet. Allein in diesem Jahr kommen noch mehrere hinzu.

Starmed wurde 1998 gegründet und hat sich auf die Entwicklung und Produktion von Systemen für den Patienten- und Gerätetransport im Rahmen der Intensivmedizin spezialisiert. So entwickelte das Unternehmen das erste, seriell produzierte Intensiv-Transportsystem. Außerdem agiert das neunköpfige, interdisziplinäre Team als Entwicklungsdienstleister für Rettungsdienste, für Kliniken oder Medizingerätehersteller. Gründer René Stern kann auf jahrelange eigene Erfahrungen in der boden- und luftgebundenen Rettung zurückgreifen.

www.starmed.eu

RENÉ STERN — MANAGING DIRECTOR, STARMED GMBH

It sounds very complex.
Development was extremely fast. The Trauma Cover was ready to go after eighteen months. We naturally worked closely with medical specialists and were very close to putting it into production. However, we believe in incorporating improvements whenever possible. We have now developed a transparent curtain that attaches magnetically and protects the transporter and equipment from blood splashes.

The red colour immediately catches the eye of a non-medical person.
Patients sometimes lose a lot of blood in the trauma room, most of which accumulates on the trauma cover. A white cover would look pretty horrific. Red, on the other hand, minimises the impact because the contrast is less. The colour also signals that this is the heart of the trauma room. Incidentally, we use a gelcoat coating, which makes cleaning easier, allows blood to run off better and protects the cover's carbon fibre composite material.

Why carbon fibre?
Simple: it's light and extremely tough. The Trauma Cover weighs 28 kilogrammes and can withstand a load of up to 280 kilogrammes. That doesn't mean that patients are ever that heavy, but it is not unusual for a doctor to kneel on the cover in an emergency. So, the weight can add up.

Can you easily modify a coating typically used in boatbuilding for medical use?
We think creatively and often look for solutions outside the medical field. It doesn't have to be sterile because the injured persons aren't sterile either. Sterility is only needed when a surgical procedure is taking place.

How many units do you expect to produce?
We currently have one in use and are still collecting feedback and making small improvements, such as the splash guard I just mentioned. We will start marketing it this year in combination with the Heavystar transporter. We can't accurately predict demand at this time because there is no comparable product on the market. We are also moving into a new market segment, the "intra-hospital" sector. So far, most of our activity has been outside the hospital sector itself, i.e. in the rescue chain prior to the trauma room.

The cover is already protected by a patent – why?
We are a small company, driving innovation in an important niche market. We need to protect our achievements. We've filed numerous patent applications since we began. We expect to add several more this year alone.

Founded in 1998, Starmed specialises in the development and production of intensive care patient and equipment transport systems. The company developed the first intensive care transport system to be produced in quantity. The nine-strong interdisciplinary team also acts as a development service provider for emergency services, hospitals and medical device manufacturers. Founder René Stern has extensive experience in ground and air rescue operations.

www.starmed.eu

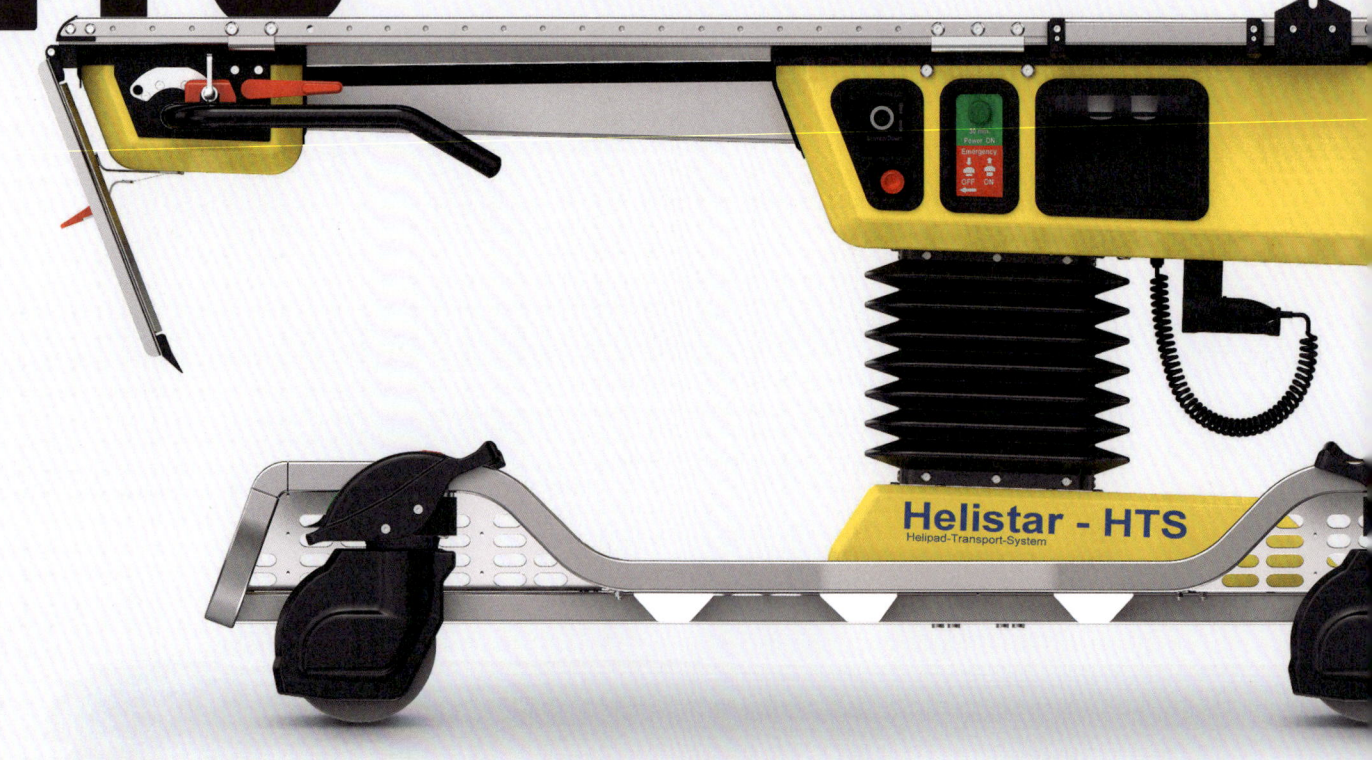

GOLD HELISTAR-HTS LANDEPLATZTRANSPORTER
HELIPAD TRANSFER PLATFORM

HELISTAR–
HTS

LANDEPLATZ
TRANSPORTE

HEALTHCARE
HEALTHCARE

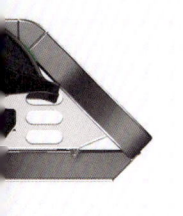

FOCUS
GOLD

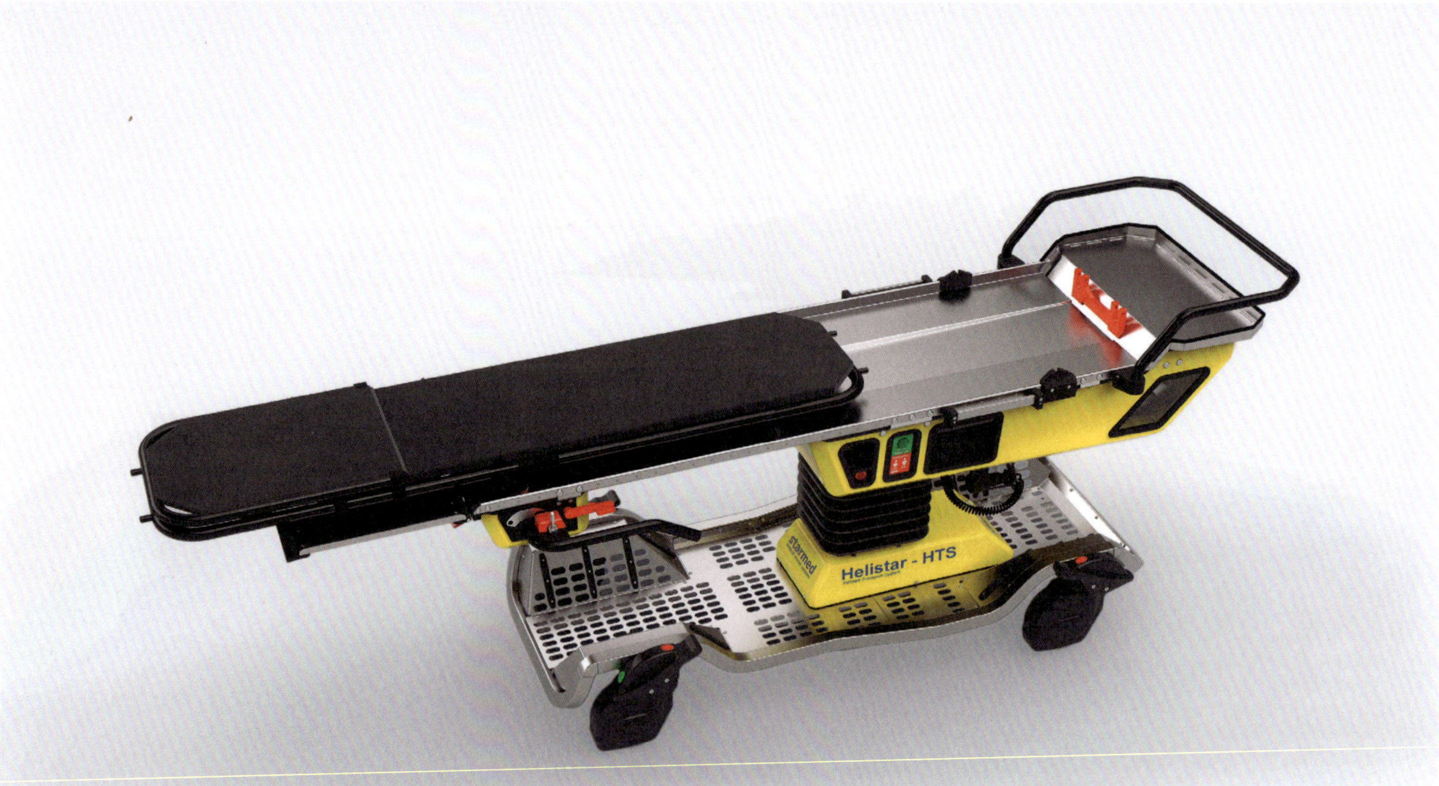
starmed
Helistar - HTS

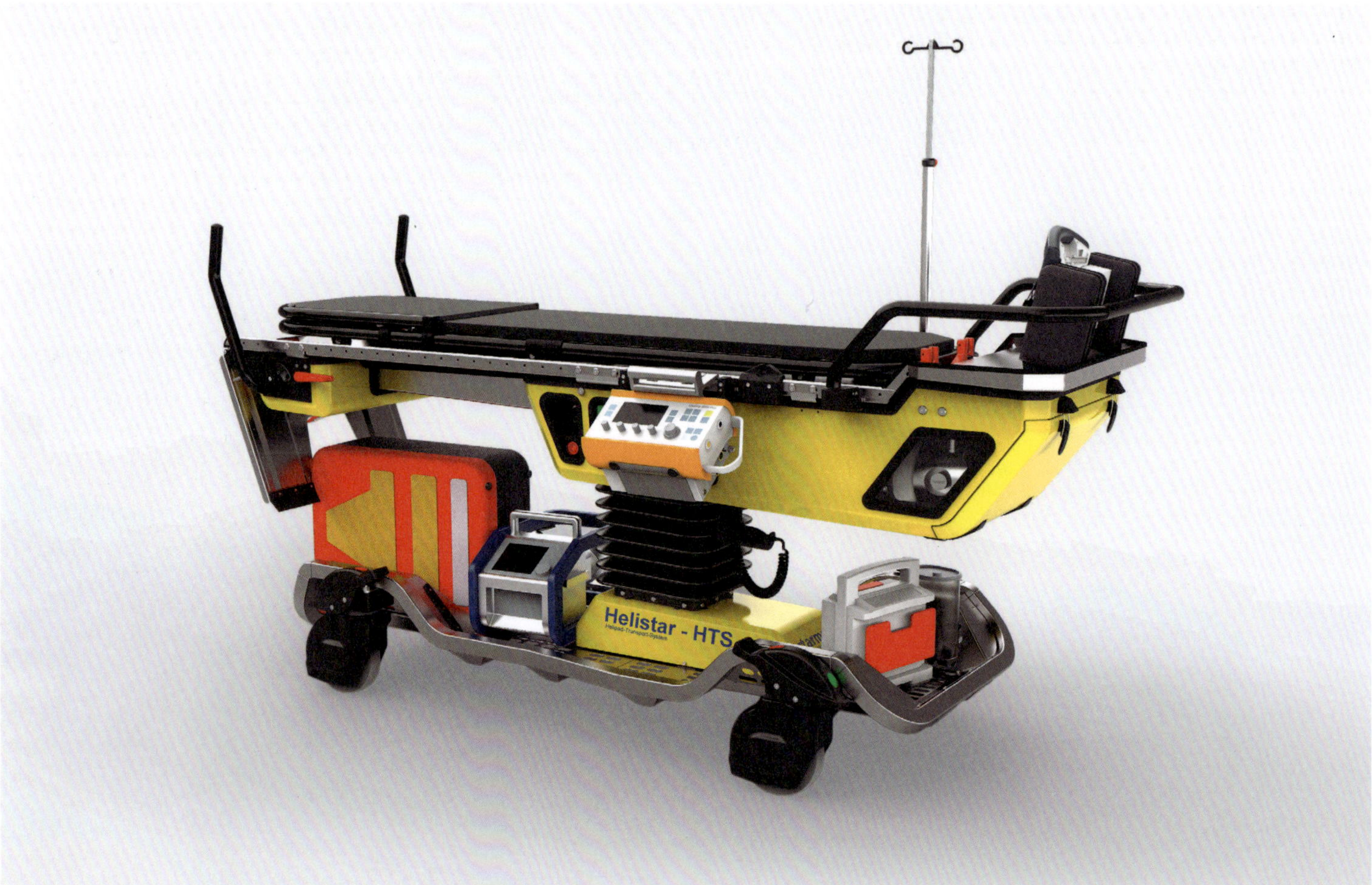
Helistar - HTS

GOLD — HELISTAR-HTS — LANDEPLATZTRANSPORTER / HELIPAD TRANSFER PLATFORM

JURY STATEMENT

Ein sehr beeindruckendes Produkt – nichts ist hier zufällig, alles anwendungsbezogen durchentwickelt und gestaltet. Trotz der komplexen Funktionalitäten und der Forderung nach möglichst flexibler Nutzung wirkt das System optisch aufgeräumt, vermittelt Robustheit und Sicherheit. Es zeigt, dass Design gerade in Produktnischen erhebliche Verbesserungen bewirken kann.

A very impressive product. Nothing here is random; every element has been carefully designed for this specific application. Despite its advanced features and versatility, the system boasts a clear design that inspires confidence in its reliability and safety. It shows that smart design can drive major gains, especially in niche markets.

HERSTELLER/MANUFACTURER
StarMed GmbH –
medical rescue systems
Stetten am Bodensee

DESIGN
Inhouse/In-house

Ist der Rettungshelikopter an der Klinik gelandet, werden die meist schwer traumatisierten Patientinnen und Patienten samt jenem Equipment, das sie konstant versorgt, umgeladen. Und zwar auf Landeplatztransporter, wie die höhenverstellbaren Fahrgestelle genannt werden. All dies passiert unter hohem Zeitdruck und oft rauen Witterungsbedingungen. Aktuell sind die Transportgeräte funktional nicht durchdacht, unergonomisch und bieten wenig Platz für die Medizingeräte.

All diesen Problemen trägt das neu entwickelte und inzwischen patentierte System Rechnung: Es bietet definierte Plätze für Geräte, den Notfallrucksack sowie Sauerstoffflaschen. Die Bedienung und das Handling wurden ergonomisch optimiert, alle Elemente lassen sich auch mit Handschuhen bedienen und sind in weiten Teilen selbsterklärend. Gewicht, Robustheit und Reinigungsfähigkeit sind wesentliche Kriterien für Werkstoffwahl und Formdetails. Auf der Ladefläche finden unterschiedlichste Tragen sicheren Halt, damit lässt sich das System nahezu universell verwenden.

Once they have landed on the helipad, critically injured patients must be swiftly transferred to hospital along with the medical equipment needed to ensure uninterrupted care. These critical patients are transferred using special height-adjustable platforms. Every second counts as the team works under great time pressure and often in brutal weather conditions. Today's medical transport platforms often fall short in terms of ergonomics and functionality and offer limited space for essential medical equipment.

This newly developed, patented system tackles these limitations head-on and features dedicated compartments for essential equipment, the emergency backpack and oxygen cylinders. The intuitive and ergonomic design enables medical personnel to operate all functions even when wearing gloves. Weight, durability and ease of cleaning were key criteria for the selection of materials and design details. The platform's compatibility with a wide array of stretchers means it can be deployed in virtually any scenario.

RENÉ STERN GESCHÄFTSFÜHRER,
STARMED GMBH

»Uns treibt eine Mischung aus Erfahrung und Ideenfreudigkeit.«

»We are driven by real-world experience and a passion for innovation.«

RENÉ STERN   **MANAGING DIRECTOR, STARMED GMBH**

Herr Stern, was eigentlich ist ein Landeplatztransportsystem?

Kurz gesagt: Es dient als Schnittstelle zwischen dem Rettungshubschrauber und der Klinik. Der Helikopter landet auf oder neben der Klinik, dann muss die Patientin oder der Patient sicher, schnell und auch kräftesparend zur Weiterbehandlung gebracht werden. Das ist nicht immer einfach, denn die Verletzten werden durch umfangreiches medizinisches Equipment begleitet, das unterbrechungsfrei mit umgeladen werden muss.

Es ist schon überraschend, wie optimierungsfähig manche medizinische Bereiche noch sind. Wie sind Sie auf den Helikopter-Usecase gestoßen?

Uns treibt eine Mischung aus Erfahrung und Ideenfreudigkeit. Das Angebot an Systemen, mit denen die Verletzten vom Landeplatz in die Klinik gebracht werden, ist im Grunde nicht zeitgemäß. Die aktuell erhältlichen Transporter sind ergonomisch schlecht, optisch nicht ansprechend, unflexibel und entsprechen nicht den aktuellen Anforderungen. So bieten sie zum Beispiel zu wenig Platz für die Ausrüstung, also für mobile Versorgungsgeräte. Das führt dazu, dass einzelne Geräte nicht nur im Helikopter, wo gleiche Platzprobleme herrschen, sondern auch bei der Übergabe auf den Patientinnen und Patienten abgelegt werden.

Der Helistar verbindet zwei spezielle Sphären – die Klinik am Boden und das Rettungsvehikel aus der Luft. Auf welcher Seite waren die Herausforderungen größer?

Unsere Ansprechpartner waren die Kliniken, hier sind die Anforderungen komplexer. Landeplätze sind zwar prinzipiell normiert, aber nicht immer direkt neben oder auf der Klinik. Also müssen mitunter längere Wege mit unterschiedlichen Belägen oder Querrillen zurückgelegt werden. Das bedeutet großen Kraftaufwand und gefährliche Erschütterungen für die Patientinnen und Patienten. Unser Helistar ist bewusst schwer, denn mehr Masse bedeutet weniger Vibrationen. Die Anbindung an den Helikopter ist weniger herausfordernd. Es gibt zwar unterschiedliche Typen mit abweichenden Beladehöhen sowie Heck- oder Seitenbeladung. Aber das lässt sich vergleichsweise einfach abbilden.

Mr Stern, what exactly is a helipad transfer system?

In a word, it's a system that facilitates the movement of patients between a rescue helicopter and a hospital. When a rescue helicopter lands on or near a hospital, the patient has to be transported safely, quickly and efficiently to the hospital for further treatment. Patient transfers are often complex due to the extensive life-sustaining equipment that must accompany the patient throughout the process.

It's surprising how much some areas of medicine can be improved. How did you come across the helicopter use case?

We are driven by real-world experience and a passion for innovation. The systems currently being used to transport patients from helipads to hospitals are basically outdated. The transport systems currently available are ergonomically inadequate and visually unappealing. They also lack flexibility and don't meet current requirements. For example, they don't provide enough space for the equipment needed to provide proper patient care. As a result, some of the equipment must be stored in the helicopter, which also lacks space, and on the patients themselves during patient transfer.

The Helistar bridges the gap between ground-based medical care and airborne rescue. Which environment presented the greatest design challenges?

We were in direct contact with hospitals, whose requirements are more complex. Although helipads are generally standardised, they aren't always located right next to or on the hospital building. This means that sometimes long distances have to be covered across varying terrain, including uneven surfaces that require a great deal of effort to negotiate and generate harmful vibrations for the patients. Our Helistar is purposely heavy because more mass means less vibration. The helicopter environment is less challenging. While there are many types of helicopters with different loading heights and rear or side access, developing a solution that accommodates these differences is relatively straightforward.

RENÉ STERN GESCHÄFTSFÜHRER, STARMED GMBH

Nämlich wie?
Durch eine elektrische Höhenverstellung der Trageaufnahmeplatte um 40 Zentimeter. Mit ihr kommen wir auch dem eigentlichen Ziel näher, die Übergabe rascher und reibungsloser zu machen. Das ist gut für die Verletzten und der Hubschrauber steht schneller für den nächsten Einsatz bereit.
Die Problematik der Querrillen haben wir übrigens mit einer neuen, patentierten Rolle gelöst, die aus drei Rädern besteht und das Eintauchen in die Vertiefungen verhindert. Insgesamt lässt sich das System sehr agil bewegen.

Was haben Sie aus den Erprobungen vor Ort einfließen lassen?
Wir sind mit unseren Entwicklungen immer schon sehr nahe an der Serientauglichkeit, lernen aber immer wieder dazu. Zum Beispiel haben wir festgestellt, dass wir trotz unseres Ansatzes, möglichst viel selbsterklärend zu gestalten, diesbezüglich noch mehr tun müssen. Hingegen hatten wir die Bedienbarkeit mit Handschuhen schon früh im Blick, schließlich passiert das alles unter rauen Witterungsbedingungen. Auch das Gerät selbst musste möglichst robust ausgelegt werden.

Wie lange braucht es für die Entwicklung eines so komplexen Gerätes?
Insgesamt dürften das um die fünf Jahre gewesen sein, aber wir haben zwischenzeitlich mehrmonatige Unterbrechungen gehabt, weil andere Themen anstanden und wir diese nicht parallel abarbeiten konnten.

Sie produzieren möglichst viel in Deutschland, warum?
Wir sind ein kleines Unternehmen, das keine Großserien produziert. Daher arbeiten wir mit Partnern zusammen, die möglichst aus der Region kommen und flexibel sind. Da die deutsche Industrie primär auf Großserien ausgelegt ist, suchen wir oft lange nach passenden Lieferanten. Parallel dazu haben wir unsere eigene Fertigungstiefe ausgebaut. Und wir vermeiden bestimmte Produktionstechniken, zum Beispiel Spritzguss, weil die Stückzahlen zu gering sind. Stattdessen setzen wir auf 3D-Druckverfahren, vor allem bei Anbauteilen.

Mit welchen Stückzahlen rechnen Sie?
Das ist nicht so einfach, aber ich gehe davon aus, dass wir etwa 100 Einheiten in sechs Jahren verkaufen werden. Auf diesen Wert skalieren wir auch die Produktion.

Starmed wurde 1998 gegründet und hat sich auf die Entwicklung und Produktion von Systemen für den Patienten- und Gerätetransport im Rahmen der Intensivmedizin spezialisiert. So entwickelte das Unternehmen das erste, seriell produzierte Intensiv-Transportsystem. Außerdem agiert das neunköpfige, interdisziplinäre Team als Entwicklungsdienstleister für Rettungsdienste, für Kliniken oder Medizingerätehersteller. Gründer René Stern kann auf jahrelange eigene Erfahrungen in der boden- und luftgebundenen Rettung zurückgreifen.

www.starmed.eu

RENÉ STERN — MANAGING DIRECTOR, STARMED GMBH

How?
By electrically adjusting the height of the stretcher support by up to 40 centimetres. This also helps us achieve our goal of making the transfer quicker and smoother. It is good for the patients and the helicopter can be made ready for its next mission more quickly.

Incidentally, we have solved the problem of negotiating laterally groove surfaces with a new, patented, three-wheeled roller system that prevents the Helistar from dipping into the grooves. On the whole, the system is exceptionally manoeuvrable.

What have you incorporated as a result of your on-site trials?
Even when our products are on the brink of being production-ready, we consistently uncover new areas for improvement. For example, despite our strong focus on intuitive product design, we still identified opportunities to elevate the user experience. However, we focused at an early stage on good usability with gloves because the product is frequently used in harsh weather conditions. We also had to make sure the unit was as robust as possible.

How long does it take to develop such a complex device?
It probably took around five years in total, but there were gaps of several months when we had other issues to deal with and couldn't work on everything at the same time.

Why do you concentrate production primarily in Germany?
We are a small company with small production runs. That's why, whenever possible, we prefer to work with partners who are local and flexible. Finding suitable suppliers can often prove time-consuming because German industry is geared primarily towards mass production. At the same time, we have increased vertical integration within the company. And we avoid certain techniques, such as injection moulding, because our production quantities are too small. We use 3D printing instead, especially for ancillary equipment.

How many units do you expect to sell?
That's not easy to say, but I reckon we'll sell around 100 units over six years. We are also scaling our production accordingly.

Founded in 1998, Starmed specialises in the development and production of intensive care patient and equipment transport systems. The company developed the first intensive care transport system to be produced in quantity. The nine-strong interdisciplinary team also acts as a development service provider for emergency services, hospitals and medical device manufacturers. Founder René Stern has extensive experience in ground and air rescue operations.

www.starmed.eu

| SPECIAL MENTION | CITYCADDY
→ SEITE/PAGE 64 | GEHHILFE
MOBILITY AID |

SPECIAL MENTION OKUSTIM NEUROSTIMULATOR NEUROSTIMULATOR

→ SEITE/PAGE 65

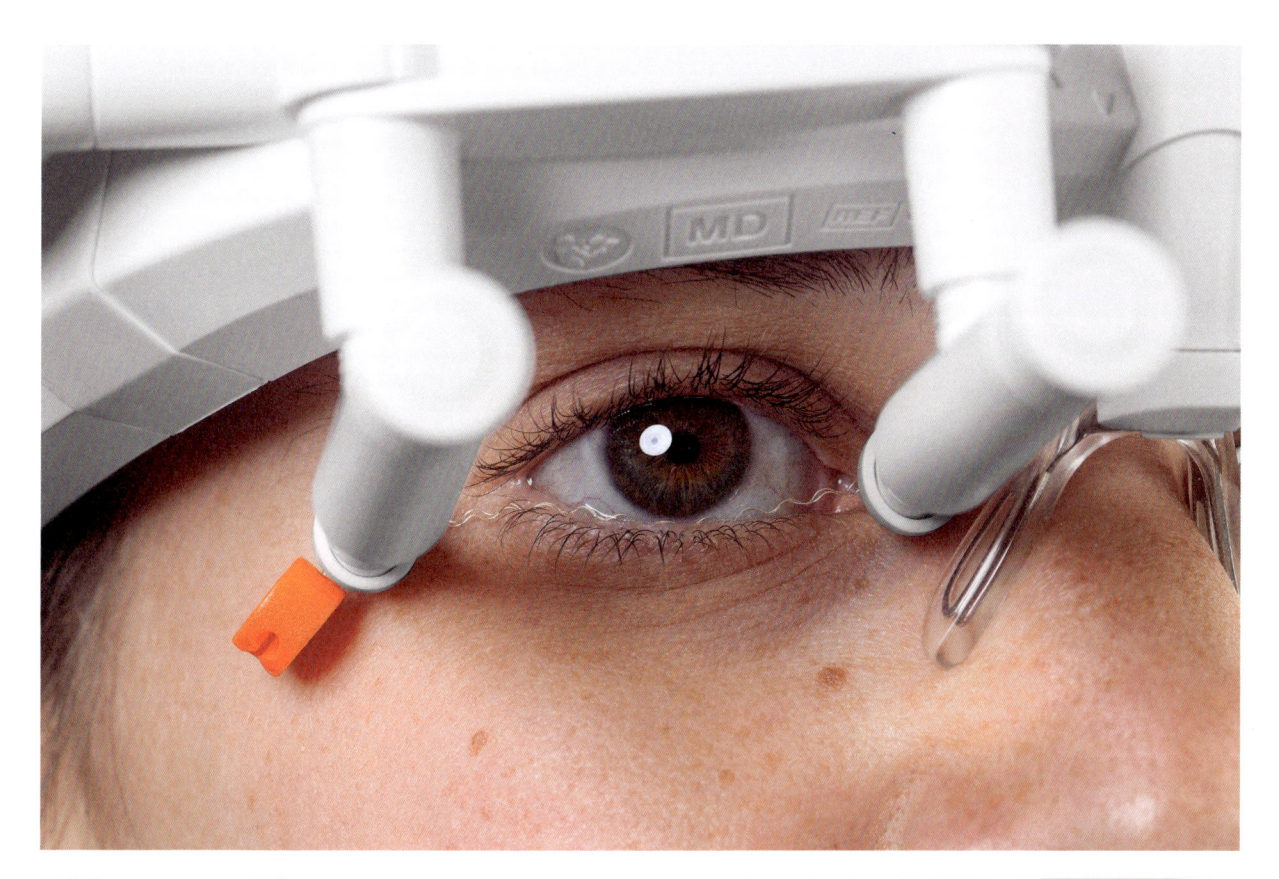

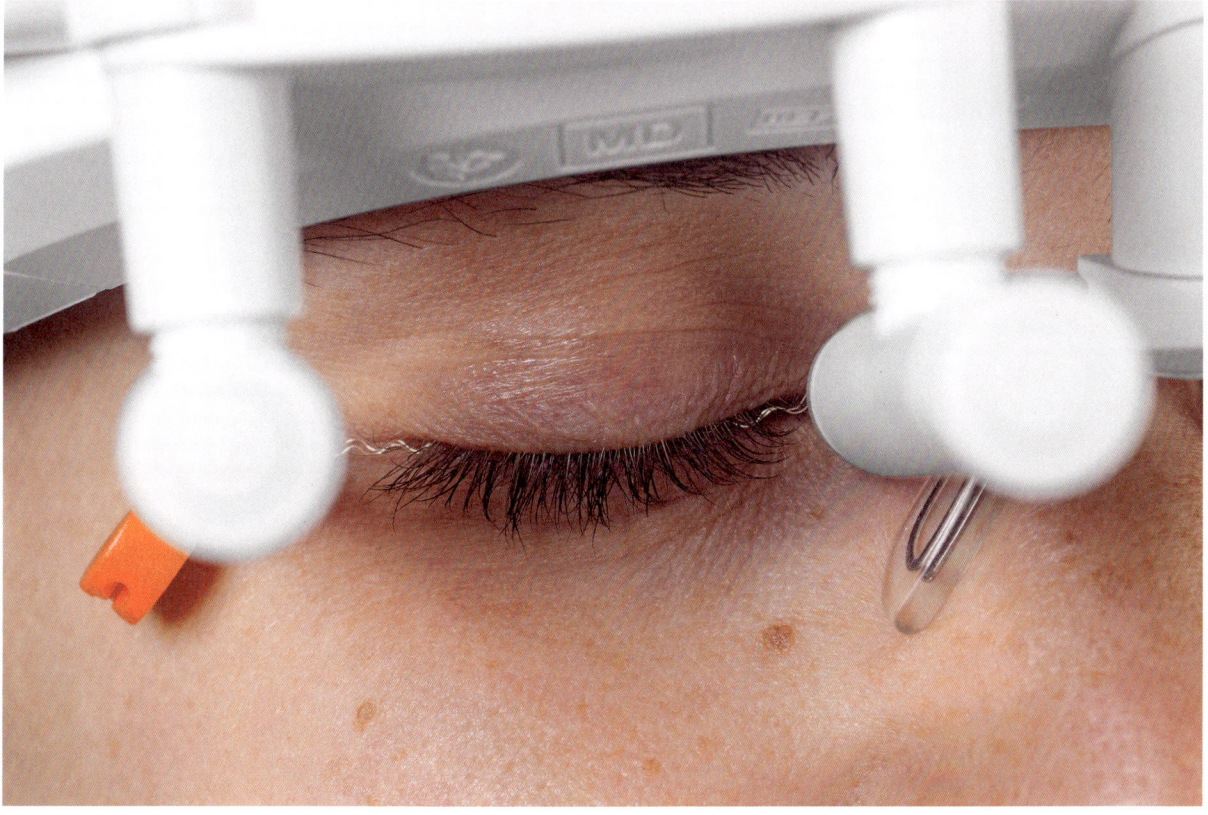

SPECIAL MENTION **CITYCADDY** **GEHHILFE
MOBILITY AID**

> **JURY STATEMENT**
>
> Ein positives Produkt, entstigmatisierend, würdevoll und praktisch. Der CityCaddy beweist, wie man Rollatoren anders entwickelt und dass Unterstützungsprodukte für ältere Menschen ästhetisch sein können, ja müssen. Verwundert es, dass die Gestalterin selbst Nutzerin ist?
>
> An empowering product, confidence-boosting and elegantly functional. The CityCaddy breaks the stereotype of mobility aids and shows that support products for older adults can – indeed must – be aesthetically pleasing. It is perhaps unsurprising that the designer is a user herself.

HERSTELLER/MANUFACTURER
CityCaddy UG (haftungsbeschränkt)
Hamburg

DESIGN
Elke Jensen
Hamburg

Unsere Gesellschaft altert zunehmend. Doch viele Produkte und Angebote, die auf die Bedürfnisse einer älteren Zielgruppe zugeschnitten sind, lassen es noch an Innovationsfreude, gutem Design und Gestaltungswillen fehlen. Nach wie vor zeigen sich beispielsweise viele ältere Menschen nicht gern mit einem Rollator – zu sehr haftet ihm das Stigma der Gebrechlichkeit an. Der CityCaddy verfolgt hier einen neuen Ansatz: Er ist zwar sichtbar eine Gehhilfe, fördert aber durch seine neu gedachte Form, hochwertige Materialien und starke Farben ein positives Altersbild. Der Caddy besteht aus einem Trolley samt abnehmbarer Tasche und kann sowohl geschoben als auch gezogen werden. Er ist höhenverstellbar, der ovale, lederbezogene Griff erlaubt den Händen ermüdungsfreies Greifen. Bei der Fertigung kommen so gut wie keine Verbundstoffe zum Einsatz, der Fokus liegt auf der Möglichkeit des Reparierens und Wiederaufarbeitens.

We are living in a world with an increasingly ageing population. However, many products and services tailored to the needs of an older target group still lack innovation, good design and creative flair. Many older people are reluctant to make use of a rollator because of the stigma of frailty attached to it. The CityCaddy takes a fresh look at this problem. Although it is clearly a mobility aid, its re-imagined form, high-quality materials and strong colours promote a positive image of older adults. The caddy, which consists of a trolley and a removable bag, can be pulled as well as pushed. The height-adjustable design features an oval, leather-covered handle for comfortable, fatigue-free use. For easy repair and future recycling, the product is built with minimal composite materials.

SPECIAL MENTION   **OKUSTIM**   **NEUROSTIMULATOR**
NEUROSTIMULATOR

JURY STATEMENT

Auf den ersten Blick ist das Gerät von einer visuellen Vielfalt geprägt, die aber den vielen Justierungsoptionen geschuldet ist. Hervorzuheben ist die sehr einfach handhabbare Platzierung der Elektroden. Insgesamt ein System, das die Selbstbestimmung von Patientinnen und Patienten beispielhaft voranbringt.

The device may seem complex at first but this is because it offers so many adjustment options. The quick and easy placement of the electrodes deserves special mention. All in all, this system empowers patients to confidently manage their condition at home.

HERSTELLER/MANUFACTURER
Okuvision GmbH
Reutlingen

DESIGN
defortec GmbH
Dettenhausen

Rund drei Millionen Menschen leiden weltweit unter Retinitis pigmentosa, einer Netzhautdegeneration, die meist genetisch bedingt ist und als häufigste Ursache für den Sehverlust im mittleren Alter gilt. Mit dem OkuStim-System steht nun eine nicht-invasive Therapiemethode bereit, die den Verlauf zumindest verlangsamen kann. Die transkorneale Elektrostimulation aktiviert mit schwachen Stromimpulsen entzündungshemmende Prozesse in der Netzhaut.

Mit dem neuen OkuStim-System lässt sich diese Stimulation regelmäßig und ohne medizinische Assistenz durchführen. Kern ist das Headset, das den eigentlichen Neurostimulator wie auch die vielfach justierbaren Schwenkeinheiten für die Elektroden integriert. Die fadenartigen Elektroden werden vor der Anwendung frisch eingesetzt und dafür, hygienisch optimiert, speziellen Blisterverpackungen entnommen. Orangefarbene Plomben und magnetische Fixierungen gewährleisten die richtige Positionierung.

An estimated three million people globally have retinitis pigmentosa, an inherited retinal disease that is the leading cause of vision loss in middle age. The OkuStim system offers a non-invasive therapy method designed to slow the progression of the disease. Transcorneal stimulation is a therapy that delivers weak electrical impulses that activate anti-inflammatory processes in the retina.

The new OkuStim system allows this low-level electrical stimulation to be carried out regularly and without the need for medical assistance. The centrepiece is the headset, which incorporates the neurostimulator and the adjustable electrode holders. The thread-like electrodes are supplied in special blister packs for single use. Orange-coloured seals and magnetic fixings ensure correct positioning.

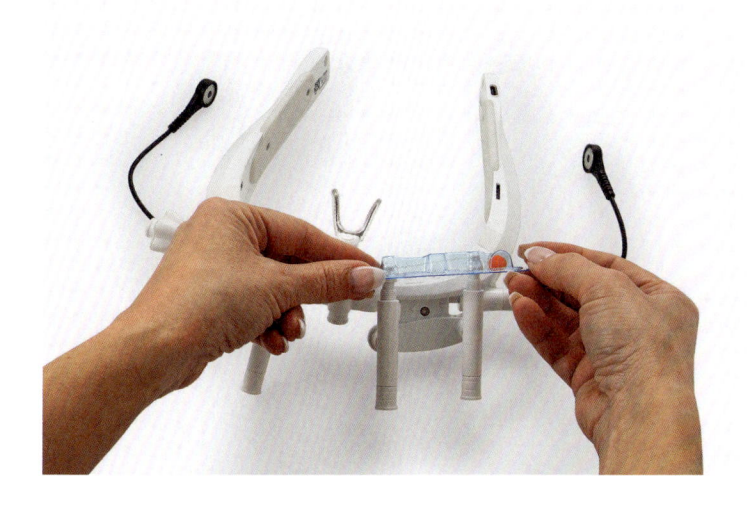

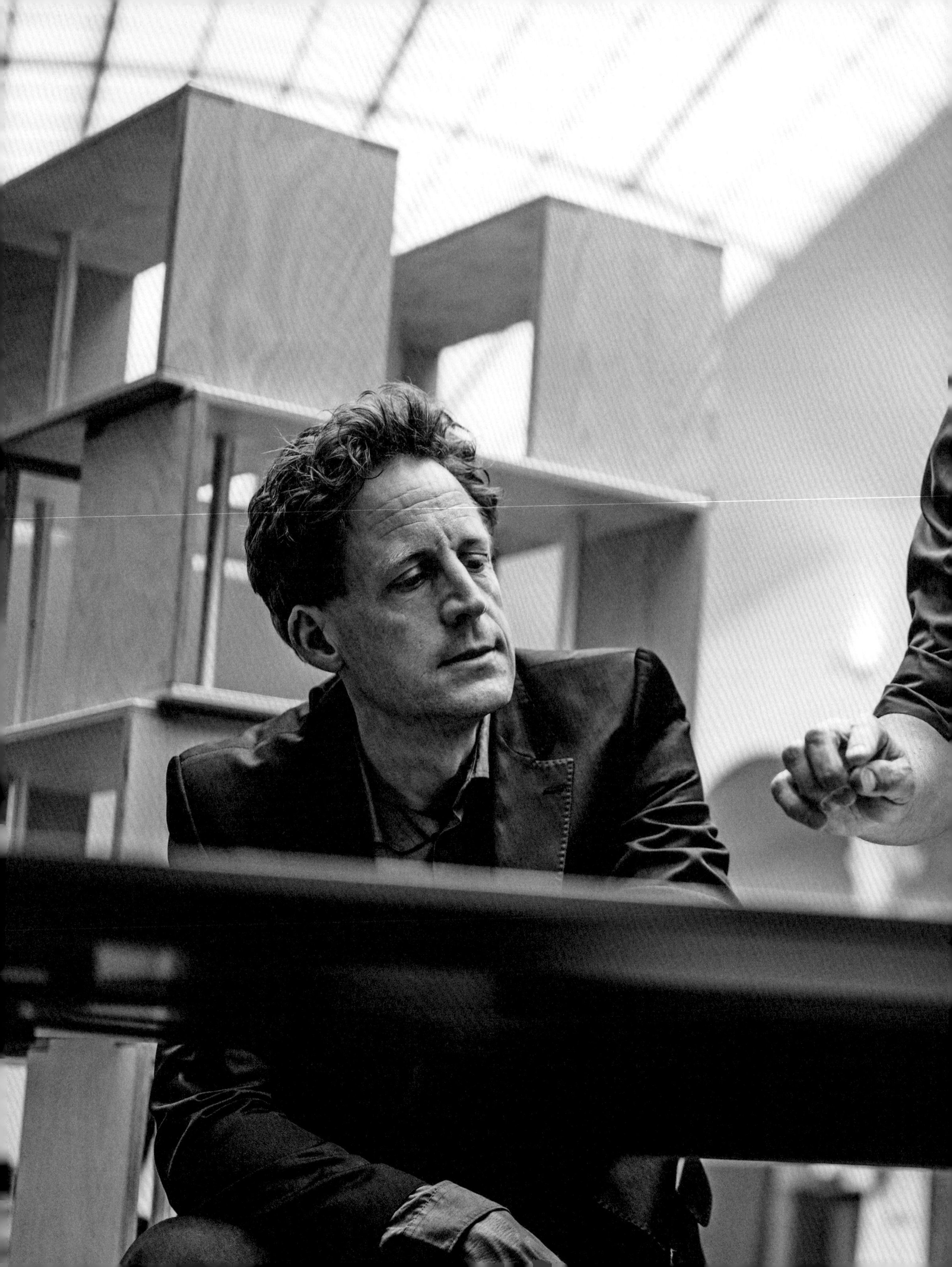

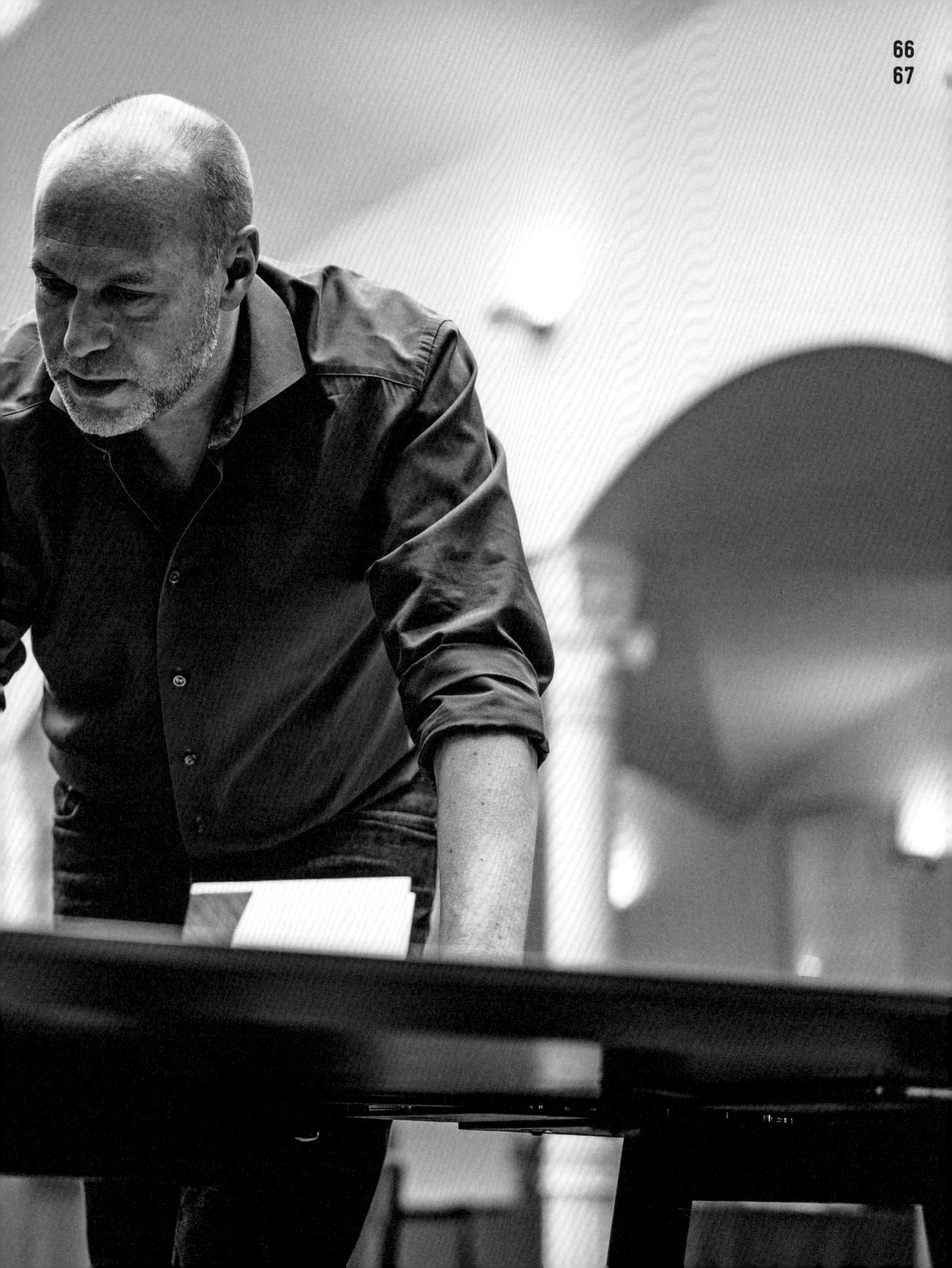

1 → SEITE/PAGE
70–71

KÜCHE, HAUSHALT, TISCHKULTUR
KITCHEN, HOUSEHOLD, TABLE

SPECIAL MENTION:
1 **BLUE FIZZ STATION**
Grohe AG
Düsseldorf

Die Technisierung des Haushalts schreitet weiter voran, dabei brillieren hier Produkte, die den Alltag mit neuen Lösungen erleichtern und nutzungsorientiert konzipiert sowie gestaltet sind. Design sorgt hier für emotionale Aufladung und Zugänglichkeit.

The home technology sector is constantly innovating and introducing new products and solutions designed and engineered to make our lives easier. Here, design not only prioritises user-centred concepts but also fosters a strong emotional connection while maintaining accessibility.

4

SPECIAL MENTION

BLUE FIZZ STATION
→ SEITE/PAGE 71

WASSERSPRUDLER
WATER CARBONATOR

SPECIAL MENTION — BLUE FIZZ STATION — WASSERSPRUDLER / WATER CARBONATOR

JURY STATEMENT

Ein sauber durchgestaltetes Produkt, das sich formal geschickt zurücknimmt. Damit passt es problemlos in unterschiedlichste Küchen- oder Wohnumgebungen, ohne dabei laut oder gar aufdringlich zu wirken. Praktisch ist die Anzeige der Restmenge in der Kartusche.

This product's clean lines and subtle design allow it to blend effortlessly into a wide variety of kitchen and room aesthetics. The CO_2 level indicator is a useful feature.

HERSTELLER/MANUFACTURER
Grohe AG
Düsseldorf

DESIGN
LIXIL Global Design
Düsseldorf

Kistenweise schwere Sprudelflaschen nach Hause zu schleppen, davon haben sich mittlerweile viele Haushalte verabschiedet. Wassersprudler, die Leitungswasser durch eine Karbonisierung per Knopfdruck in ein sprudelndes Getränk verwandeln, liegen im Trend. Hier setzt der Blue Fizz in Sachen Handling und Individualität neue Maßstäbe: Über einen Drehknopf oben am Gerät können Nutzerinnen und Nutzer vorab die Menge an CO_2 wählen, mit der das Wasser aufgesprudelt werden soll – von leicht über medium bis stark sprudelnd. Die One-Push-Technology sorgt dafür, dass für die Karbonisierung des Wassers ein einzelner Knopfdruck ausreicht, die verbleibende Kapazität des CO_2-Zylinders lässt sich über ein Display ablesen. Mit seiner schlanken, minimalistischen Formgebung und drei zurückhaltenden Farbvarianten fügt sich der Wassersprudler in jede Küchenumgebung ein.

Carrying heavy crates of sparkling water home is now a thing of the past for many households, as water carbonators continue to gain popularity as a convenient and eco-friendly alternative. Blue Fizz, with its innovative features, takes water carbonators to the next level. For example, a rotary knob conveniently located on top of the machine allows the user to preset the carbonation level – from light to medium to highly sparkling. Thanks to the station's one-push technology, a single push carbonates the water perfectly, while a built-in display shows how much CO_2 is left in the gas cylinder. With its sleek, minimalist design and three understated colour options, this sparkling water maker blends seamlessly into any kitchen environment.

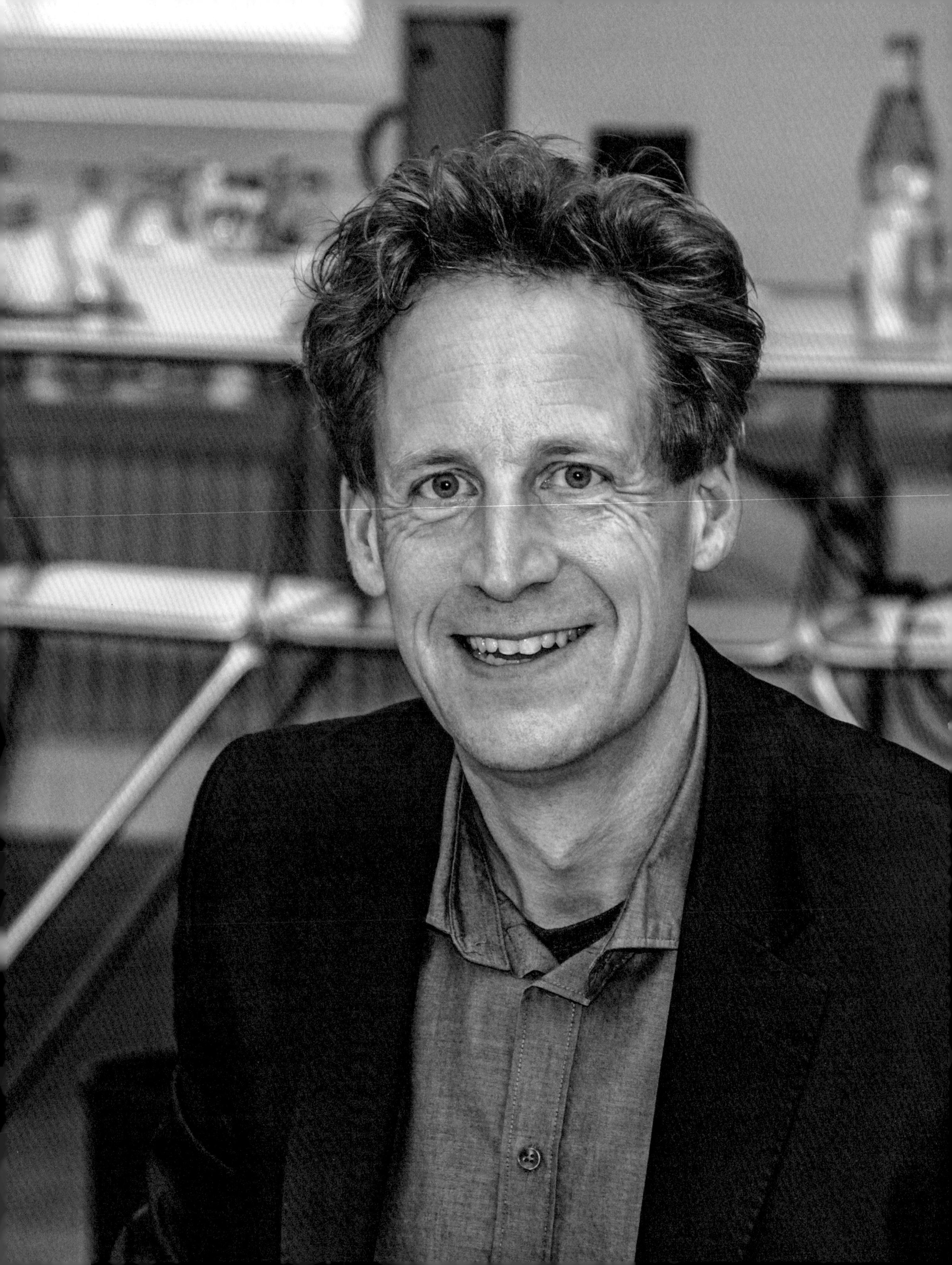

ANDREAS BRUNKHORST — **BRAUN-STEINE GMBH, AMSTETTEN**

»Beim FOCUS OPEN setzt man sich als Jury intensiv und leidenschaftlich mit dem Thema Innovation auseinander. Das macht den Award so reizvoll.«

»The FOCUS OPEN jury meticulously evaluates the innovative qualities of each entry. That's what makes the award so appealing.«

Andreas Brunkhorst studierte an der Dualen Hochschule in Mosbach Bauingenieurwesen. Er sammelte über viele Jahre Erfahrung in der Betonstein- und Keramikbranche; seit 2016 arbeitet er bei braun-steine als Leiter des Innovationsmanagements, um in der Forschung neue, konstruktive Materiallösungen für mineralische Bauelemente zu finden.

www.braun-steine.de

Andreas Brunkhorst studied civil engineering at the Baden-Wuerttemberg Cooperative State University in Mosbach. With many years of experience in the concrete block and ceramic industry, he has been head of the innovation management department at braun-steine since 2016, focusing on research into new constructive material solutions for mineral building elements.

www.braun-steine.de

1 → SEITE/PAGE
76, 80

2 → SEITE/PAGE
77, 81

3 → SEITE/PAGE
78, 82

4 → SEITE/PAGE
79, 83

INTERIOR
INTERIORS

SILVER:
1 **MORPH**
   dBcover Solutions® S.L.
   Elda, Spanien/Spain

SPECIAL MENTION:
2 **SLIDE CONNECT**
   Wilhelm Renz GmbH + Co. KG
   Böblingen

3 **THEHOCKER**
   PARO DESIGN®
   Stuttgart

4 **BOOL**
   UnternehmenForm GmbH & Co. KG
   Stuttgart

Ein Stuhl, ein Tisch, ein Bett und ein Regal – was braucht man mehr? Und doch ist das Universum der Möbel immens weit, wandelt sich stetig, erneuert sich und spielt mit Volumina, Materialien, Oberflächen, Farben. Möbeldesign ist eine der populärsten Gestaltungsdisziplinen, die heutzutage von den Prämissen Flexibilität, Nachhaltigkeit und Funktionalität gefordert wird.

A chair, a table, a bed and a shelf – what more could anyone want? And yet the world of furniture is huge, changes constantly, reinvents itself and plays with volumes, materials, finishes and colours. Furniture design is one of the most popular design disciplines of all – and today faces totally new challenges in terms of flexibility, sustainability and functionality.

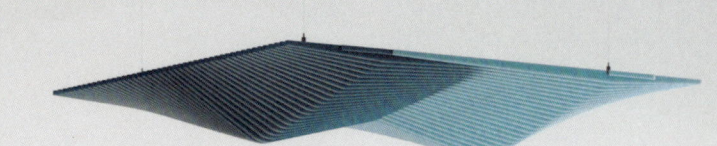

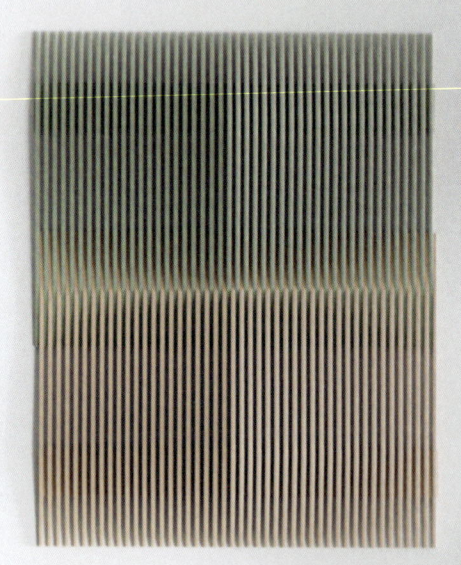

SILVER   MORPH   AKUSTIKSYSTEM
                      ACOUSTIC SYSTEM
         → SEITE/PAGE
           80

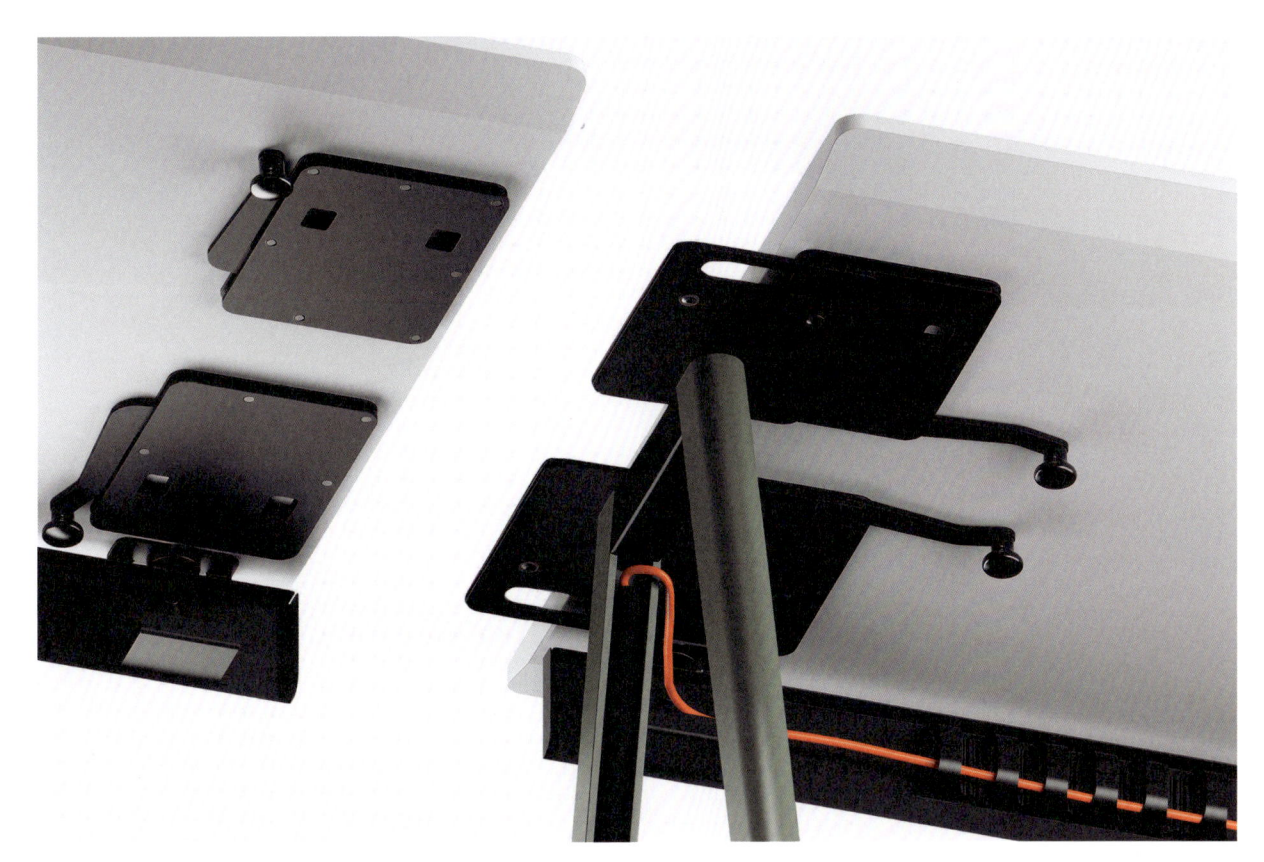

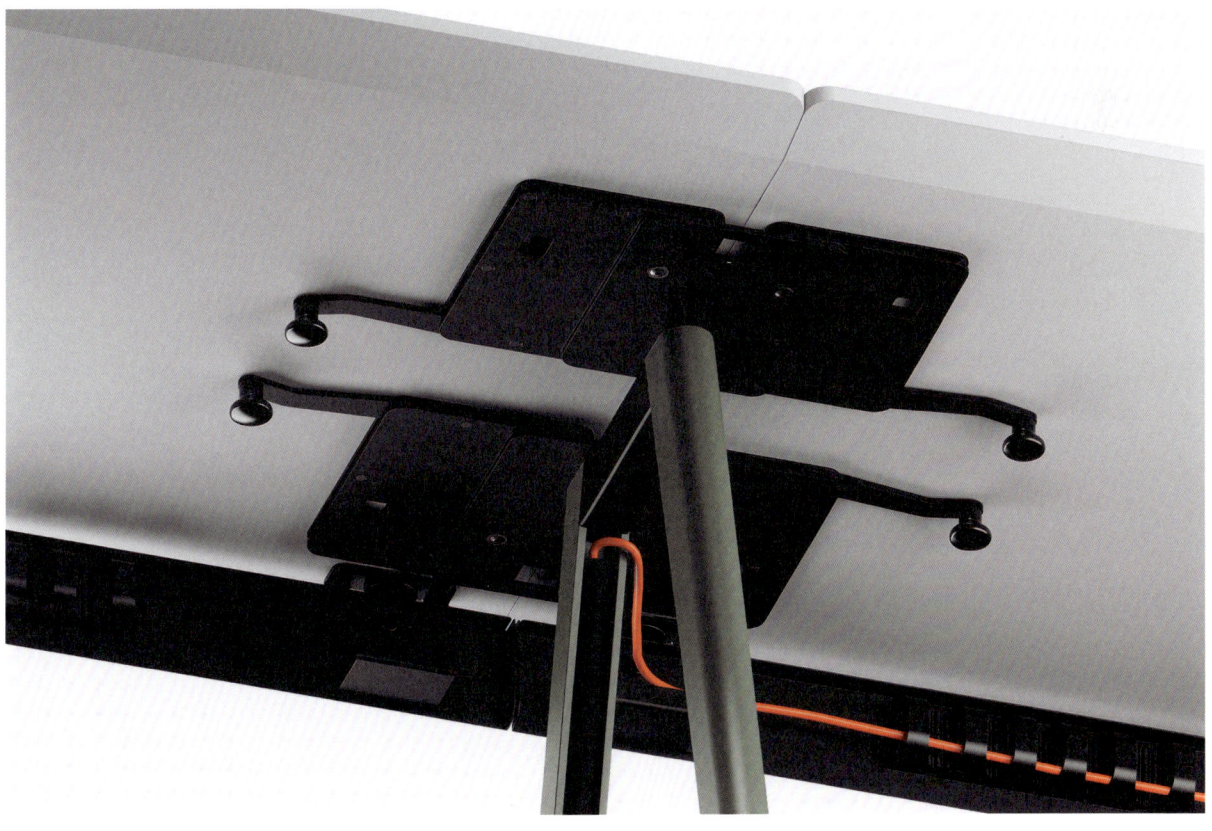

SPECIAL MENTION

SLIDE CONNECT
→ SEITE/PAGE 81

KONFERENZTISCHSYSTEM
CONFERENCE TABLE SYSTEM

| SPECIAL MENTION | THEHOCKER → SEITE/PAGE 82 | SITZMÖBEL SEATING |

| SPECIAL MENTION | BOOL | REGALSYSTEM |
| | → SEITE/PAGE 83 | SHELVING SYSTEM |

SILVER

MORPH

AKUSTIKSYSTEM
ACOUSTIC SYSTEM

> **JURY STATEMENT**
>
> Ein ästhetisch sehr ansprechendes und vielseitig verwendbares System, das aus Monomaterial besteht und in diversen Farben angeboten wird. Damit lassen sich auch freistehende Lösungen ohne zusätzliche Aussteifungen umsetzen, etwa für mobile Zonierungen.
>
> An aesthetically pleasing and versatile system made of monomaterial and available in a choice of colours. It can also be used without additional bracing to create free-standing solutions such as mobile partitions.

HERSTELLER/MANUFACTURER
dBcover Solutions® S.L.
Elda, Spanien/Spain

DESIGN
MOJA Design GmbH
Stuttgart

In modern gestalteten, großen Räumlichkeiten wie Büros, Foyers, Restaurants, Bars oder Hotellobbys finden häufig schallharte Materialien wie Beton und Glas Verwendung. Dann sind schallabsorbierende Maßnahmen und Lösungen gefragt, um die Raumakustik zu verbessern.

Dieses Akustiksystem besteht aus Wand- und Deckenpaneelen sowie Raumtrennern. Die besondere Lamellenstruktur der Elemente sorgt für hohe Absorptionswerte und ist mit unterschiedlichsten Farbvarianten gleichzeitig ästhetischer Blickfang. Mehrere Paneele können zusammengesteckt und unterschiedlich weit ineinandergeschoben werden – so lassen sie sich an unterschiedlichste Raumhöhen anpassen. In den Elementen aus PET-Vlies steckt ein hoher Anteil an wiederverwerteten Einweg-PET-Produkten.

Modern, open spaces like offices, foyers, and restaurants often feature hard surfaces like concrete and glass that can contribute to poor acoustics. Sound-absorbing treatments are essential to mitigate these issues and create a comfortable acoustic environment.

This acoustic treatment system consists of wall and ceiling panels as well as room dividers. In addition to providing exceptional sound absorption, the unique lamella structure of the elements offers a visually striking appearance with a diverse colour palette. Multiple panels can be combined and adjusted to various heights, accommodating a wide range of room sizes. The PET fleece used in the panels contains a high proportion of recycled PET products.

SPECIAL MENTION **SLIDE CONNECT** **KONFERENZTISCHSYSTEM / CONFERENCE TABLE SYSTEM**

JURY STATEMENT

Ein optisch sehr ansprechendes System mit interessanter Materialität und Farbigkeit. Trotz der reduzierten Formensprache bringt das System eine hochwertige, neue Atmosphäre mit Wohncharakter ins Büro.

A visually attractive system with interesting materials and colours. Despite its minimalist aesthetic, the system is capable of creating a premium office environment that feels like home.

HERSTELLER/MANUFACTURER
Wilhelm Renz GmbH + Co. KG
Böblingen

DESIGN
KASCHKASCH GbR
Köln

Nach wie vor sind physische Meetings der Goldstandard, wenn es um neue Ideen oder Konzepte geht. Speziell für agile Teams wurde dieses System entwickelt, das unterschiedlichste Konfigurationen erlaubt. Dazu gehören verschiedene Plattenformen, drei Tiefen, skalierbare Breiten sowie zwei Höhen. Mit diesen Komponenten können Einzeltische, Konferenztische und auch lange Teamtische in Stehhöhe realisiert werden. Die optisch leichten, A-förmigen Tischgestelle nehmen Kabel auf, Auslässe für Energie und Daten befinden sich zentral in den Tischplatten. Beine und Platten stehen farblich identisch oder bewusst kontrastierend zur Auswahl.

Physical meetings remain the best platform for developing and refining innovative concepts. This conference table system was developed specifically for meetings by agile teams. It allows for countless configurations, including customisable top shapes, three depth options, adjustable widths, and two height choices. Whether you need an individual workspace, a collaborative conference table or a high-standing team table, this system has you covered. The visually open, A-shaped table frames incorporate cable management, with power and data outlets conveniently positioned at the centre of the table. Legs and tabletops are available in matching or contrasting colours.

SPECIAL MENTION | THEHOCKER | SITZMÖBEL / SEATING

JURY STATEMENT

Ein klassisches Designobjekt, sehr einfach gedacht, aber auch sehr schlüssig auf das Minimum reduziert. Der Zusammenbau macht Spaß, der Prototyp mutet noch etwas roh an – aber vielleicht macht dies den besonderen Charme aus.

A classic design object, unpretentious but defined by its logical reduction to the purest form. Assembly is fun, although the prototype still looks slightly unfinished. That might be what gives it its special charm.

HERSTELLER/MANUFACTURER
PARO DESIGN®
Stuttgart

DESIGN
Inhouse/In-house

Werden schnell zusätzliche Sitzmöglichkeiten benötigt, kommt meist der universelle Hocker ins Spiel. Nicht selten ist das ein zwar nützliches, aber sperriges Möbel. Ganz anders dieser Hocker: Sein Charme liegt in der einfachen, werkzeuglosen Montage und der Möglichkeit des platzsparenden Aufbewahrens bei Nichtgebrauch. Beine und Sitzplatte bestehen aus FSC-zertifiziertem Multiplex, für den Einsatz werden sie ganz einfach zusammengesteckt. Mit 2,7 Kilogramm ist der Hocker fast ein Leichtgewicht, trägt aber bis zu 150 Kilogramm Gewicht. Gefertigt wird er in Baden-Württemberg.

When you need additional seating in a hurry, a multi-purpose stool is often a good choice. But while they are useful, stools can also be cumbersome. This one is different. The convenience of tool-free assembly combined with its space-saving design make it a desirable item of furniture. The legs and seat are made of FSC-certified plywood and simply slot together. At 2.7kg, the stool is relatively lightweight but can still support a weight of up to 150kg. It is manufactured in Baden-Württemberg.

SPECIAL MENTION BOOL REGALSYSTEM / SHELVING SYSTEM

JURY STATEMENT

Das Konzept spielt mit Sprüngen in Tiefe und Breite, die Böden laufen seitlich offen aus. Diese Lebendigkeit und die Simplizität des Strebenprinzips machen das Regal bemerkenswert.

A modern take on shelving with a captivating interplay of depth and width; the shelves are open and accessible from the side. The vibrant simplicity of the strut principle makes this shelf exceptional.

HERSTELLER/MANUFACTURER
UnternehmenForm GmbH & Co. KG
Stuttgart

DESIGN
Inhouse/In-house

Die klassische Büro-Arbeitswelt hat weitgehend ausgedient: Veränderte Arbeitsbedingungen wie agile Teams, flexible Raumnutzungen oder schnell wechselnde Aufgaben erfordern heute Büromöbel, die den Bedürfnissen derjenigen angepasst sind, die damit leben und arbeiten. Das Regalsystem, bestehend aus MDF-Platten und Verbindungselementen aus Aluminium, ist modular aufgebaut, lässt sich folglich zerlegen und in immer neuen Konfigurationen zusammenbauen. In Höhe und Breite ist es skalierbar, verschiedene Versteifungselemente erlauben eine sowohl offene als auch geschlossene Gestaltung als Raumteiler, freistehendes oder deckenhoch eingespanntes Regal. Die Produktion erfolgt nachhaltig und regional zu 90 Prozent in Süddeutschland.

The traditional office environment is becoming obsolete. As workstyles evolve with agile teams, flexible spaces and rapidly changing tasks, office furniture must adapt to meet the dynamic needs of today's workforce. This modular shelving system, constructed from MDF panels and aluminium connectors, allows for endless customisation through easy disassembly and reassembly. Scalable in both height and width, the system can be configured with stiffening components to create open or closed structures such as room dividers, for example, and free-standing or floor-to-ceiling shelving. 90 per cent of production is rooted in sustainable practices in southern Germany.

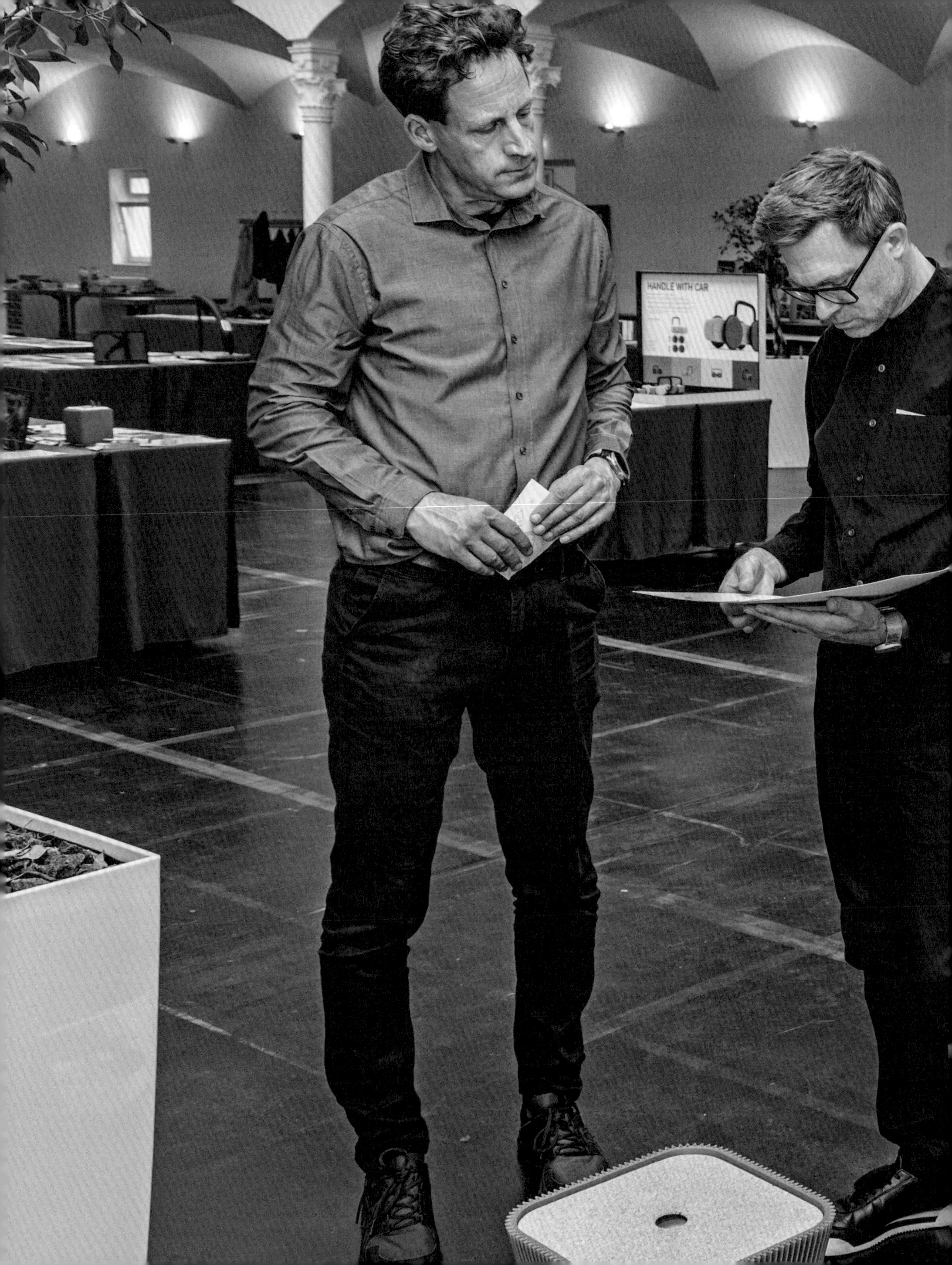
HANDLE WITH CAR

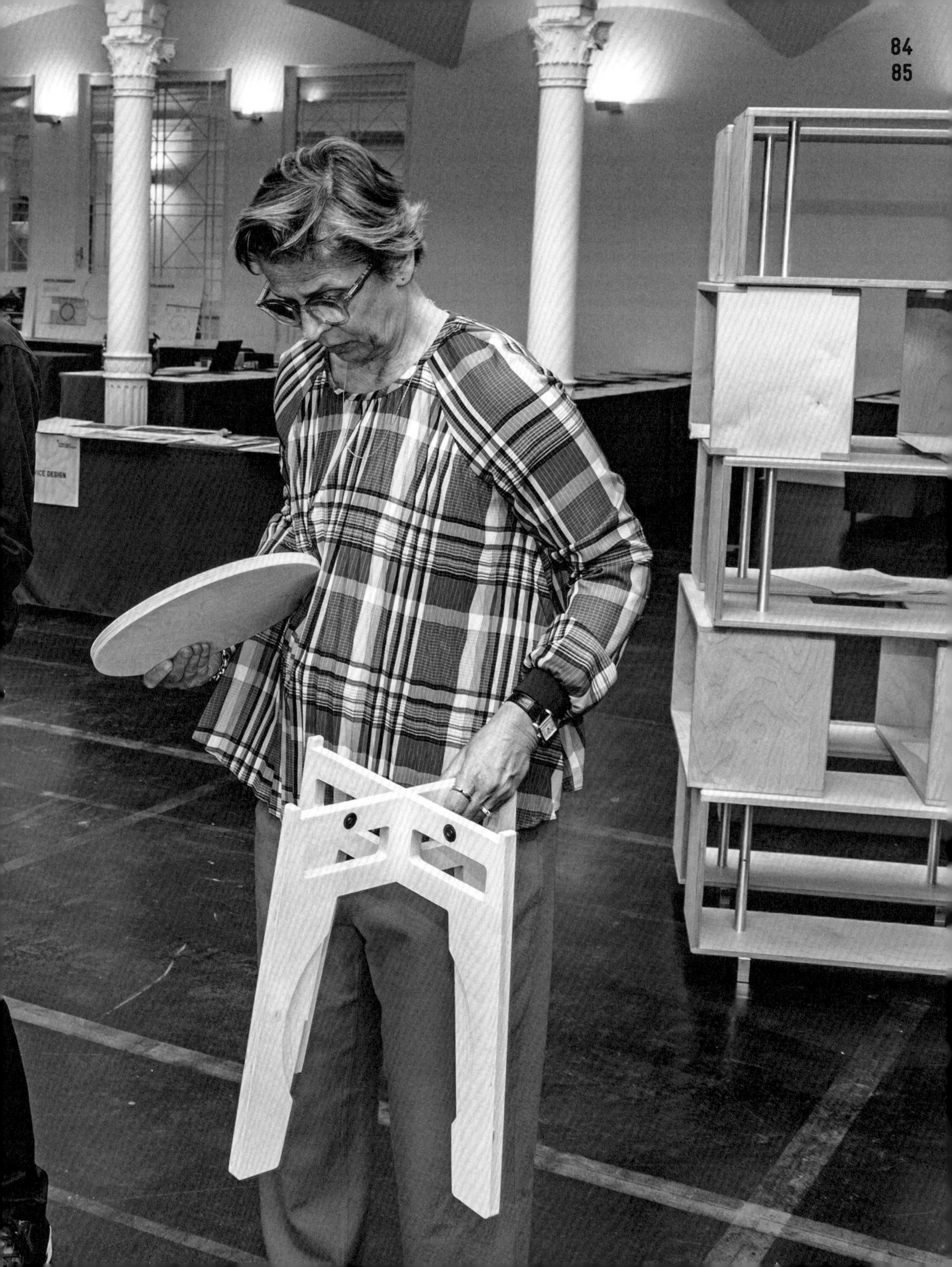

1 → SEITE/PAGE
88–95

2 → SEITE/PAGE
98, 102

3 → SEITE/PAGE
99, 103

4 → SEITE/PAGE
100, 104

LICHT
LIGHTING

GOLD:
1 **REFLEX² WALL**
serien Raumleuchten GmbH
Rodgau

SILVER:
2 **C1-MICRO-VL**
corporate friends® GmbH
Kamenz

SPECIAL MENTION:
3 **LUKULI LOUNGE**
Lukuli Design GmbH
Esslingen

4 **AFL 100**
WE-EF LEUCHTEN GmbH
Bispingen

Licht aus der Leuchtdiode ist längst Standard – denn sie bietet nicht nur Energieeffizienz, sie ermöglicht auch ganzheitlich konzipierte Leuchtensysteme. Neben der Ergänzung mit zusätzlichen Features oder der faszinierenden Miniaturisierung bietet das Halbleiter-Leuchtmittel auch im Außenbereich spannende neue Optionen.

Light-emitting diodes have long been a standard light source. Not only are they highly efficient but they also make it easier to design integrated lighting solutions. Besides enabling additional features and a fascinating degree of miniaturisation, the semiconductor light source also offers exciting new possibilities for outdoor use.

7

GOLD   REFLEX² WALL   WANDLEUCHTE
WALL LIGHT

REFLEX² WALL

WANDLEU

LICHT
LIGHTING

88
89

FOCUS
GOLD

CHTE

GOLD   REFLEX² WALL   WANDLEUCHTE / WALL LIGHT

JURY STATEMENT

Die Leuchte vermittelt eine entspannte Zurückhaltung, wirkt ausgesprochen elegant und ist physisch nur minimal präsent. So reduziert kann sie sich in jeden Kontext einfügen, sogar in ein Barockschloss würde sie bestens passen. Explizit positiv zu erwähnen ist zudem der ausgeklügelte und perfektionierte Montageprozess.

With its minimal profile and air of sophistication, the luminaire exudes understated elegance. Thanks to the minimalist approach, it fits perfectly into any environment — even a baroque palace. The ingenious and well-thought-out installation process also deserves a positive mention.

HERSTELLER/MANUFACTURER
serien Raumleuchten GmbH
Rodgau

DESIGN
Inhouse/In-house

Das jüngste Mitglied der Leuchtenfamilie ergänzt die Tisch-, Decken- und Bodenvariante um ein Modell für die Wandmontage. Auch hier gibt das puristische Rahmenprinzip die formale Erscheinung vor, allerdings wird nun der Rahmen zum Leuchtkörper selbst und integriert das 12 Watt leistende und tauschbare LED-Modul besonders smart. Trotz ihrer kompakten Abmessungen – sie greift nur 120 Millimeter in den Raum aus – produziert die Wandleuchte einen Lichtstrom von bis zu 1470 Lumen. Die satinierte Glasabdeckung sorgt für blendfreie Abstrahlung, sowohl bei der Nutzung als Up- wie auch als Downlight.

Praxisgerecht mitgedacht wurde auch die Montage. Nach der Anbringung des wandseitigen Adapters wird die Elektronik sowie die Leuchte selbst einfach aufgesteckt, die elektrischen Verbindungen stellen sich dabei selbst her.

This wall-mounted model joins the company's growing luminaire family, offering a versatile option alongside their table, ceiling, and floor models. The sleek frame format is retained, but this time the frame functions as the luminaire thanks to the replaceable 12-watt LED module cleverly integrated into the unit. Despite its compact dimensions – it protrudes a mere 120 millimetres into the room – the wall light delivers a light output of up to 1470 lumens. A frosted glass cover ensures glare-free illumination when used as an uplight or a downlight.

Due consideration has been given to ease of installation. You simply attach the adapter to the wall and plug in the electronics and luminaire. The connections are made automatically.

JEAN-MARC DA COSTA   MANAGING DIRECTOR,
                       SERIEN.LIGHTING

»Unser Ansatz heißt:
So viel wie nötig und so wenig
wie möglich.«

»Our approach is:
as little as possible, as much
as necessary.«

JEAN-MARC DA COSTA   MANAGING DIRECTOR, SERIEN.LIGHTING

Was steht am Anfang einer neuen Leuchte – die Designidee oder die Lichttechnik?

Je nachdem. Die Reflex-Familie geht auf das Jahr 1984 zurück, als die Halogentechnik ganz aktuell war und wir die Chance sahen, eine filigrane, indirekt wirkende Deckenleuchte entwickeln zu können. Wir haben einen einfach herstellbaren Reflektor gestaltet, der mit vertikalen Streben mit Abstand zur Decke montiert wird und das Licht des Halogenstabs nach oben richtet. Das war damals ein sehr erfolgreiches Produkt. Mit der LED-Technologie bekamen wir dann die Option an die Hand, die damalige Idee gründlich zu überarbeiten und eine andere formale Lösung zu finden. Geblieben sind die Streben, die dort integrierte Stromführung, die Nutzung des Deckenanschlusses und das indirekte Licht.

Die Reflex²Wall ist formal extrem reduziert – schränkt dieser Ansatz das Design nicht sehr ein?

Nein, denn tatsächlich sehen wir das nicht als Einschränkung, sondern positiv, als Herausforderung. Wir streben nach der maximalen formalen Reduktion, unser Ansatz heißt: So viel wie nötig und so wenig wie möglich. Im Prinzip feilschen wir um jeden Millimeter, aber am Ende muss die Technik reinpassen und alles produktionstechnisch umsetzbar sowie skalierbar sein. Das gelingt uns, weil wir im Prinzip alles inhouse entwickeln und gestalten. Dazu gehört auch die durchdachte, einfache Montage. Bei der Reflex²Wall kommt noch die komfortable Möglichkeit zur Nivellierung der Leuchte hinzu.

Viele Ihrer Leuchten erlauben die stufenlose Veränderung der Lichttemperatur. Wie relevant ist dieses Feature?

Tuneable White ist so relevant, weil Sie damit die Lichtfarbe und damit das Farbklima im Raum nach Ihren Wünschen verändern können. Daneben trägt in vielen unserer Produkte die Dim-to-Warm-Regelung auch zur Lichtqualität bei: Sie sorgt dafür, dass sich beim Herunterdimmen das Spektrum der LEDs in einen wärmeren Bereich verschiebt.

What is the starting point for a new luminaire – the design idea or the lighting technology?

It depends. The original Reflex family dates back to 1984, when halogen technology was the latest thing and we saw an opportunity to develop a slim, indirect ceiling light. We designed an easy-to-manufacture reflector which, when mounted using vertical struts below the ceiling, directed the light from the halogen rod upwards. It proved to be a very successful product at the time. LED technology enabled us to completely rethink the original concept and develop a new aesthetic. We retained the struts, the built-in power supply, the ceiling connector and the indirect lighting.

The Reflex²Wall is extremely minimalist in form. Doesn't this approach restrict your design options?

No. Far from being a restriction, we see this as a positive challenge. We aim to eliminate all unnecessary design elements. Our approach is "as little as possible, as much as necessary". We scrutinise every millimetre, but the technology has to fit inside, and we also have to consider the practical aspects of production feasibility and scalability. We can do this because we basically conceive and develop everything in-house. This includes designing for easy installation. So, the Reflex2Wall also offers a convenient way of levelling the luminaire.

Many of your luminaires allow for stepless variation of the colour temperature. How important is this feature?

Our Tuneable White technology is important because it lets you change the colour temperature and thus the colour scheme of your room. Moreover, the dim-to-warm technology in many of our products also enhances light quality by shifting the LED colour to a warmer spectrum when the light is dimmed.

JEAN-MARC DA COSTA MANAGING DIRECTOR, SERIEN.LIGHTING

Ihre Produkte sind langlebig und zudem reparierbar. Was bedeutet letzteres für das Design?
Die Reparaturfähigkeit ist für uns schon immer ein selbstverständlicher Aspekt. Das heißt, wenn eine Komponente tatsächlich einmal defekt sein sollte, beispielsweise eine LED-Platine oder ein Treiber, so können diese ausgetauscht werden. Außerdem vergießen wir keine Komponenten, alles ist reversibel. Die meisten unserer Leuchten sind minimalistisch im Design, in der Konstruktion aber durchaus komplex. Reparaturfähigkeit und Design schließen sich also keineswegs aus.

Der Leuchtenmarkt kennt viele Akteure – wo ordnen Sie sich dort ein?
Nach 40 Jahren am Markt sind wir schon sehr etabliert – das zeigt auch die Einladung des Museums für Angewandte Kunst in Frankfurt, uns in diesem Jahr mit einer Retrospektive zu präsentieren. Wir sind ein vielfach ausgezeichneter, international bekannter Familienbetrieb mit Manufaktur-Charakter. Wir sind sehr effizient und flexibel, weil wir eben fast alles selbst entwickeln. Zugleich konzentrieren wir uns auf das, was für uns machbar ist. Im Gegensatz zu den großen Playern im Markt können wir Individualisierungen anbieten, ja sogar Unikate herstellen. Das ist für Planer sehr wichtig, entsprechend häufig werden wir angefragt. Mit dieser Expertise fahren wir seit Jahren sehr gut.

Dennoch können Sie nicht alles selbst fertigen – wie wichtig sind zuverlässige Lieferanten?
Natürlich sehr, insbesondere bei den elektronischen Bauteilen, für die wir stets nur beste Zutaten verwenden. Andere Komponenten unserer Leuchten werden in der Regel speziell für uns produziert. Zum Teil sind die Lieferanten seit unserer Gründung dabei, das pflegen wir gezielt. Auch bei der Auswahl neuer Lieferanten suchen wir uns Partner, die verstehen, was wir tun, was wir benötigen und uns auf dem Weg zum anspruchsvollen Endprodukt eng begleiten. Kontinuität ist dabei enorm wichtig, denn vieles basiert auf Menschen. Ein gutes Beispiel sind unsere mundgeblasenen Glasschirme. Sie werden stets von denselben Glasbläsern produziert, weil es dabei auf das passende Lungenvolumen ankommt. Da kann man nicht einfach auf andere Quellen ausweichen. Und wir bleiben bei unseren Lieferanten, auch wenn sie ihre Preise wegen steigender Energiepreise anpassen müssen.

Apropos Jubiläum. Wie hat sich das Leuchtendesign rückblickend verändert?
Wenn ich für uns spreche, dann sind unsere Entwürfe immer minimalistischer geworden, was vor allem die industrielle Fertigung ermöglicht. Bei unseren ersten Leuchten ist erkennbar, dass unsere Freiheiten damals vergleichsweise eingeschränkt waren: Wir griffen häufig auf Halbzeuge zurück und kombinierten sie additiv. Später kamen neue Technologien und Materialien hinzu, Druckgussteile, Aluminiumschaum beispielsweise oder Glas. Insbesondere der Einsatz von LEDs brachte einen enormen Schub, weil sie neue formale und funktionale Ideen triggerten. Dennoch haben wir nach wie vor Leuchten im Programm, die wir vor 25 Jahren konzipierten, das sind fast schon Ikonen.

Heute steht bei uns primär die Lichtqualität, die Effizienz und die Entblendung im Vordergrund. Die Formensprache der Leuchten selbst ist teils super reduziert. Zum guten Leuchtendesign gehört für uns heute stets die einfache Montage sowie die Vielseitigkeit, dank der sich unsere Produkte auch in großen Projekten einsetzen lassen.

Die Serien Raumleuchten GmbH – 1983 gegründet und seit 1985 am Markt – beschäftigt aktuell 35 Mitarbeiterinnen und Mitarbeiter im hessischen Rodgau. Das von Manfred Wolf und Jean-Marc da Costa geführte Unternehmen konzentriert sich auf Entwicklung, Design und Produktion hochwertiger sowie langlebiger Leuchten mit ausgefeilter Lichtwirkung für unterschiedlichste Raumszenarien. Dazu gehören auch projektbezogene Sonderlösungen. Viel Wert legt das Unternehmen auf regionale Lieferantenbeziehungen, manuelle Montage, hochwertige Materialien und Komponenten sowie Repair-by-Design.

www.serien.com

JEAN-MARC DA COSTA   **MANAGING DIRECTOR, SERIEN.LIGHTING**

Your products are both durable and repairable. How does this affect the design process?
We have a long-standing commitment to making repairable products. If a component like an LED board, for example, or a driver becomes defective, you can replace it. We don't pot any components either; everything can be taken apart. Most of our luminaires are minimalist in design but complex in construction. Repairability and good design are therefore not mutually exclusive

There are many players in the lighting market – where do you fit in?
After 40 years on the market, we are already well established – as can be seen by the invitation from the Museum of Applied Arts in Frankfurt to stage a retrospective on our products this year. We are a multi-award-winning, internationally recognised family-owned manufacturer. Our in-house development capabilities allow us to be exceptionally efficient and flexible. At the same time, we focus on the things we do best. In contrast to the big players on the market, we can offer customisation and even produce one-offs. This is especially important for planners, which is why we are frequently asked about it. Our expertise in this area has served us well for years.

Nevertheless, you can't manufacture everything yourself. How important are reliable suppliers?
Very important, of course, especially when it comes to electronic components because we insist on using only the very best parts. The other components in our lights are usually made specially for us. Some of our suppliers have been with us ever since the company started, and we look after them. When selecting new suppliers, we look for partners who understand what we do and what we need, and who are prepared to collaborate closely with us on the development of highly advanced end products. Continuity is extremely important here because so much depends on people. Our mouth-blown glass shades are a good example. These are always produced by the same glassblowers because consistent lung capacity is crucial for this process. You can't simply switch to other sources. And we stick with our suppliers, even when they have to adjust their prices to meet rising energy prices.

Speaking of anniversaries, how has luminaire design changed over the years?
As far as serien.lighting is concerned, our designs have moved towards greater minimalism, a trend that has been helped by industrial-scale production. We had comparatively little design freedom with our first luminaires and would often use a combination of different semi-finished products. Later, we began to make use of new technologies and materials such as die-cast parts, aluminium foam and glass. The use of LEDs in particular provided a huge boost because they encouraged the development of new shapes and features. That said, our product range still includes luminaires we designed 25 years ago and which have gained near-iconic status.

Today, our primary focus is on quality, efficiency and glare control. Some of our luminaires feature starkly minimalist designs. For us, good luminaire design always prioritises ease of installation and versatility, enabling our products to be used in large projects.

Established in 1983, Serien Raumleuchten GmbH began its operations in 1985 and currently employs 35 people in Rodgau, Hesse. The company, managed by Manfred Wolf and Jean-Marc da Costa, specialises in the design, development and production of durable, high-quality luminaires incorporating advanced lighting effects for a wide variety of room scenarios. This also includes project-specific customised solutions. The company places a high priority on its regional supplier relationships, manual assembly, high-quality materials and components, and repair-by-design.

www.serien.com

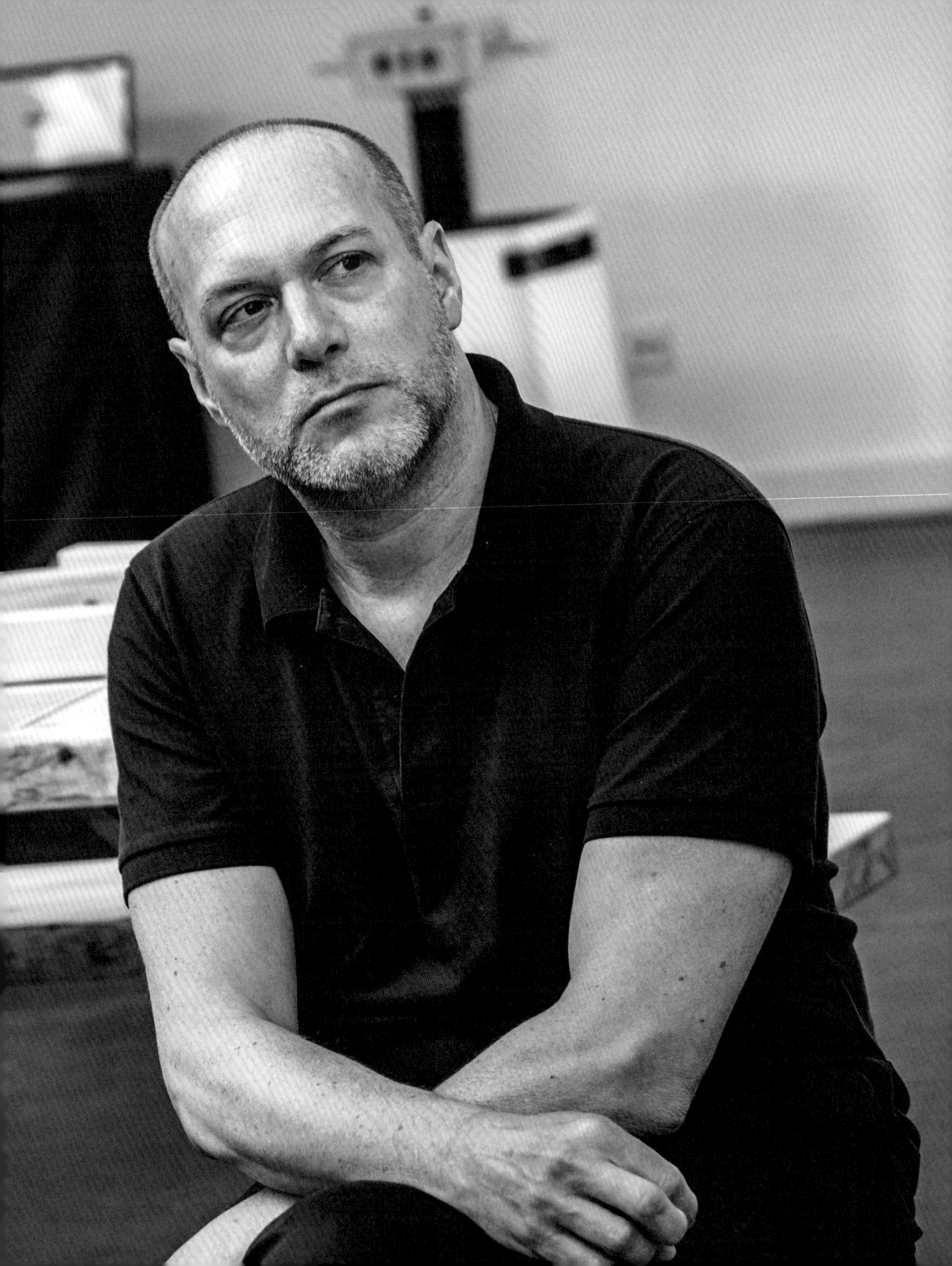

HENNING RIESELER **STUDIO F.A. PORSCHE, BERLIN**

»Da Produkte immer komplexer werden, nimmt die Relevanz von Design zu. Erst gutes Design macht Produkte und Services verständlich.«

»As products and services grow ever more complex, good design is becoming increasingly important for user understanding.«

Henning Rieseler verantwortet als Design Director von Studio F. A. Porsche alle Projekte für externe Kunden und leitet die entsprechenden Designteams an allen Standorten. Henning Rieseler studierte in Kiel technisches Produktdesign und ist seit 2002 bei Studio F. A. Porsche beschäftigt, ab 2013 als Studioleiter in Berlin und seit 2020 als Design Director.

As design director at Studio F. A. Porsche, Henning Rieseler oversees all projects for external clients and leads the design teams across all locations. He studied technical product design in Kiel and has been with Studio F. A. Porsche since 2002 – from 2013 as studio manager in Berlin and since 2020 as design director.

www.studiofaporsche.com

www.studiofaporsche.com

SILVER	C1-MICRO-VL	LED-SPOTLEUCHTE
	→ SEITE/PAGE	LED SPOTLIGHT
	102	

SPECIAL MENTION	LUKULI LOUNGE	STEHLEUCHTE
	→ SEITE/PAGE 103	FLOOR LAMP

SPECIAL MENTION AFL 100 AUSSENLEUCHTE
→ SEITE/PAGE EXTERIOR LIGHTING
104

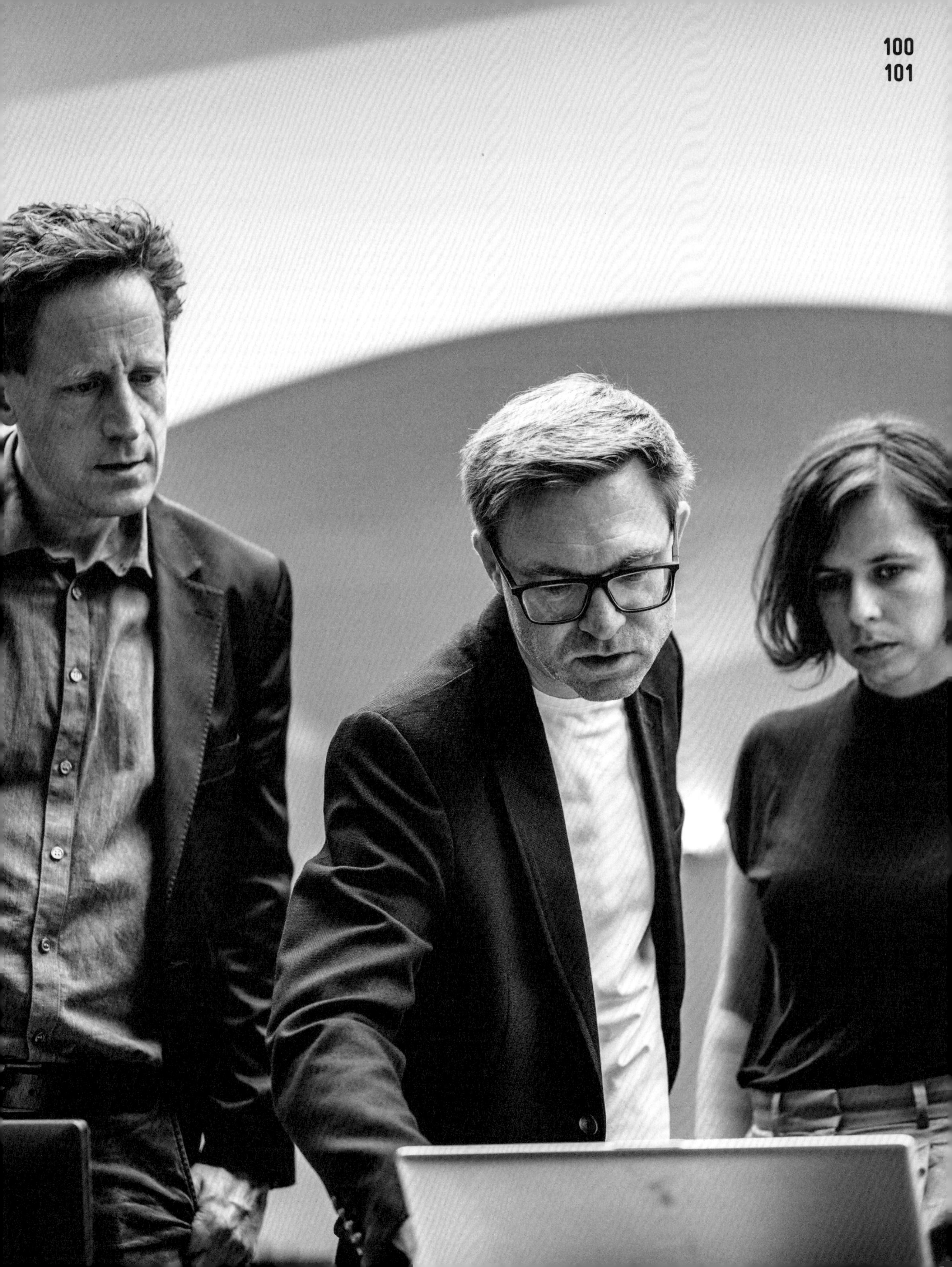

SILVER

C1-MICRO-VL LED-SPOTLEUCHTE
LED SPOTLIGHT

> **JURY STATEMENT**
>
> Reduktion ist auch hier das bestimmende Moment, vor allem hinsichtlich der Dimensionen, aber auch in Sachen Design. Damit bleibt das hochwertige und extrem variable Vitrinenlicht formal im Hintergrund und lässt den Exponaten den Vortritt.
>
> Minimalism is the defining characteristic here, evident in both size and design. This ensures that the high-quality and highly adjustable showcase lighting system remains unobtrusive while allowing the exhibits to command attention.

HERSTELLER/MANUFACTURER
corporate friends® GmbH
Kamenz

DESIGN
Inhouse/In-house

Speziell für die Beleuchtung von Exponaten in Vitrinen wurde diese Miniatur-Leuchte entwickelt. Sie setzt sich aus der vertikalen Lichtschiene und den andockbaren LED-Spots zusammen, die variabel justierbar und mit verschiedenen Abstrahloptiken ausrüstbar sind. Trotz ihres nur 14 Millimeter großen Durchmessers produzieren die dimmbaren Spots 90 Lumen bei nur 1,4 Watt Leistung. Die freistehende Stromschiene lässt sich in vorhandene Vitrinen nachrüsten und misst acht Millimeter im Durchmesser. Fünf verschiedene Lichtfarben sowie zusätzliche Raster und Blenden ermöglichen sehr spezifisch abgestimmte Lichtwirkungen.

This miniature luminaire was developed specifically for illuminating items in display cabinets. It consists of a vertical lighting track and adjustable LED spotlights that can be configured with various beam optics. Despite being just 14 millimetres in diameter, the dimmable spots produce 90 lumens and consume a mere 1.4 watts. The free-standing track measures 8 millimetres in diameter and can be retrofitted into existing display cabinets. Five different lighting colours as well as optional accessories such as honeycomb grids and anti-glare tubes enable carefully tailored lighting effects.

SPECIAL MENTION | **LUKULI LOUNGE** | **STEHLEUCHTE**
 | | **FLOOR LAMP**

JURY STATEMENT

Die batteriebetriebene Leuchte ist vergleichsweise leicht und damit sehr mobil. Auf die wesentlichen Elemente reduziert, bleibt sie selbstbewusst im Hintergrund. Samt Scharnier macht sie einen sehr stabilen und wertigen Eindruck, sie lässt sich als Wallwasher genauso gut nutzen wie als Leselicht.

The lightweight design makes the battery-operated luminaire highly portable. The minimalist form factor helps it to merge seamlessly into the background with understated confidence. With a robust, high-quality build and hinged construction, it serves equally well as a wall washer or reading light.

Bar jeder formalen Allüren präsentiert sich diese Stehleuchte, die, rein akkubetrieben, bis zu 100 Stunden Licht spendet. Möglich machen dies 87 breit abstrahlende LEDs im Leuchtenkopf, der zwischen vertikaler und horizontaler Position dank Friktionsscharnier stufenlos neigbar ist. Die aus pulverbeschichtetem Aluminium individuell produzierte Leuchte erzeugt einen Lichtstrom von bis zu 870 Lumen bei 3000 K Lichttemperatur. Aktiviert und gedimmt wird die Leuchte berührungslos per Gestensensor.

This minimalist cordless floor lamp provides up to 100 hours of light when fully charged. This is possible thanks to the 87 wide-beam LEDs built into the head of the luminaire, which is equipped with a friction hinge that allows the unit to be continuously adjusted vertically and horizontally. Each luminaire is constructed from powder-coated aluminium and generates a luminous flux of up to 870 lumens with a light temperature of 3000 K. A gesture sensor allows users to switch it on, off, or adjust its brightness with a simple hand movement.

HERSTELLER/MANUFACTURER
Lukuli Design GmbH
Esslingen

DESIGN
Inhouse/In-house

SPECIAL MENTION **AFL100** **AUSSENLEUCHTEN
EXTERIOR LIGHTING**

> **JURY STATEMENT**
>
> Das Design dieser Leuchte ist maximal reduziert und gerade deshalb auszeichnungswert. Dank der formalen Zurückhaltung sowie der modularen Konzeption eignet sich die Leuchte für unterschiedlichste öffentliche Räume. Hervorzuheben sind die durchdachten technischen Features.
>
> This luminaire's stripped-back aesthetic makes it particularly award-worthy. Thanks to its restrained form and modular design, it is suitable for a wide variety of public spaces. The thoughtfully designed technical features deserve special mention.

HERSTELLER/MANUFACTURER
WE-EF LEUCHTEN GmbH
Bispingen

DESIGN
Inhouse/In-house

Die Beleuchtung von Straßen, Wegen oder Plätzen ist längst zu einer komplexen Thematik geworden. Vor allem die Aspekte Energiebedarf und Lichtverschmutzung treiben die Entwicklung voran. Mit den drei Typen der Leuchtenfamilie werden beide Aspekte gezielt adressiert – und auch das Recycling der langlebigen Produkte. Sie bestehen aus kupferarmem Aluminium, das sich ohne Qualitätseinbußen wiederverwerten lässt. Der modulare Aufbau erleichtert die individuelle Konfiguration, Reparatur und Montage. Neben der bedarfsabhängigen Aktivierung der Leuchten via Sensorik können sie Teil von Smart-City-Systemen werden. Die warme Lichtfarbe mindert zudem Auswirkungen auf die Tierwelt.

The task of lighting streets, paths and town squares has become increasingly challenging, due largely to energy consumption and light pollution concerns. This lighting range offers three types of luminaire that address both of these concerns while also being cognisant of the product's extended lifespan and end-of-life impact. The luminaires are made from low-copper aluminium, a material that can be recycled endlessly without degradation. The modular design simplifies customisation, repair and installation. These luminaires are not only sensor-activated for energy efficiency but have also been designed to work with smart city systems. The warm light colour reduces the impact on wildlife.

104
105

1 → SEITE/PAGE
108, 112

2 → SEITE/PAGE
109, 113

3 → SEITE/PAGE
110, 114

FREIZEIT, SPORT, SPIELEN
LEISURE, SPORTS, PLAY

SILVER:
1 **ATC/STC**
SWAROVSKI OPTIK AG & Co. KG
Absam
Österreich/Austria

SPECIAL MENTION:
2 **MOON**
höfats GmbH
Kempten

3 **TRAKTOR MIT ANHÄNGER**
Schleich GmbH
Schwäbisch Gmünd

Entspannung und Rekreation, Herausforderung und Challenge – die Freizeit ist prall gefüllt mit verschiedensten Aktivitäten. Längst unterstützen innovative Produkte die jeweiligen Spielfelder der Freizeit – daheim, unterwegs oder in der Natur.

Leisure time offers a world of relaxation, recreation, goals and challenges. From home to the great outdoors, innovative products have long enhanced our enjoyment of a wide range of leisure activities.

SILVER ATC/STC KOMPAKT-TELESKOPE
COMPACT TELESCOPES
→ SEITE/PAGE
112

| SPECIAL MENTION | MOON
→ SEITE/PAGE 113 | FEUERKORB
FIRE BASKET |

SPECIAL MENTION

TRAKTOR MIT ANHÄNGER
→ SEITE/PAGE 114

SPIELZEUG
TOY

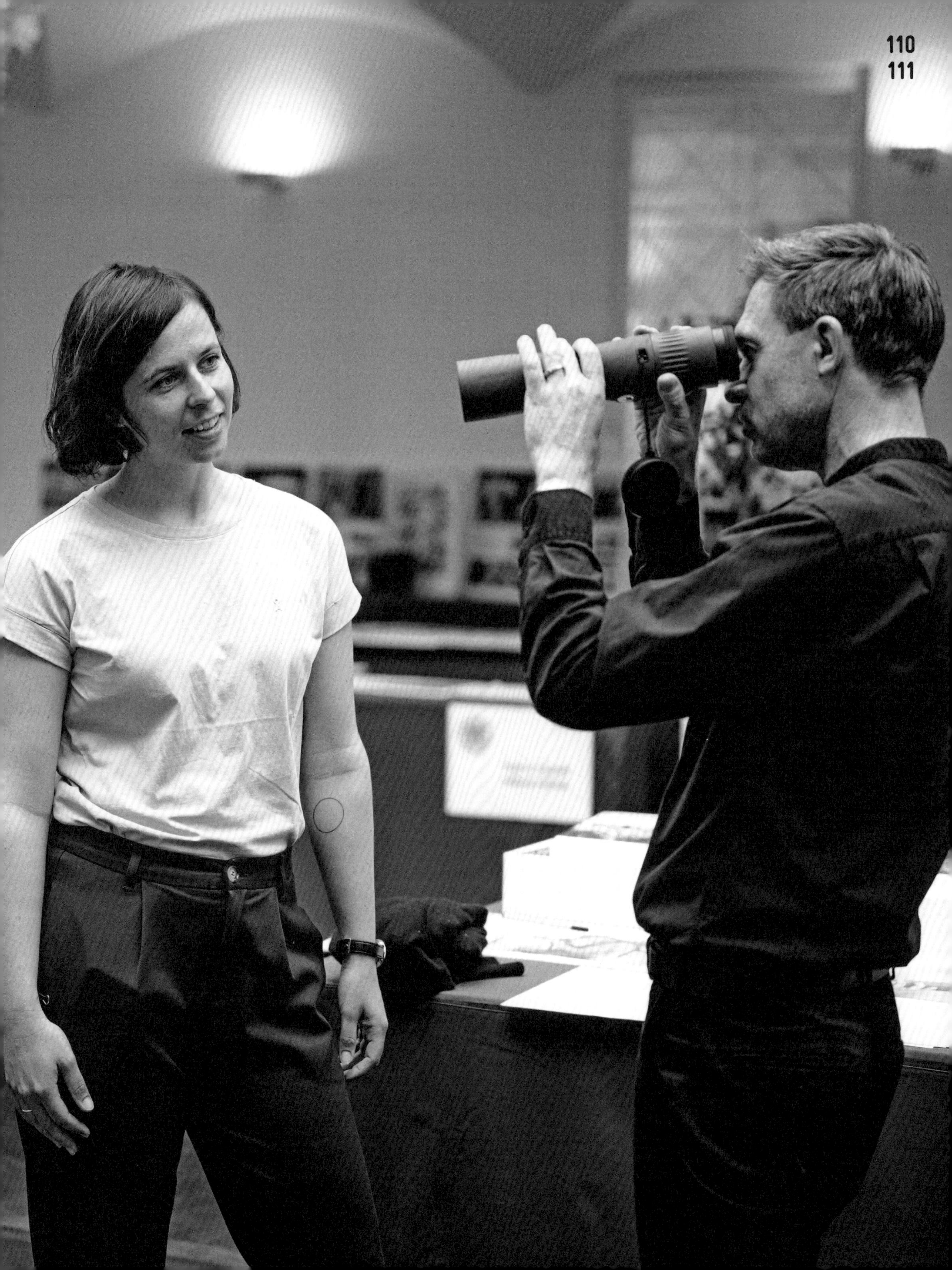

SILVER	ATC/STC	**KOMPAKT-TELESKOPE**
COMPACT TELESCOPES

> **JURY STATEMENT**
>
> Die beiden Teleskope sind perfekt durchgestaltet, das Design vermittelt, dass es sich hier um höchst präzise Geräte handelt. Neben der Ästhetik sind auch die Haptik sowie die Bedienung positiv hervorzuheben.
>
> The meticulous design of both telescopes clearly signifies their status as high-precision instruments. Besides their visual appeal, the tactile quality and functionality deserve special mention.

HERSTELLER/MANUFACTURER
SWAROVSKI OPTIK AG & Co. KG
Absam
Österreich/Austria

DESIGN
formquadrat GmbH
Linz
Österreich/Austria
Julian Pröll
Stefan Degn

Um Tiere in der Natur zu beobachten, braucht es passendes Equipment, konkret: leistungsstarke Ferngläser oder Teleskope. Die sollten zugleich auch leicht und kompakt sein, schließlich wollen sie ja erst an den Ort der Beobachtung getragen werden. Genau dieses Profil erfüllen die beiden neuen Teleskope: Sie wiegen unter 1000 Gramm und verfügen über eine Zoom-Optik mit großem Linsendurchmesser. Zoom- und Fokussierrad sind bedienoptimiert dimensioniert – eine zusätzliche Halbschale verbessert das Handling des Teleskops auch beim Fehlen eines Stativs. Und mit einem optionalen Adapter lässt sich an das Okular direkt ein Smartphone andocken. Das Teleskop wird in einer geraden und einer abgeknickten Version angeboten.

If you want to observe animals in their natural surroundings, you'll need the right equipment, including high-power binoculars or telescopes. You'll also want them to be light and compact for easy transport to the observation site. These two new telescopes satisfy these requirements perfectly. They weigh less than 1000 grams and have zoom optics and a large diameter lens. The zoom and focusing wheel is optimised for ease of use. An additional half shell improves handling even when a tripod is not available. An optional adapter allows a smartphone to be docked directly onto the eyepiece. The telescopes are available in both straight and angled versions.

SPECIAL MENTION — MOON — FEUERKORB / FIRE BASKET

JURY STATEMENT

Der Feuerkorb weist mit seiner Kugelform nicht nur formal einen neuen, eleganten Weg. Die Luftführung im Gehäuse optimiert den Verbrennungsvorgang und reduziert – im Gegensatz zu offenen Feuerschalen – die Emission problematischer Partikel und Verbrennungsgase.

The spherical shape of the fire basket is more than simply a new, elegant design approach. The optimised airflow within the basket enhances combustion and – compared to traditional open fire bowls – significantly reduces the emission of harmful particles and gases.

HERSTELLER/MANUFACTURER
höfats GmbH
Kempten

DESIGN
Inhouse/In-house

Während Heizsysteme im heimischen Haushalt immer effizienter oder sogar weitgehend unsichtbar werden, fasziniert uns Menschen nach wie vor die archaische Kraft des offenen Feuers. Ein solches anzufachen, verbietet sich in dicht besiedelten Lebensräumen schon allein durch die Rauchentwicklung von selbst. Abhilfe verspricht der Feuerkorb mit neuartiger Holzvergaser-Technologie, der mit Pellets oder Brennholz befeuert werden kann. Die doppelschalige, kugelförmige Wand des Feuerkorbs ermöglicht dabei eine zweigeteilte Verbrennung, die zwei Stunden lang für ununterbrochenes Feuer ohne Nachlegen sorgt. Wird mit Pellets befeuert, entsteht eine rauchfreie Flamme. Das filigran wirkende, aber äußerst standfeste Fußgestell ist in zwei Höhen erhältlich.

While modern technology renders home heating systems increasingly effective and unobtrusive, our primal attraction to the dramatic power of an open flame persists. In densely populated living spaces, lighting a fire is simply not possible because of the smoke it produces. This fire basket, whose innovative wood gasifier technology can be fuelled with pellets or firewood, offers a solution to the problem. The basket's double-walled spherical design enables two-stage combustion, providing an uninterrupted two-hour flame without refuelling. When fuelled with pellets, a smokeless flame is produced. The slim but extremely stable support stand is available in a choice of two heights.

SPECIAL MENTION

TRAKTOR MIT ANHÄNGER

SPIELZEUG TOY

> **JURY STATEMENT**
>
> Das Produkt ist nicht komplett neu, aber maßgeblich überarbeitet worden und nach aktuellen Maßstäben optimiert. Vor allem die Reduktion des Materials ist beispielhaft, aber auch das didaktisch interessante und Reparaturen ermöglichende Bausatz-Konzept.
>
> Although the product is not completely new, it has been significantly upgraded and optimised to meet the latest standards. The reduced material use, together with the educational and easy-to-repair design, is especially impressive.

HERSTELLER/MANUFACTURER
Schleich GmbH
Schwäbisch Gmünd

DESIGN
whiteID GmbH & Co. KG
Schorndorf

Im Re-Design eines Produktes liegen immer besondere Herausforderungen: Einerseits sollen marken- und produktspezifische Merkmale erhalten bleiben, andererseits bieten neue Designansätze oder auch der Wunsch nach einer nachhaltigeren Produktion neue Gestaltungsperspektiven.

So behält auch die Neuauflage eines der Klassiker des Spielzeugherstellers seine archetypischen Merkmale und damit seinen Wiedererkennungswert bei, geht aber konstruktionstechnisch neue Wege. Anders als bisher ist der Traktor zerlegbar, wird also in Einzelteilen geliefert und kann von den Kindern selbst zusammengebaut werden. Möglich machen dies eine Reduktion der Anzahl an Einzelteilen sowie ausgeklügelte Verbindungstechniken – das spart Material und erlaubt zudem, effizienter zu produzieren.

Redesigning a product is always a challenge. On the one hand, preserving core brand identity and product features is essential, while on the other, exploring innovative design approaches and more sustainable production methods can offer exciting design opportunities.

The latest version of one of this toy manufacturer's classics retains its typical features and therefore its recognition value, while at the same time breaking new ground in terms of design. Unlike the previous model, this tractor can be dismantled. It is supplied in individual parts that can be assembled by the children themselves. This has been achieved by reducing the number of component parts and incorporating some clever fastening technology. This saves on material and allows for more efficient production.

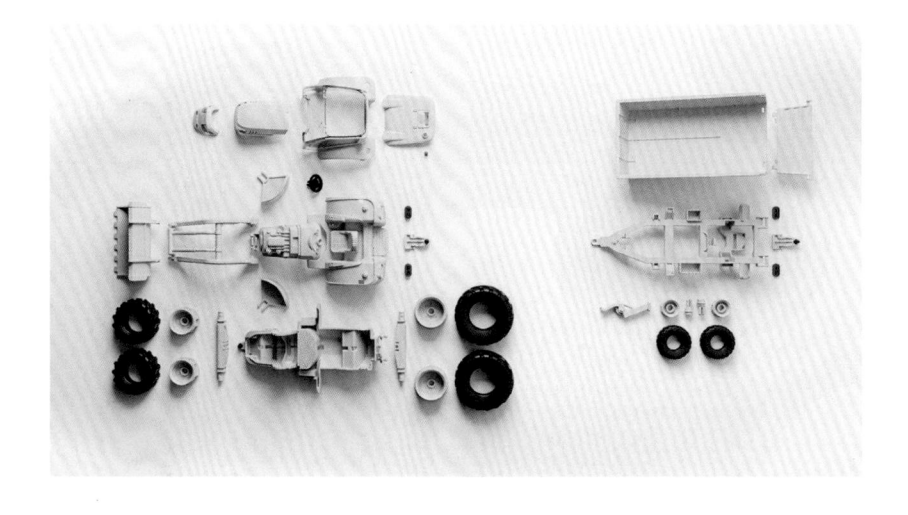

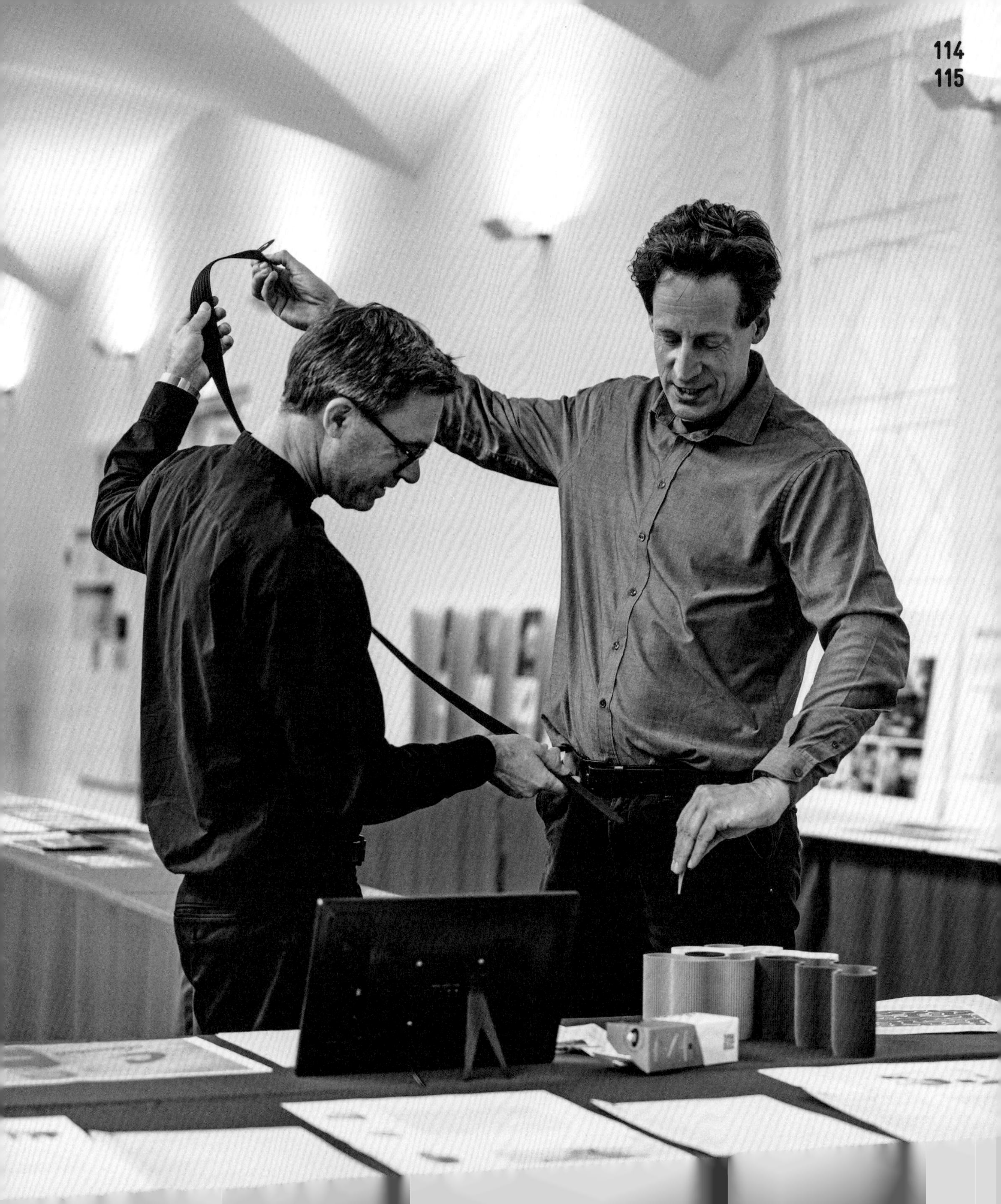

1 → SEITE/PAGE
118–125

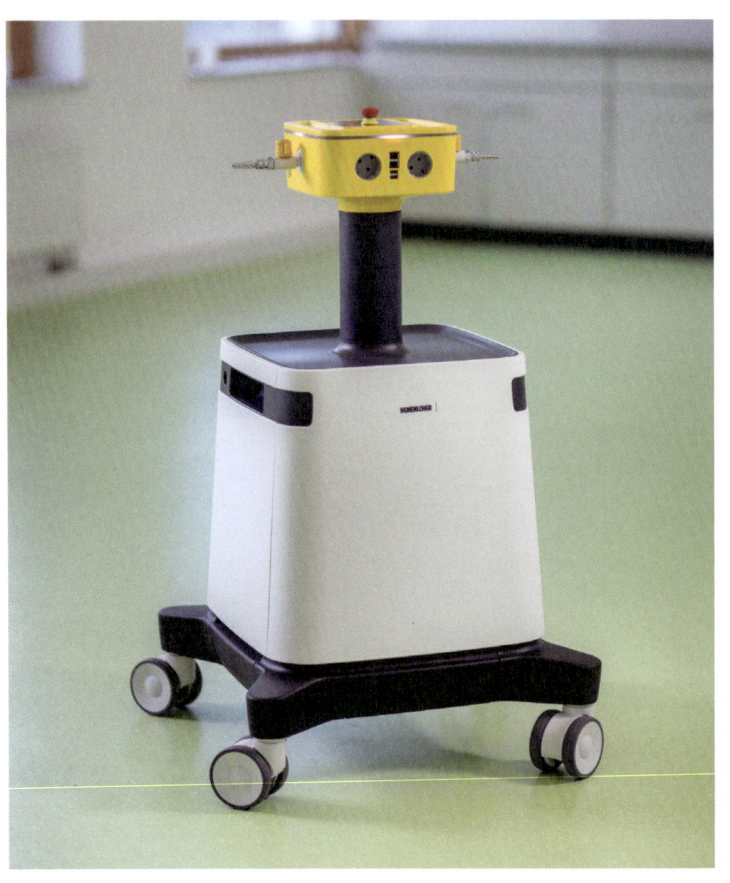

2 → SEITE/PAGE
128, 130

3 → SEITE/PAGE
129, 131

GEBÄUDETECHNIK
BUILDING TECHNOLOGY

GOLD:
1 **MEDIENBUDDY**
Hohenloher Schuleinrichtungen GmbH & Co. KG
Öhringen

SPECIAL MENTION:
2 **BUSCH-ART LINEAR/ALBA**
Busch-Jaeger Elektro GmbH
und/and ABB Niessen
Lüdenscheid

3 **BUSCH-ROOMTOUCH 4"**
Busch-Jaeger Elektro GmbH
Lüdenscheid

Design unterstützt Architektur in ihrem Bestreben, ästhetische und zugleich funktionale, effiziente sowie zukunftstaugliche Gebäude zu realisieren. Dazu gehören die weiten Welten der Haustechnik und Gebäudesteuerung, die in Bezug auf die Energiewende auch im industriellen Umfeld von großer Bedeutung sind.

Design supports architecture in its endeavours to create aesthetic buildings that are nevertheless functional, efficient and futureproof. These include the vast worlds of building technology and building control, which are also of great importance to energy transition in the industrial environment.

10

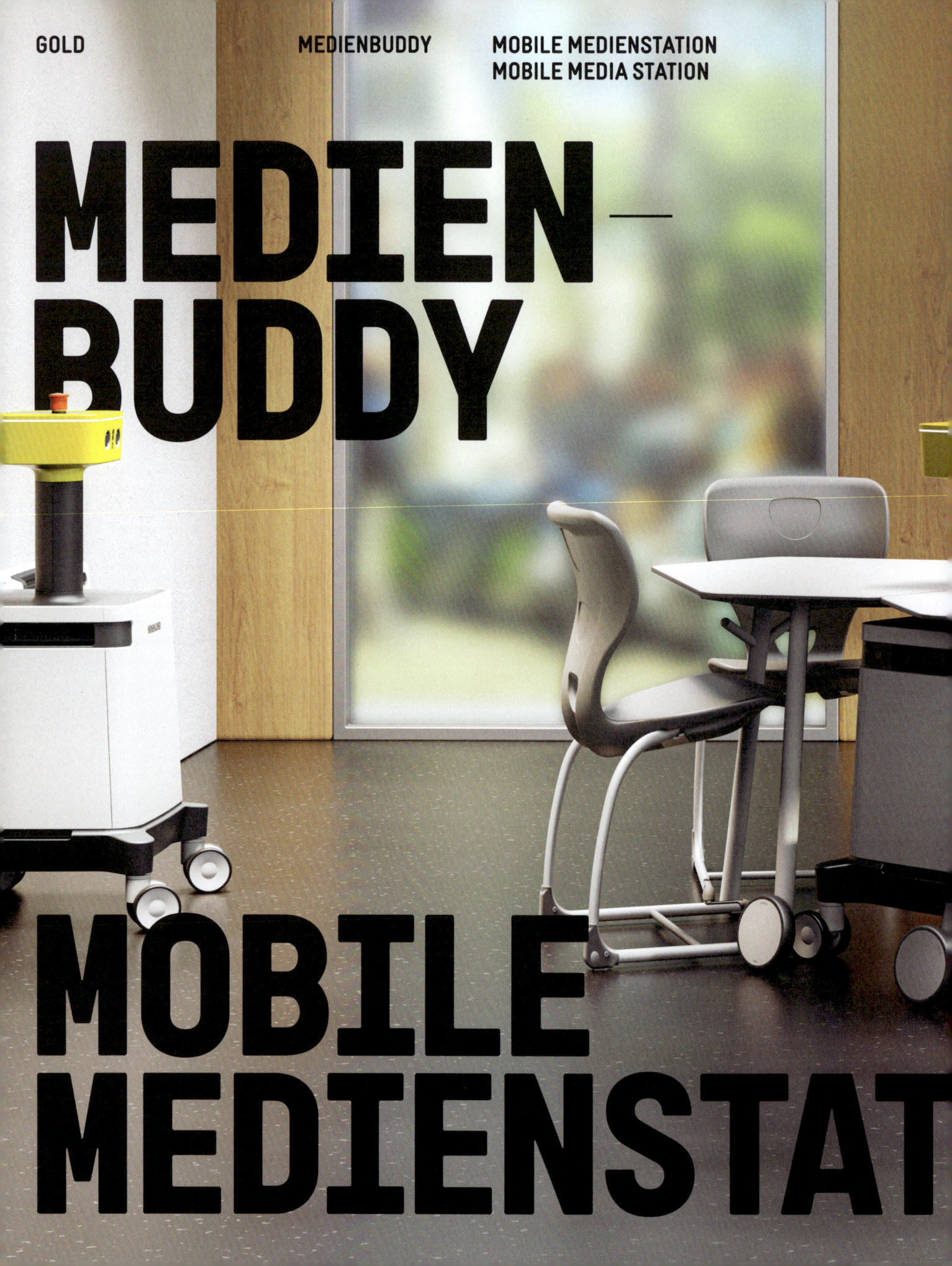

GOLD | MEDIENBUDDY | MOBILE MEDIENSTATION
MOBILE MEDIA STATION

MEDIEN—
BUDDY

MOBILE
MEDIENSTAT

GEBÄUDETECHNIK
BUILDING TECHNOLOGY

118
119

FOCUS
GOLD

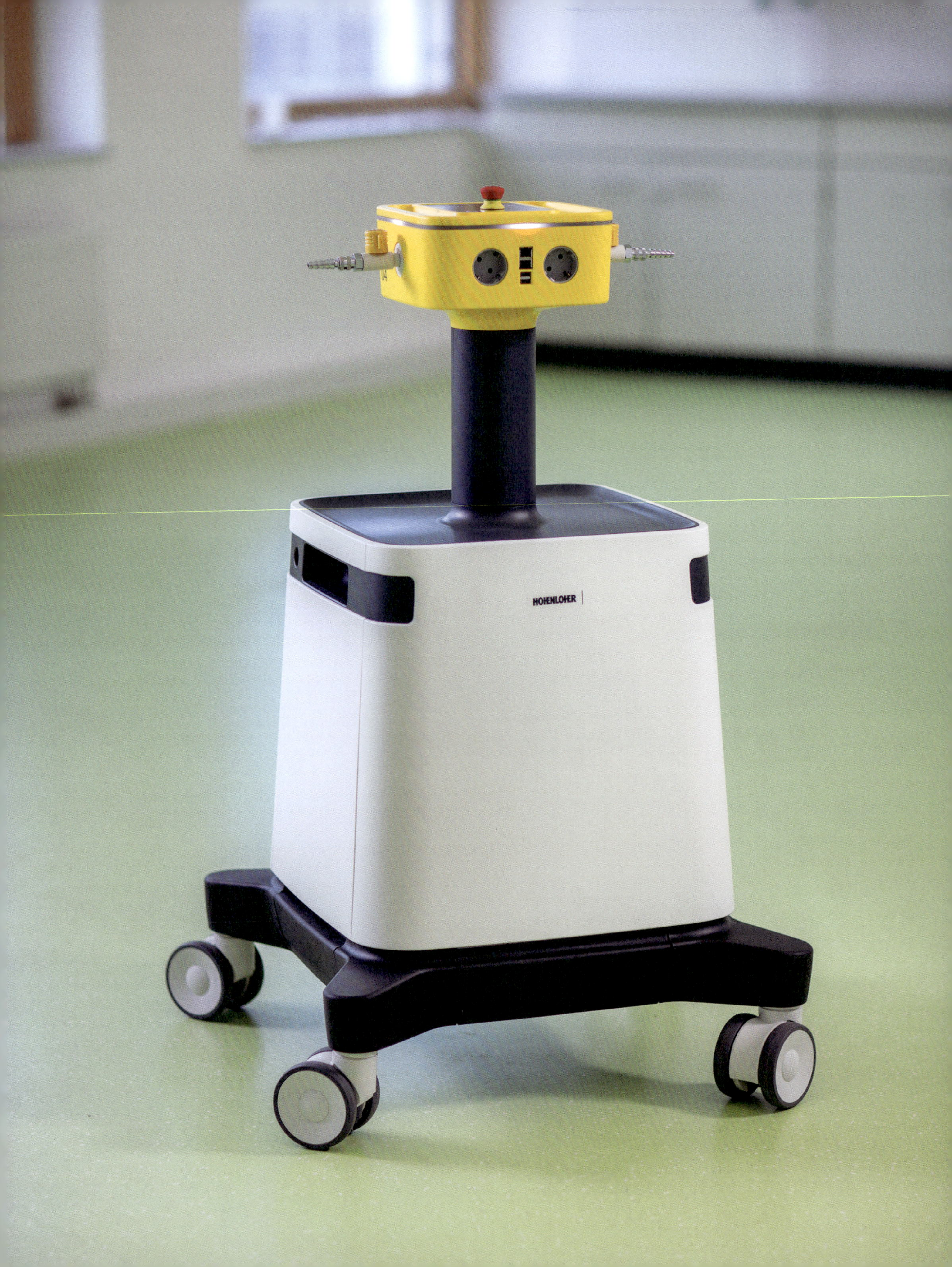
HOHENLOHER

MEDIENBUDDY
MOBILE MEDIENSTATION / MOBILE MEDIA STATION

GOLD

JURY STATEMENT

Ein total schlüssiges Konzept für einen zeitgemäßen Unterricht, der sinnlich erfahrbare Experimente einbezieht. Die dezente humanoide Anmutung ist nicht aufgesetzt, sondern ergibt sich aus der logischen Anordnung der Elemente – die halsähnliche Verbindung zum Medienkopf beispielsweise erleichtert das Heranrücken an Tische.

A powerful concept for sensory-based science teaching in the digital age. The discreet humanoid appearance is not contrived but results from the logical arrangement of the elements; the neck-like connection to the media head, for example, makes it easier to position the station closer to tables.

HERSTELLER/MANUFACTURER
Hohenloher Schuleinrichtungen GmbH & Co. KG
Öhringen

DESIGN
UP Designstudio GmbH
Stuttgart

Während der Frontalunterricht in vielen Schulfächern ausgedient hat, ist er in naturwissenschaftlichen Fächern nach wie vor präsent. Das liegt unter anderem an der für Experimente notwendigen Infrastruktur, die bislang feste Raumstrukturen erforderte. Der mobile MedienBuddy dreht die Verhältnisse um und stellt Strom, Gas und Internet genau dort bereit, wo die Medien von den Lerngruppen gebraucht werden – auch im Außenbereich.

Die Medienports befinden sich auf Augenhöhe der Nutzenden im humanoid inspirierten Gerätekopf. Für gutes Handling sorgen große Griffmulden, Feststellrollen sowie ein Interface, das über den Status der Verbindungen sowie Füllstände informiert. Sämtliche Funktionen werden vom Lehrpersonal per RFID freigeschaltet.

While many school subjects can now be taught online, the value of face-to-face instruction remains undiminished in science education. One of the reasons for this is the infrastructure required for experiments, which until now has relied on fixed room structures. However, the Mobile MediaBuddy eliminates the limitations of traditional learning by providing electricity, gas, and internet access exactly where students need it – even outdoors.

The media ports in the station's humanoid-inspired head are conveniently positioned at user eye level. Ease of use is ensured by the large, recessed handles, locking castors and an interface that provides information on the status of the connections and fill levels. All functions are enabled by teaching staff using RFID.

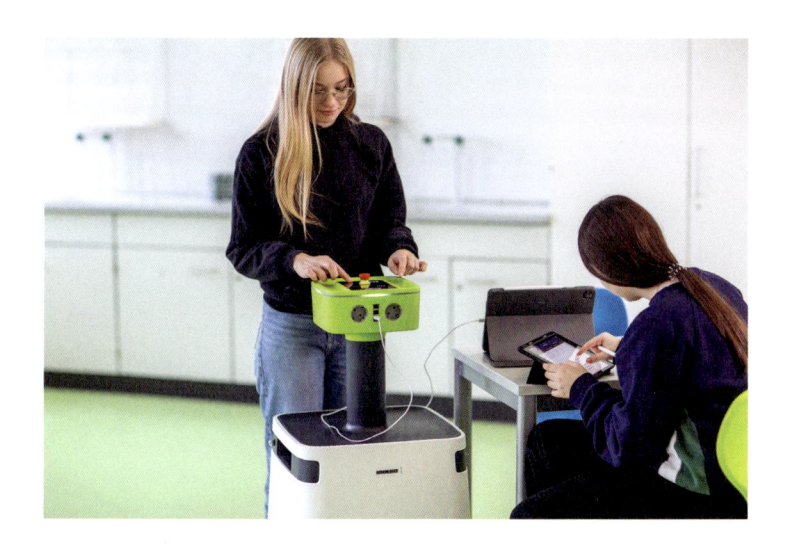

SEBASTIAN RIEGER — HEAD OF PRODUCT DESIGN, UP DESIGNSTUDIO GMBH

»Es ist generell von Vorteil, wenn Konstruktion und Design parallel laufen und sich gegenseitig inspirieren.«

»When engineering and design are undertaken simultaneously, it usually leads to mutual inspiration and improved outcomes.«

SEBASTIAN RIEGER   **HEAD OF PRODUCT DESIGN, UP DESIGNSTUDIO GMBH**

Der Medienbuddy hat eindeutig humanoide Züge. Warum?

Die Nüchternheit und Rationalität der Naturwissenschaften schrecken manche Kinder ab. Der Medienbuddy bietet als freundlicher und sympathischer Lernbegleiter einen emotionalen Zugang. So erleichtert er den Einstieg in die ersten eigenen Experimente, motiviert zum Mitmachen und weckt Neugierde. Das Produkt stellt nicht nur die Medien zur Verfügung, sondern macht den Versuch mit.

Stand das so auch als Anforderung im Lastenheft?

Die Produktvision war ein mobiles Medienmodul, das unabhängig von der Raumstruktur das Experimentieren im MINT-Unterricht ermöglicht. Denn der Trend in Schulen geht zu flexibleren Raumnutzungen, teils temporären Schulräumen und zu Notlösungen in Containern.

Also muss das Modul alle Medien an Bord haben, Strom und Gas, in Form eines Akkus und einer Gasflasche. Zu Beginn war auch noch Druckluft angedacht. Jetzt haben wir zwei Buddies, einen für Strom und einen für Strom und Gas. Rollen für den flexiblen Einsatz waren auch logisch. Grundfläche und Größe wurden nicht genau bestimmt, sollten sich aber an den bestehenden Standardtischen von Hohenloher orientieren. Es waren also noch viele Punkte offen.

Praktisches Experimentieren scheitert oft an einem übersteigerten Sicherheitsdenken – was kann der Medienbuddy da leisten?

Dieser besonderen Herausforderung war sich Hohenloher als Spezialist für die Ausstattung von Bildungseinrichtungen von Anfang an bewusst und ihr auch gewachsen. Da es ein Produkt wie den Medienbuddy noch nicht gab, mussten wir ganz unterschiedliche Sicherheitsvorgaben erfüllen und verbinden. Das begann bei den Größen der Gaskartuschen und Batterien und reichte bis zum Schutz vor Kippen oder Wegrollen.

Das Sicherheitskonzept berücksichtigt sowohl die zentrale Freigabe der Medien durch die Lehrkraft als auch die elektronische Feststellbremse. Mittels RFID-Technologie können alle Medienbuddies gleichzeitig ausgeschaltet werden. Für den Ernstfall wurde auch eine zusätzliche Notaussäule entwickelt, die die Buddies stilllegt.

Die getrennten Kammern für Gaskartusche und Batterie können nur per Schlüssel geöffnet werden.

The Medienbuddy has clear humanoid traits. Why is that?

Some children are put off by the seriousness and rationality of science. The Medienbuddy, on the other hand, is a friendly and likeable learning companion who offers a more emotional approach. This makes it easier for children to start their first experiments, while at the same time arousing their curiosity and encouraging them to join in. The product not only provides the service media but also takes an active part in the experiment.

Was this also part of the requirements specification?

The product vision was a mobile service media module that supports experiments in STEM lessons irrespective of room layout. The trend in schools is towards more flexible room utilisation, temporary classrooms and emergency solutions using containers.

The module must therefore be self-powered, with electricity in the form of a rechargeable battery and gas from a cylinder. Compressed air was also considered at the beginning. Now we have two Buddies, one electric-powered and one powered both by electricity and gas. Castors were also a logical choice, as they improve flexibility. The footprint and size were not precisely defined originally but were to be based on the sector-standard tables from Hohenloher. So, there were were still many open points.

Practical experiments often fail due to excessive safety concerns. What can the Medienbuddy do to help?

As a specialist educational equipment provider, Hohenloher was aware of and capable of meeting this particular challenge from the outset. As a product like the Medienbuddy did not yet exist, we had to satisfy and combine quite different safety requirements. These considerations began with the size of the gas canisters and batteries and extended to preventing the device from tipping or rolling away.

The safety concept includes both the centralised release of the media by the teacher and the electronic parking brake. RFID allows all Medienbuddies to be switched off simultaneously. We have also developed an additional emergency stop column that will immobilise the Buddies in the event of an emergency.

The gas cartridge and battery are housed in separate, key-locked containers.

SEBASTIAN RIEGER **HEAD OF PRODUCT DESIGN, UP DESIGNSTUDIO GMBH**

Sie haben bei der Entwicklung ausgiebige Tests durchgeführt. Welche Erkenntnis war für Sie überraschend?
Die Bestätigung von Seiten der Lehrkräfte und Bildungsträger hatten wir so nicht erwartet. Dass sich Schülerinnen und Schüler auf den Medienbuddy stürzen und Lust auf die Anwendung haben, war uns klar, aber dass sich wirklich alle Beteiligten sofort hinter das Projekt stellten und die Sinnhaftigkeit und Anwendbarkeit verstanden, hat uns sehr begeistert. Die Lösung eignet sich für akute Bedarfe in Hinblick auf flexible Raumnutzung. Und bei der Planung neuer Schulen ist das Produktsystem perfekt integrierbar.

Kann der Medienbuddy Vorbild für andere mobile Lern- oder Arbeitsplätze sein?
Der Trend weg von starren Strukturen und Systemen bleibt. Es spricht vieles für eine mobile Medienversorgung und die flexible Raumnutzung. Das macht den Medienbuddy zum Vorbild für die agile Zusammenarbeit in unterschiedlichen Gruppengrößen und die aufgabenbezogene Raumausstattung bei vollem Funktionsangebot. Zugleich beweist der Medienbuddy, dass ein emotionaleres Design Vertrauen in innovative Technologie aufbauen kann. Der Buddy bewährt sich zum Beispiel auf Messen wunderbar als Gesprächsanlass und weckt durch sein freundliches Gesicht schon im Vorbeigehen das Interesse.

Wie intensiv waren Sie in die technische Produktentwicklung des Herstellers involviert?
Auch wenn es im Grund um Laboreinrichtung geht und damit das Kerngeschäft von Hohenloher betrifft, war der Medienbuddy doch ein Schritt ins Unbekannte. Dass wir das Engineering und Produktdesign aus einer Hand bieten konnten, erleichterte die Umsetzung. Kurze Abstimmungswege und ein gemeinsamer Blick aus beiden Perspektiven beschleunigten den Entwicklungsprozess. So fanden wir schnell herstellbare Lösungen für die technische Vorkonstruktion und entwickelten den Touchscreen sowie das zugehörige Interface.

Es ist generell von Vorteil, wenn Konstruktion und Design parallel laufen und sich dabei gegenseitig inspirieren. Die Konstruktion muss keine Designentscheidung treffen und umgekehrt auch nicht. Jede Disziplin kann zielgerichtet ihre Aspekte einbringen. Wie sich beim Buddy zeigt, werden so die Lösungen mutiger und unkonventioneller.

Das UP Designstudio mit Sitz in Stuttgart wurde in der Vergangenheit bereits mehrfach mit dem FOCUS OPEN ausgezeichnet – für Consumer-Produkte ebenso wie für Investitionsgüter. 1994 von Stefan Lippert gegründet, firmierte das Büro lange Jahre als ipdd, seit 2017 ist es als UP Designstudio präsent.

www.updesignstudio.de

SEBASTIAN RIEGER   **HEAD OF PRODUCT DESIGN, UP DESIGNSTUDIO GMBH**

You carried out extensive tests during development. What did you find that surprised you?
We hadn't expected the positive reaction from teachers and educational establishments. We were confident that pupils would embrace the Medienbuddy, but we were thrilled by the immediate and unanimous support from all stakeholders, who clearly recognised the value and potential of the project. The solution effectively addresses an urgent need for adaptable room usage and can be seamlessly integrated into the planning of new schools.

Could the Medienbuddy be a role model for other mobile learning or work places?
The current trend is away from rigid structures and systems and towards the mobile supply of energy sources and flexible room utilisation. This makes Medienbuddy perfect for flexible collaboration among varying group sizes, offering a comprehensive suite of room equipment to support diverse tasks. At the same time, the Medienbuddy shows that a more human-centred design can build trust in innovative technology. The Buddy has proven to be a wonderful conversation starter at trade fairs, for example, and its friendly face arouses interest as soon as you walk past.

How closely were you involved with the technical product development by the manufacturer?
Despite being within Hohenloher's core competency of laboratory equipment, we were venturing into uncharted territory with the Medienbuddy. The fact that we have engineering and product design in-house simplified the development process. Short coordination channels and a shared view from both perspectives accelerated the development process. We quickly found workable solutions for the preliminary design and then developed the touchscreen and associated interface.

When engineering and design are undertaken simultaneously, it usually leads to mutual inspiration and improved outcomes because engineering doesn't have to make any design decisions, and vice versa. Each specialism can contribute its expertise where it is required. As the Buddy shows, this makes solutions bolder and more unconventional.

UP Designstudio, based in Stuttgart, has previously been a recipient of several FOCUS OPEN awards – for consumer products as well as capital equipment. Founded in 1994 by Stefan Lippert, the company operated under the name of ipdd for many years before being rebranded as the UP Designstudio in 2017.

www.updesignstudio.de

MIRJAM ROMBACH HOCHPARTERRE AG,
ZÜRICH

»Es geht nicht darum, Bedürfnisse zu befeuern, sondern wichtige Fragen zu adressieren – und über das Ende des life cycle hinaus zu denken.«

»It's not about meeting immediate needs but about tackling important questions – and thinking beyond the end of the life cycle.«

Mirjam Rombach hat Textildesign an der Hochschule Luzern – Design & Kunst studiert. Nach Praxisjahren am Theater sowie in der Textil- und Modebranche hat sie als Texterin, Redakteurin und freie Journalistin gearbeitet. Seit Januar 2021 verantwortet sie das Ressort Design bei Hochparterre, einem schweizerischen Verlag für Architektur, Planung und Design.

www.hochparterre.ch

Mirjam Rombach studied textile design at the Lucerne School of Art and Design. Prior to her career as a copywriter, editor and freelance journalist, she spent a number of years working in the theatre and the textile and fashion industry. Since January 2021, she has been head of the design department at Hochparterre, a Swiss publishing house for architecture, planning and design.

www.hochparterre.ch

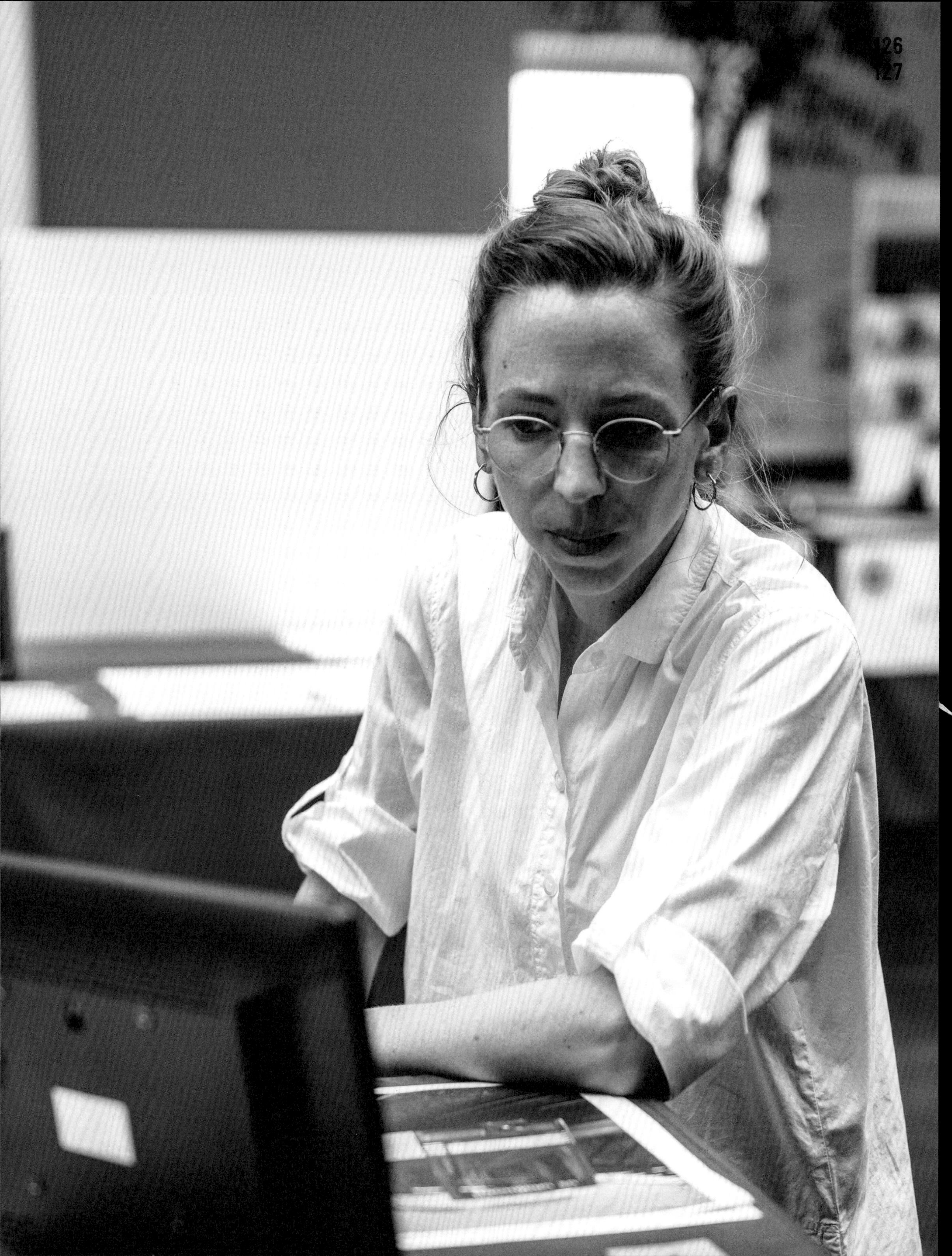

SPECIAL MENTION

ALBA
→ SEITE/PAGE 130

SCHALTERSERIE
LIGHT SWITCH RANGE

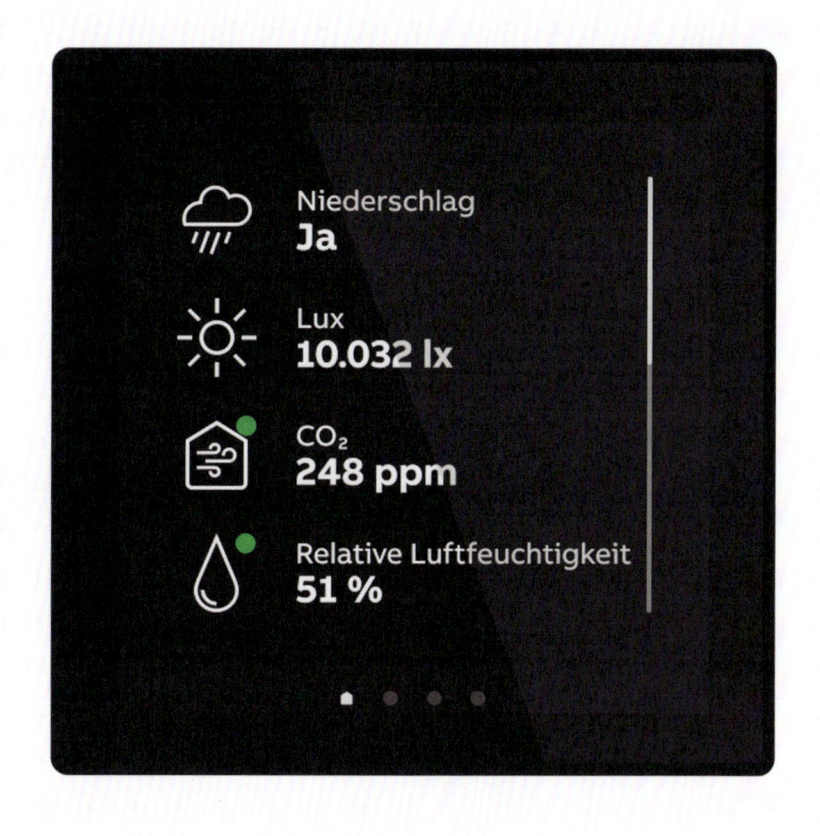

SPECIAL MENTION | ROOMTOUCH 4" | TOUCHDISPLAY | 128
| → SEITE/PAGE 131 | TOUCH DISPLAY | 129

Niederschlag
Ja

Lux
10.032 lx

CO_2
248 ppm

Relative Luftfeuchtigkeit
51 %

SPECIAL MENTION

BUSCH-ART LINEAR/ALBA

SCHALTERSERIE LIGHT SWITCH RANGE

> **JURY STATEMENT**
>
> Mit den schwebend erscheinenden Schalterflächen entsteht eine zweite Ebene über dem Rahmen, der nicht mehr als Umfassung, sondern als Hintergrund wahrgenommen wird. Das ist neu und durch seine formale Reduktion eine spannende Alternative zu etablierten Systemen. Dazu kommt die dezidierte Verwendung von Recyclaten.
>
> The way the rocker switches appear to float over the faceplate gives a 3-D effect that transforms the faceplate into a background element. This new, minimalist form offers an exciting alternative to conventional systems. The conscious choice of recycled materials is a welcome bonus.

HERSTELLER/MANUFACTURER
Busch-Jaeger Elektro GmbH
und/and ABB Niessen
Lüdenscheid

DESIGN
Entwurfreich GmbH
Düsseldorf

Recyclingmaterial wird gern mit ästhetischen Kompromissen gleichgesetzt – dass dem nicht so sein muss, zeigt diese neue Schalterserie. Statt natives Polycarbonat einzusetzen, produziert der Hersteller die weißen Elemente aus 92 Prozent, die schwarzen Teile sogar aus 98 Prozent rezykliertem Polycarbonat. Das spart Ressourcen und reduziert den CO_2-Fußabdruck um 82 Prozent, wie das seit 2019 per Cradle-to-Cradle-Certified®-Unternehmen berechnet hat.

Formal zeichnet sich die Serie durch klare Kanten und Schaltflächen aus, die über dem Rahmen schweben – damit wird das traditionelle Prinzip des umfassenden Rahmens ins Gegenteil verkehrt. Elemente aus Glas und Metall sowie Dekorrahmen erweitern die gestalterische Vielfalt des rund 200 Varianten umfassenden Programms. Die Unterputzeinsätze sind mit anderen Serien des Herstellers kompatibel.

While the use of recycled material often goes hand in hand with aesthetic compromises, this new range of light switches shows that this doesn't have to be the case. Rather than use native polycarbonate, the manufacturer makes its white components from 92 per cent and its black components from 98 per cent recycled polycarbonate. This saves resources and reduces the company's carbon footprint by 82 per cent, as calculated internally. The company has been Cradle to Cradle certified® since 2019.

The styling breaks away from the traditional all-round faceplate look and is characterised by clearly defined contours and rocker switches floating above the faceplate. Glass, metal, and decorative faceplate options create a customisable programme with over 200 unique combinations. The flush-mounted inserts are compatible with the manufacturer's other product ranges.

SPECIAL MENTION — BUSCH-ROOMTOUCH 4" — TOUCHDISPLAY / TOUCH DISPLAY

JURY STATEMENT

Dieses Display kann ein großes Problem lösen – die funktionale Überfrachtung von Steuerpanels im Smart Home. Dafür sprechen auch die KNX-Kompatibilität sowie die einfache Installation. Angenehm ist die geringe Latenzzeit des kapazitativen Screens und das haptische Feedback.

This display can solve a major problem – the lack of functionality of control panels in the smart home. KNX compatibility and ease of installation are additional benefits. The low latency of the capacitive screen and the haptic feedback are nice to have.

HERSTELLER/MANUFACTURER
Busch-Jaeger Elektro GmbH
Lüdenscheid

DESIGN
Inhouse/In-house

Bis zu zwölf Funktionen der Home-Automation lassen sich mit diesem kompakten Touchdisplay ansteuern – beispielsweise Heizung, Klimatisierung, Jalousien, Beleuchtung sowie individuell konfigurierbare Szenerien. Das vier Zoll große Display bietet mit 480 Pixeln eine HD-Auflösung, ist aus verschiedenen Perspektiven lesbar und blendet nicht im Dunkeln.

Mittels Wischbewegungen gelangt man von einer Ebene zur nächsten – dies und die eindeutigen Icons machen das flache Steuerelement intuitiv bedienbar. Technisch gesehen kommuniziert es per universellem KNX-Standard oder über das herstellereigene Protokoll mit den angeschlossenen Sensoren, Aktuatoren und Geräten. Für den Einbau reicht eine Standardschalterdose.

This compact touch display can control as many as twelve home automation functions, such as heating, air conditioning, blinds, lighting and other individually configurable functions. The four-inch display has an HD resolution of 480 pixels, is easily read from any angle and features a glare-free mode for use in the dark.

Swiping gestures seamlessly transition between levels, while clear icons make the flat control panel intuitive to use. It uses either the universal KNX standard or the manufacturer's own protocol to communicate with the linked sensors, actuators and devices. For ease of installation, the display is compatible with standard switch boxes.

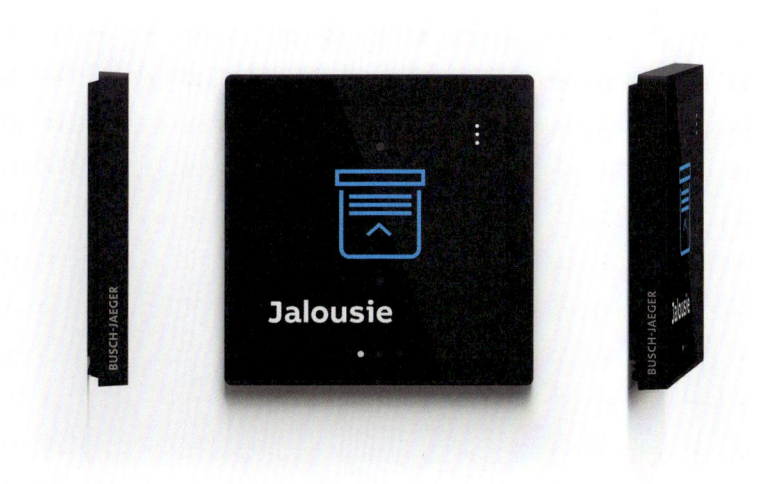

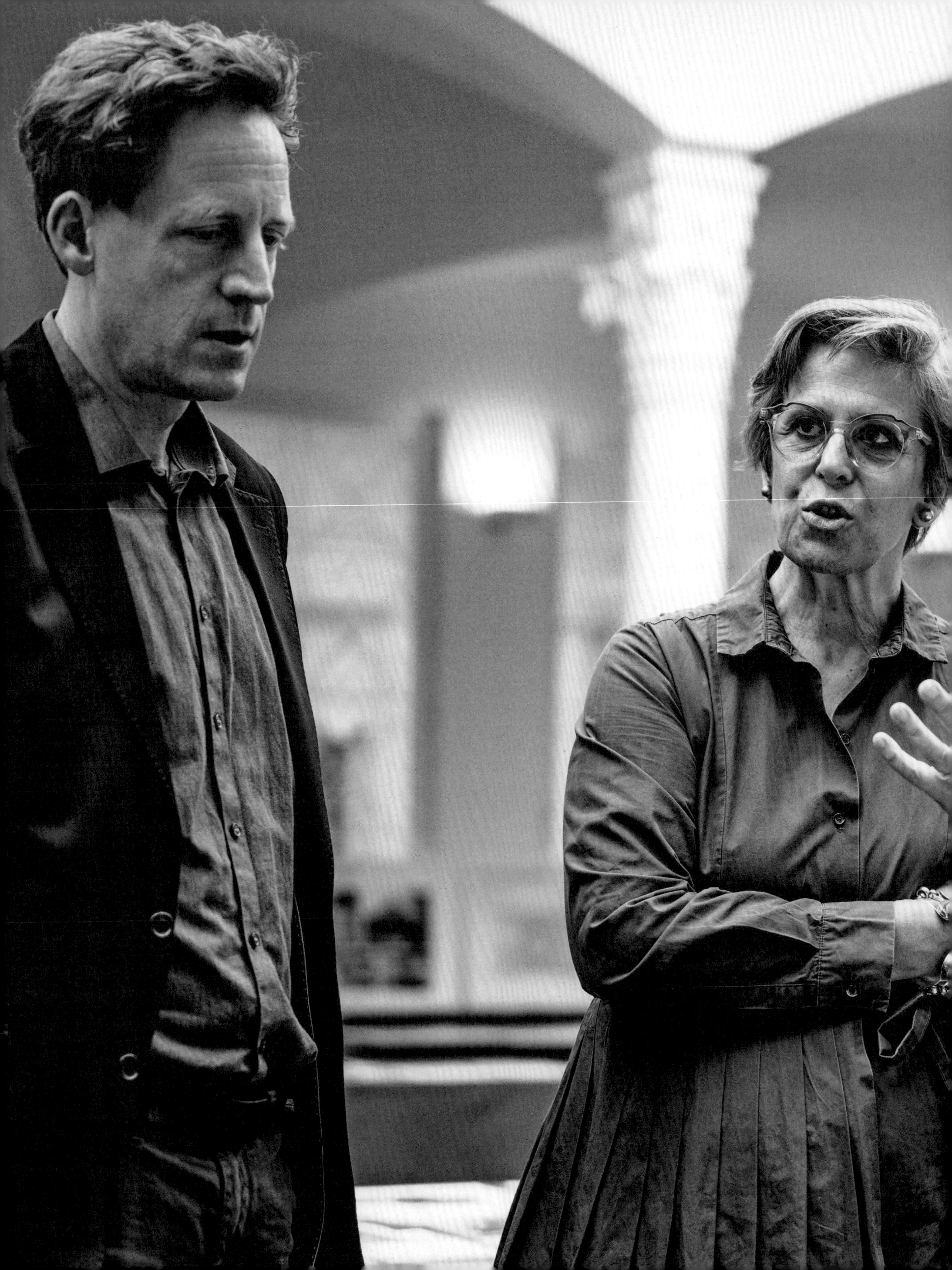

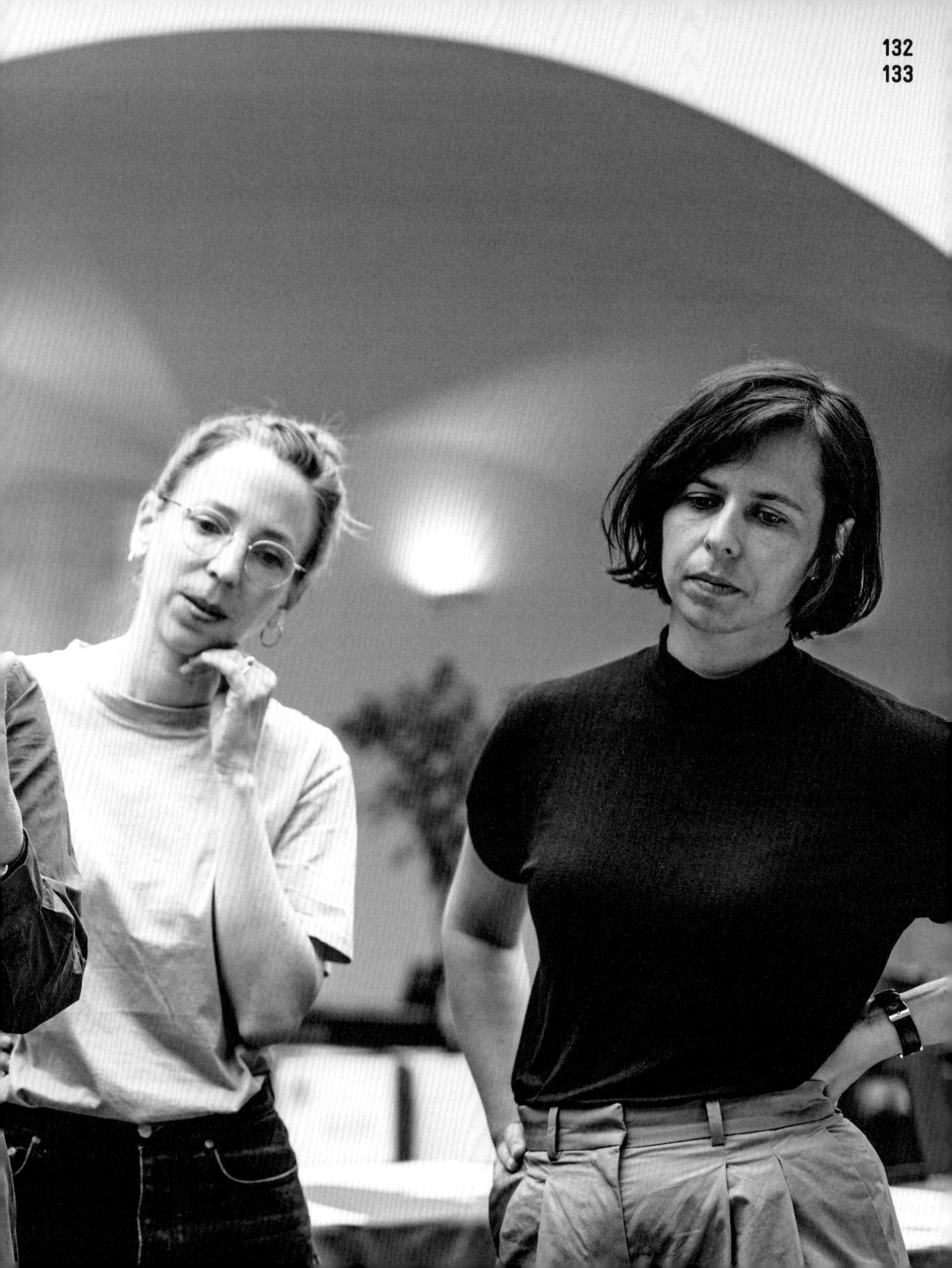

1 → SEITE/PAGE
136–143

2 → SEITE/PAGE
146, 150

3 → SEITE/PAGE
147, 151

4 → SEITE/PAGE
148, 152

PUBLIC DESIGN, URBAN DESIGN

GOLD:
1 **OBSTBAUMUSEUM GLEMS**
Förderverein Obstbaumuseum Glems e.V.
Metzingen-Glems

SILVER:
2 **STIHL MARKENWELT**
ANDREAS STIHL AG & Co. KG
Waiblingen

SPECIAL MENTION:
3 **GALERIESYSTEM**
Galerie Sammlung Amann
NO W HERE | Architekten Designer
Volpp Amann GbR
Stuttgart

4 **TINY BOXX**
Klaiber + Oettle Architekten
und Ingenieure GbR
Schwäbisch Gmünd

Gestaltung für die Öffentlichkeit ist immer auch von der Inszenierung geprägt – besonders Ausstellungskonzepte mit ihren multimedialen Präsentationen von Exponaten und Geschichten bedienen sich dieses Prinzips, um die Besuchenden für das jeweilige Thema zu gewinnen.

Design for public spaces invariably incorporates some element of staging, with exhibition concepts in particular likely to adopt this principle in the form of multimedia exhibits and narratives designed to attract visitors.

11

GOLD | OBSTBAUMUSEUM GLEMS | AUSSTELLUNGSKONZEPTION
EXHIBITION CONCEPT

OBSTBAUMUSEUM GLEMS

AUSSTELLUNGS KONZEPTION

PUBLIC DESIGN, URBAN DESIGN
PUBLIC DESIGN, URBAN DESIGN

FRÜHLING

PFLANZEN SCHUTZ

STREUOBSTBAU

KARREN SPRITZE

RÜCKEN SPRITZE

GOLD

OBSTBAUMUSEUM GLEMS
AUSSTELLUNGSKONZEPTION / EXHIBITION CONCEPT

JURY STATEMENT

Ein herausragendes Beispiel für die zeitgemäße und zugleich hochwertige Ausgestaltung eines regionalen Museums, das sich in einer alten Hülle befindet. Die Präsentation verzichtet bewusst auf digitale Medientechnik und setzt auf analoge, sinnliche Mitmach-Erlebnisse.

An outstanding example of the contemporary yet high-quality design of a regional museum housed in an old building. The presentation deliberately avoids the use of digital media and focuses on delivering a sensory, hands-on analogue experience.

HERSTELLER/MANUFACTURER
Förderverein Obstbaumuseum Glems e.V.
Metzingen-Glems

DESIGN
VISUELL – Studio für Kommunikation GmbH
Stuttgart
Annika Köhnlein
Laureen Seider
Aline Wißmann
Luis Seider

Seit vielen Generationen wird am Rand der Schwäbischen Alb der Obstbau in Form von Streuobstwiesen mit hoher biologischer Diversität betrieben. Um dieses immaterielle Kulturerbe zu bewahren, informiert das Obstbaumuseum in Glems bei Metzingen in einer neu konzipierten Ausstellung über die regionale Bedeutung, die Pflege der Baumwiesen, ihre Rolle für die Biodiversität und die typischen Obstsorten selbst.

Installiert in der ehemaligen, inzwischen denkmalgeschützten Kelter, nutzt die Ausstellung analoge, haptische und interaktive Exponate samt spielerischer Anreize. Dazu gehört beispielsweise die Figur der Biene Glemmy, die Kinder durch das 150 Quadratmeter große Museum begleitet. Ergänzend zu dieser Dauerschau kann der Betreiberverein mittels eines modularen Systems auch temporäre Ausstellungen selbst aufbauen.

For generations, fruit trees have been cultivated on the edge of the Swabian Alb in orchards with a high level of biological diversity. To preserve this intangible cultural heritage, the fruit-growing museum in Glems near Metzingen has created a new exhibition which explores the regional significance of fruit trees, their cultivation in orchards, their role in biodiversity and the typical fruit varieties grown.

Located in a former wine press, which is now a listed building, the exhibition uses analogue, haptic and interactive exhibits, including attractions for children such as Glemmy the bee, who accompanies them through the 150 square metre museum. Besides the permanent exhibition, the operating association is also able to host temporary exhibitions, using a modular display system.

LAUREEN UND LUIS SEIDER GESCHÄFTSFÜHRENDE, VISUELL GMBH

»Besuchende werden nicht mit Informationen überladen, sondern an die Hand genommen.«

»Visitors are not overloaded with information, but taken by the hand.«

LAUREEN AND LUIS SEIDER — MANAGING DIRECTORS, VISUELL GMBH

Das Obstbaumuseum Glems wird von einem Verein betrieben. Hat dies Ihre Arbeitsweise beeinflusst?

Der Förderverein engagiert sich stark für das Obstbaumuseum. Bisher wurde das Museum von den Vereinsmitgliedern getragen, die ihre Expertise in Führungen lebendig an Besuchende weitergegeben haben. Ihr wertvolles Wissen haben die Mitglieder im Rahmen verschiedener Workshops auch mit uns geteilt und somit in die Ausstellung integriert. Insbesondere der Vorstand Willy Müller war treibende Kraft des Projekts. Die inhaltliche und gestalterische Neuausrichtung des Museums war ein intensiver, über knapp drei Jahre laufender Prozess. Es war nicht immer einfach, die Kritik des Vereins in konstruktive und realisierbare Lösungen zu bringen.

Mit welcher Grundidee sind Sie in die Konzeption gestartet?

Ganz nach dem Motto ‚man schützt nur, was man kennt', sollen insbesondere junge Menschen für den Streuobstbau begeistert werden. Denn nur wenn das Wissen rund um den Streuobstbau weitergegeben wird, kann diese einzigartige Kulturlandschaft bewahrt werden. Die Grundidee ist, die Inhalte so aufzubereiten, dass Besuchende das Museum selbstständig erkunden können.

Sie haben bewusst auf übermäßige multimediale Interaktionen verzichtet. Warum?

Es geht uns nicht darum, möglichst viel digitale Technik in eine Ausstellung zu integrieren, sondern sie an sinnvollen Stellen einzusetzen. Im Obstbaumuseum gibt es beispielsweise einen Touchscreen, über den Informationen zu zahlreichen Obstarten und -sorten abgerufen werden können. Diese Sammlung kann über die Zeit kontinuierlich wachsen. An einer anderen Stelle haben wir bewusst Audio eingesetzt, um Tierstimmen erlebbar zu machen. An einer weiteren Medienstation können Besuchende Handwerksberufe audiovisuell und somit emotional kennenlernen.

The Glems Fruit Tree Museum is run by an association. Has this influenced the way you work?

The association plays a significant role in the fruit tree museum's activities. It has always been run by the members of the association, who also conduct guided tours to pass their expertise on to visitors. The members also share their valuable knowledge with us in various workshops, and we have incorporated this knowledge into the exhibition. Board member Willy Müller has been instrumental in driving the project forward. The overhaul of the museum's content and design was an intensive process that took almost three years. Transforming the association's criticisms into practical and achievable solutions was not always straightforward.

What was the underlying idea behind the original concept?

True to the motto "you only protect what you know", the aim is to get people – particularly young people – interested in meadow orchards. In other words, passing on knowledge about orchards is key to protecting this unique cultural landscape. The primary goal is to present the content in a way that fosters autonomous exploration and discovery by visitors.

You have deliberately avoided excessive use of interactive multimedia. Why is that?

Our aim was to employ digital technology selectively to enhance the exhibition experience. In the fruit tree museum, for example, you'll find a touchscreen that you can use to obtain information on many types and varieties of fruit. This body of knowledge will grow continuously over time. At another location, we have deliberately chosen audio to bring animal sounds to life. At another media station, visitors can enjoy an audiovisual presentation of different skilled trades, with a focus on the human element.

LAUREEN UND LUIS SEIDER GESCHÄFTSFÜHRENDE, VISUELL GMBH

Mit der Figur der Biene Glemmy und anderen spielerischen Elementen sprechen Sie explizit Kinder an. Gelingt dies?
Seit der Wiedereröffnung waren schon einige Besucher mit Kindern da. Die Biene Glemmy begrüßt sie und führt sie mit einem Bandolino-Spiel durch das Museum. Das Spiel haben wir in zwei Schwierigkeitsstufen entwickelt. Auch wenn dieses Angebot sehr gut angenommen wird, wünschen der Förderverein und wir uns noch mehr Familien und Schulklassen im Museum.

Bei einer relativ kleinen Fläche von 150 Quadratmetern muss man sich konzentrieren.
Der Schwerpunkt des Museums liegt auf dem Streuobstbau und den heute und früher notwendigen, jahreszyklischen Tätigkeiten. Dieser Jahreszyklus dient als roter Faden, der alle Themen der Ausstellung miteinander verbindet und zusammenhält.

Immer mehr Museen machen sich Gedanken über ihren ökologischen Fußabdruck. Inwieweit beeinflusste das Ihre Konzeption?
Das Zusammenspiel aus sorgfältig ausgewählten Materialien wie regionalem Holz, transparenten Lieferketten und der Zusammenarbeit mit lokalen Handwerksbetrieben führt zu einer langlebigen Ausstellung. Durch die zeitlose Thematik des Obstbaus bleibt das Museum auch in Zukunft relevant. Die eigens für die Sonderausstellungsfläche entwickelten modularen Möbel ermöglichen die Realisierung temporärer Ausstellungen ohne Ressourcenverschwendung. Diese beleuchten immer wieder neue Themen und schaffen einen Anreiz, das Museum immer wieder zu besuchen.

Die Aufmerksamkeitsspanne sinkt, sagt man, auch in Museen. Wie reagiert man darauf als Gestaltende?
Indem wir unterschiedliche Informationsebenen schaffen. Bereits ein kurzer Besuch im Obstbaumuseum vermittelt durch die übergeordnete Informationsebene mit aussagekräftigen Exponaten, Videos, Grafiken und prägnanten Texten einen ersten Eindruck über die Tätigkeiten rund um den Streuobstbau. Besuchende werden nicht mit Informationen überladen, sondern an die Hand genommen und durch kurze Texte an das Thema herangeführt. Sie können selbst entscheiden, weiter in die Tiefe zu gehen.

Und eine letzte Frage: Warum haben Sie gerade dieses Projekt zum Focus Open eingereicht?
Als Designerinnen und Architekten tragen wir eine gesellschaftliche Verantwortung. Wir identifizieren uns stark mit dem Projekt und können absolut dahinterstehen. Über alle Leistungsphasen hinweg sind wir gemeinsam mit allen Beteiligten ans Ziel gekommen – darauf sind wir stolz.

Visuell – Studio für Kommunikation, entwickelt und realisiert emotionale Ausstellungen und Events für Museen sowie Unternehmen. Das 1986 gegründete Stuttgarter Kreativstudio hat sich auf die visuelle Kommunikation im Raum spezialisiert, das Team versammelt unterschiedlichste Gestaltungsdisziplinen.

www.visuell.de

LAUREEN AND LUIS SEIDER

MANAGING DIRECTORS, VISUELL GMBH

The Glemmy the Bee character and other playful elements appeal directly to children. Has this proven successful?
Quite a few people have visited with children since the reopening. Glemmy the Bee welcomes them and guides them through the museum with the aid of a Bandolino game. We created the game with two difficulty levels. While our offer has been very well received, both we and the association would like to attract even more families and school classes to the museum.

With a relatively small area of 150 square metres, you need to concentrate.
The museum explores the enduring seasonal cycle of orchard life and the tasks that bring fruit to our tables. This seasonal cycle serves as a common thread that links and binds together all the themes of the exhibition.

More and more museums are thinking about their ecological footprint. How did this influence your concept?
The interplay of carefully selected materials like regional wood, combined with transparent supply chains and collaboration with local craft businesses, has resulted in a timeless exhibition. The enduring appeal of fruit cultivation will maintain the museum's relevance well into the future. Thanks to the modular furniture that was custom designed for the special exhibition space, temporary exhibitions can be organised efficiently and cost-effectively. These provide information on a range of new topics and encourage repeat visits to the museum.

They say that attention spans are shrinking, even in museums. How do you react to this as a designer?
By creating different levels of information. Even a brief visit to the fruit-growing museum provides a rich introduction to the world of orcharding – through the use of engaging exhibits, informative videos, graphics and clear explanatory texts. Visitors are not overloaded with information but are taken by the hand and introduced to topics by means of short texts. They can then decide for themselves whether they would like to explore the topic in more depth.

One last question: why did you submit this particular project to Focus Open?
As designers and architects, we have a social responsibility. We strongly identify with this project and are absolutely behind it. Together, we and everyone involved successfully completed every stage of the project – and we are proud of that.

Visuell – Studio für Kommunikation, develops and stages emotionally resonant exhibitions and events for museums and businesses. Founded in 1986, the Stuttgart-based creative studio specialises in visual design for spaces. The team brings together a wide range of design disciplines.

www.visuell.de

ALEXANDER SCHLAG

YELLOW DESIGN GMBH, PFORZHEIM/TOKIO

»Design bietet in Zeiten der großen Transformation für Unternehmen die einzigartige Chance, sich zu differenzieren und die Zukunft aktiv zu definieren.«

»In times of great transformation, design offers companies the opportunity to stand out and actively shape the future.«

Alexander Schlag ist geschäftsführender Gesellschafter und seit 2024 Alleingesellschafter der in Pforzheim und Tokio ansässigen yellow design GmbH. Die Leitung des Büros hat der Industriedesigner bereits 2001 übernommen. Der Schwerpunkt seiner Arbeit liegt auf der Entwicklung von Projekten im Industrial- wie auch im Interior-Design. Dazu gehört insbesondere auch die europäisch-japanische Zusammenarbeit.

www.yellowdesign.com

Alexander Schlag is managing partner and, since 2024, the sole shareholder of yellow design GmbH based in Pforzheim and Tokyo. An industrial designer by profession, he assumed overall management of the studio in 2001. He specialises in projects involving both industrial and interior design, with a particular emphasis on European-Japanese cooperation.

www.yellowdesign.com

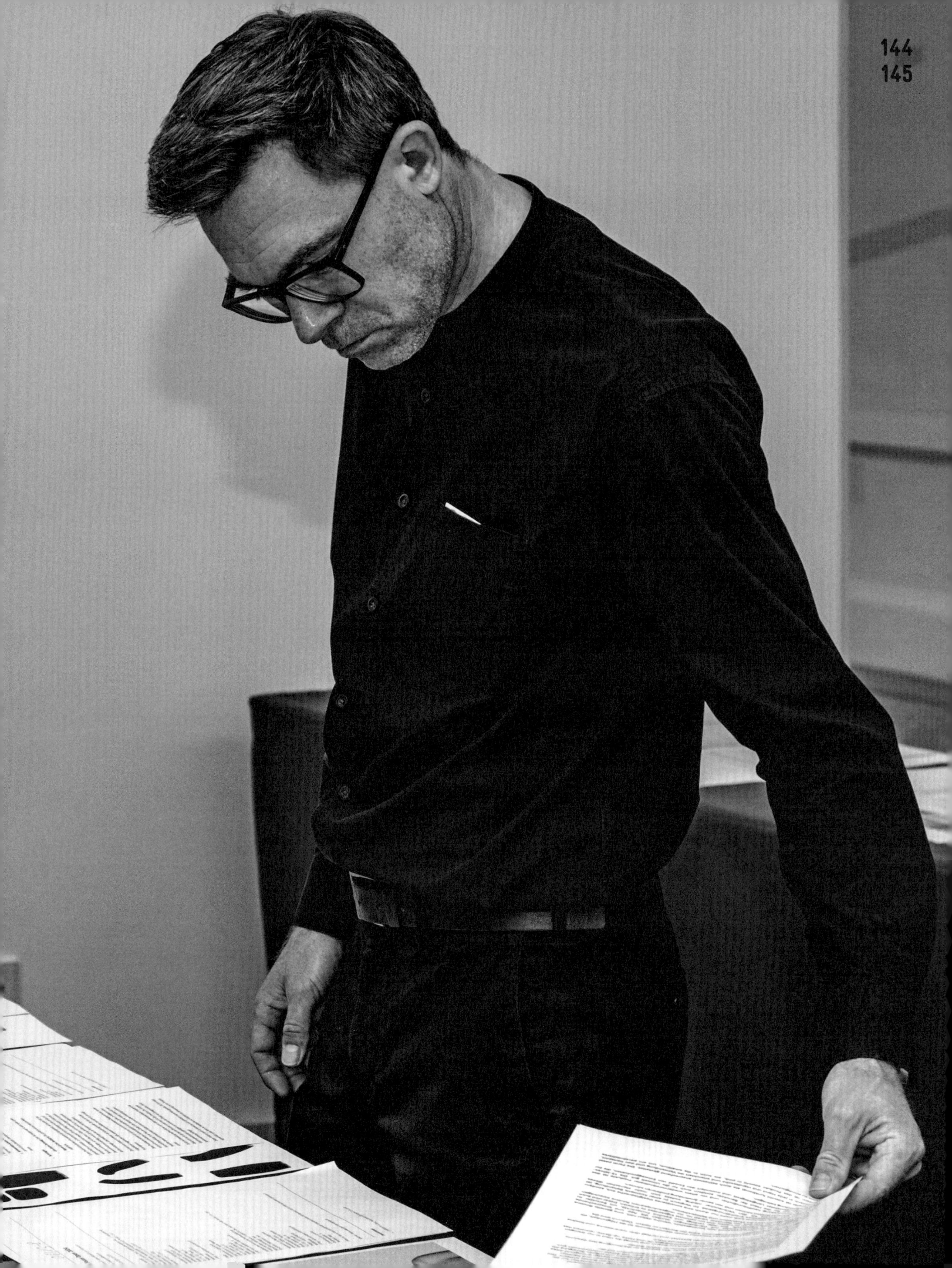

SILVER STIHL MUSEUM AUSSTELLUNGSKONZEPT
→ SEITE/PAGE EXHIBITION CONCEPT
150

| SPECIAL MENTION | GALERIESYSTEM
→ SEITE/PAGE 151 | PRÄSENTATIONSKONZEPT
PRESENTATION CONCEPT |

| SPECIAL MENTION | TINY BOXX | WALDKINDERGARTEN-GEBÄUDESYSTEM |
| | → SEITE/PAGE 152 | FOREST KINDERGARTEN BUILDING SYSTEM |

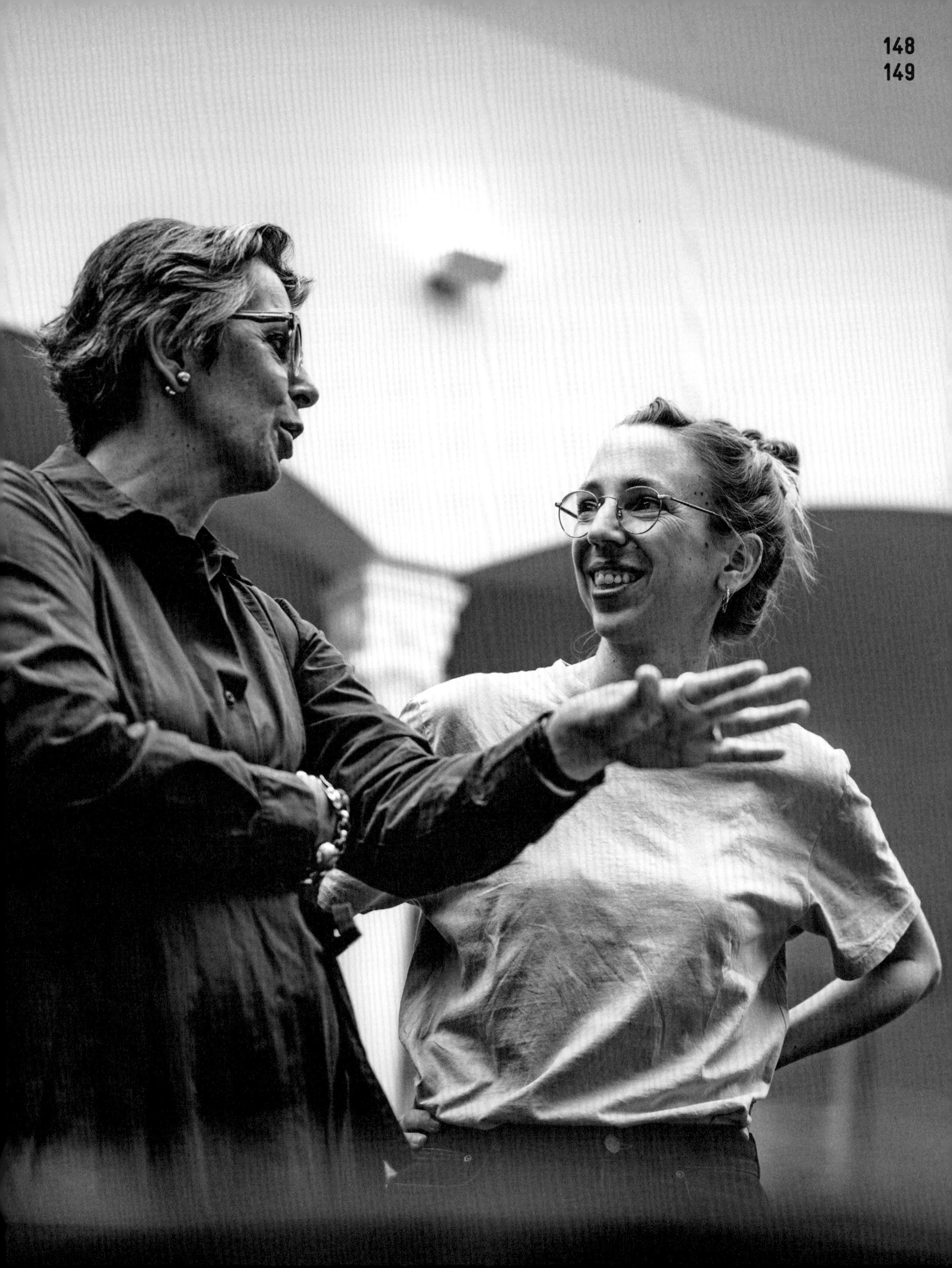

SILVER

STIHL MARKENWELT
AUSSTELLUNGSKONZEPTION / EXHIBITION CONCEPT

JURY STATEMENT

Obwohl Stihl das Synonym für Kettensägen ist, stehen die Geräte nicht aufdringlich im Vordergrund der Ausstellung. Zuerst, und das ist besonders zu erwähnen, geht es um die Natur, um den Wald, den Baum als Basis des Lebens und auch des Unternehmens. Die Schau bietet einen hohen Erlebniswert für alle Besuchergruppen.

While Stihl is synonymous with chainsaws, the exhibition is not a "hard sell" for the company's products. It should be pointed out that the emphasis here is not so much on the company but rather on nature and the forest and trees as the basis for life. The show provides a rich and rewarding experience for all visitors.

AUFTRAGGEBER/CLIENT
ANDREAS STIHL AG & Co. KG
Waiblingen

DESIGN
dreiform GmbH
Hürth
Niels Athanasiadis
Anika Biel
Katharina Böke
Philipp Frank
Clemens von Gizycki
Nadine Ledieu
Ralf Nähring

Seit Herbst 2023, knapp acht Jahre nach der Wettbewerbs-Entscheidung, lädt Stihl am Stammsitz Waiblingen in sein neues Unternehmensmuseum. Auf drei Ebenen und rund 1600 Quadratmetern Fläche präsentiert die Ausstellung nicht nur die Geschichte des Herstellers von Kettensägen, sondern thematisiert auch den Wald als Lebensraum und die nachhaltige Forstwirtschaft. Erst auf den Ebenen darüber zeigt Stihl die Historie seiner Produkte sowie Einblicke in die Entwicklung und Produktion aktueller Serien. Ergänzend dazu können sich die Besuchenden mittels VR-Exponaten sowie einer Mitmachstation im Timbersports genannten Wettkampf des Baumstammzerteilens messen. Café, Shop und eine Außentribüne runden das Museum ab.

Stihl has been inviting visitors to the new company museum at its headquarters in Waiblingen since autumn 2023, almost eight years after the announcement of the architectural competition result. Spanning three levels across approximately 1600 square metres, the exhibition not only presents the history of the chainsaw manufacturer but also focuses on the forest as a habitat and sustainable forestry. On the higher floors, Stihl shows the history of its products and provides insights into the development and production of its current product range. Visitors can also experience tree-felling in a "Timbersports" competition via VR stations and a hands-on area. A café, a brand shop and an outside lounge area complete the offering.

SPECIAL MENTION   **GALERIESYSTEM**   **PRÄSENTATIONSKONZEPT**
PRESENTATION CONCEPT

JURY STATEMENT

Eine sehr gute Lösung für Galerien, die unterschiedlichste Exponate zeigen. Das Konzept dient als neutrale, flexible Bühne, der eigentliche Raum bleibt erkennbar. Die Elemente optimieren zudem die Akustik des offenen Raumes.

A very good solution for galleries that display a wide variety of exhibits. The concept provides a neutral, adaptable space that preserves the room's identity. The modules also optimise the acoustics of the room.

AUFTRAGGEBER/CLIENT
Galerie Sammlung Amann
Stuttgart

DESIGN
NO W HERE | Architekten Designer
Volpp Amann GbR
Stuttgart

Galerieräume sollten so flexibel wie möglich nutzbar sein, andererseits braucht es aber feste Wände, um Kunst präsentieren zu können. Diesen Zielkonflikt löst die kleine Sammlergalerie mit Hilfe von Wandmodulen, die, an Deckenschienen hängend, frei im ehemaligen Abstellraum platzierbar sind. Die Elemente bestehen aus einer MDF-Tragstruktur und Oberflächen aus recyceltem PET-Filz. Den Filz fixieren sichtbare, in einem Raster angeordnete Verschraubungen, die zugleich als Hängepunkte für unterschiedliche Bildformate dienen. Da die Elemente zu schweben scheinen, entsteht eine sehr luftige Atmosphäre – werden die Wände nicht benötigt, lassen sie sich platzsparend in einer Raumecke konzentrieren.

Das Konzept ergänzt ein geschlossener Regalblock mit Filzverkleidung und ein zweites Deckenschienensystem für kleine LED-Leuchten.

While gallery spaces need to be as flexible as possible, the fundamental requirement of displaying artwork mandates permanent walls. This small collector's gallery effectively resolves this dilemma by using freely positioned wall modules suspended from ceiling rails in a former storage room. The modules consist of an MDF support structure with surfaces made from recycled PET felt. The felt is fixed in place by visible screws arranged in a grid, which also serve as hanging points for different picture formats. As the modules appear to float, a very airy atmosphere is created. Whenever the walls are not needed, they can be gathered together in a corner of the room to save space.

The concept is enhanced by a closed, felt-covered shelf block and a second ceiling track system for small LED lights.

SPECIAL MENTION TINY BOXX **WALDKINDERGARTEN-GEBÄUDESYSTEM**
FOREST KINDERGARTEN BUILDING SYSTEM

> **JURY STATEMENT**
>
> Das Holzbau-Konzept ist gut durchdacht und bietet alles, was ein Waldkindergarten braucht: einen baulichen Rückzugsort mit großen Fenstern, der autark und reversibel seinen Platz in der Natur findet. Außerdem zeigt er eine wohltuende, angemessene, ästhetische Rauheit.
>
> The thoughtfully designed timber construction concept provides everything a forest kindergarten needs: a self-sufficient, reversible structure with large windows, offering a sheltered retreat within nature. Its aesthetic roughness is both attractive and fitting.

HERSTELLER/MANUFACTURER
Klaiber + Oettle Architekten
und Ingenieure GbR
Schwäbisch Gmünd

DESIGN
Martin Kreis
Schwäbisch Gmünd

Waldkindergärten boomen – kein Wunder, sind sie doch in unserer so überaus medial geprägten Welt ein naturnaher Ort für das Lernen mit allen Sinnen.

Dabei führen nicht selten groß dimensionierte Bauwagen- oder Containermodelle mit Wasser- und Stromanschluss sowie Elektro- oder Gasheizung den Gedanken eines ressourcenschonenden, elementaren Zu- und Umgangs mit der Natur ad absurdum. Ganz anders die Konzeption der Tiny Boxx: Entstanden aus einer Zusammenarbeit zwischen Designer, Architekten und einer Elterninitiative ist die aus Holz gefertigte Basisstation autark, ohne jeden Anschluss an Versorgungssysteme. Der Innenraum gliedert sich in einen Eingangsbereich mit Garderobe und Lagerflächen, einen Bereich mit Ofen zum Aufwärmen, Malen und Spielen und einen Rückzugsraum im Dach mit Kuschelecke und Tierbeobachtungsposten. Bemerkenswert ist die Wirtschaftlichkeit: Die Baukosten reduzieren sich gegenüber einer herkömmlichen Kita auf 35 Prozent, die Betriebs- und Wartungskosten auf lediglich 10 Prozent.

Forest kindergartens are flourishing. And it's no wonder, as they provide a sensory-rich, natural learning environment and a much-needed escape from our screen-dominated world.

However, the commonly used large construction trailers and containers fitted out with water, electricity and heating are clearly at odds with the principles of sustainability and immersion in nature. The Tiny Boxx is a radically different concept. A collaborative effort by designers, architects and parents, the wooden base station is entirely self-sufficient, requiring no external utilities. The interior is divided into an entrance area with a cloakroom and storage spaces, an area with a stove in which children can warm up, paint and play, and a quiet room in the roof with a cosy corner and an animal observation post. The system offers remarkable value for money. Construction costs are 35 percent lower than a conventional daycare centre and the operating and maintenance costs are 10 percent lower.

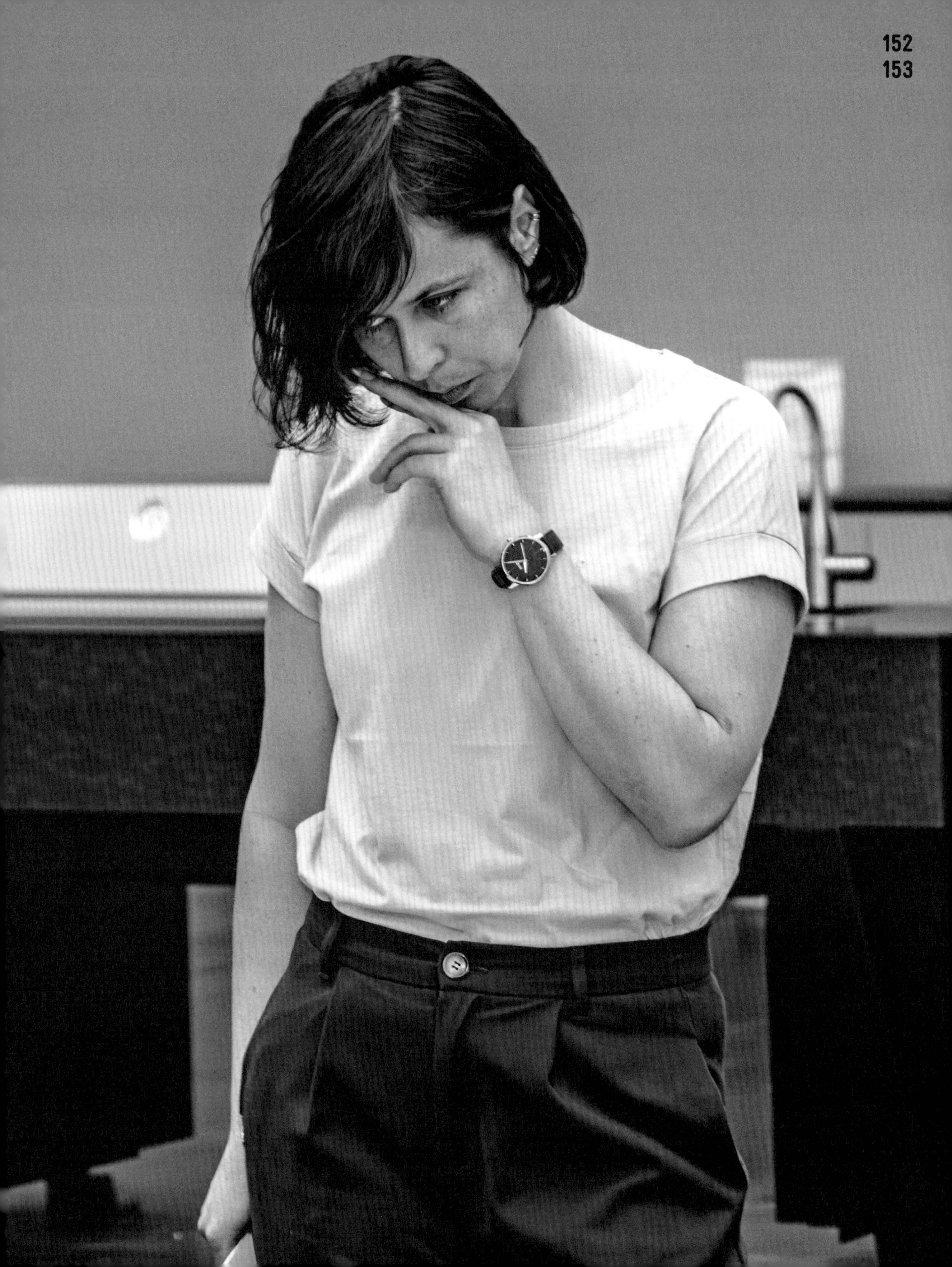

1 → SEITE/PAGE
156–163

2 → SEITE/PAGE
164, 166

3 → SEITE/PAGE
165, 167

MOBILITY
MOBILITY

GOLD:
1 **SSB DT8.16**
Stuttgarter Straßenbahnen AG
Stuttgart

SILVER:
2 **TL3Z PRO**
Supernova Design GmbH
Gundelfingen

SPECIAL MENTION:
3 **APZ 1003**
HANSA – Maschinenbau
Vertriebs- und Fertigungs GmbH
Selsingen

Die Mobilität ist ein Schlüsselthema der Moderne – und eines, das vor großen Transformationen steht. Zugleich diversifizieren sich die Mobilitätsangebote immer weiter, einschließlich spezifischer Detaillösungen für Services, Wartung oder Individualisierung. Mobility wird dreidimensional und bleibt spannend.

Mobility is a key theme of the modern age – and one that is facing major transformations. At the same time, mobility offerings are becoming increasingly diversified, including specific detail improvements to services, maintenance and customisation. Mobility is becoming three-dimensional and remains a fascinating field.

12

| GOLD | SSB DT8.16 | STADTBAHN LIGHT RAIL |

SSB DT8.16
STADTBAHN

MOBILITY
MOBILITY

156
157

FOCUS GOLD

Hauptbahnhof
Schlossplatz
SSB

GOLD SSB DT8.16 STADTBAHN
                 LIGHT RAIL

JURY STATEMENT

Es ist schon herausragend, wie modern und zeitlos eine urbane Bahn sein kann, wenn man der Versuchung widersteht, stylische Elemente einzubauen. Die Stadtbahn zeigt einen neutralen Gestaltungstenor, stellt den Nutzwert in den Vordergrund und schafft auch noch das Kunststück, an die formale Tradition der Vorgängerinnen anzuknüpfen.

It's remarkable how modern yet timeless an urban railway can be if you resist the temptation to incorporate stylish elements. This light rail system features a timeless design that prioritises functionality while also managing to echo the aesthetics of its predecessors.

AUFTRAGGEBER/CLIENT
Stuttgarter Straßenbahnen AG
Stuttgart

HERSTELLER/MANUFACTURER
Stadler Deutschland GmbH
Berlin

DESIGN
TRICON AG
Kirchentellinsfurt

Als Rückgrat des Stuttgarter Nahverkehrs dient seit Jahrzehnten die Stadtbahn – eine breitspurige Bahn, die auf eigenen Trassen sowohl ober- als auch unterirdisch unterwegs ist. Ab 2026 wird die vierte Fahrzeuggeneration auf die Schienen kommen, die optisch an ihre Vorgängerinnen anknüpfen und dennoch Eigenständigkeit vermitteln soll. So setzt vor allem die Wagenfront mit dem ergonomisch nochmals optimierten Arbeitsplatz neue visuelle Akzente. Das Interior bietet noch mehr Flexibilität – und vor allem mehr Raum für Rollstuhlfahrende, für Fahrräder, Rollatoren oder Kinderwagen. Transparenz, hochwertige Materialien und ein angenehmes, indirektes Licht erhöhen neben der Aufenthaltsqualität auch die subjektive Sicherheitswahrnehmung der unterschiedlichen Nutzergruppen. Bei der Konzeption wurde zudem viel Wert auf Reparaturfähigkeit und lange Betriebszyklen gelegt.

The light rail system – a wide-gauge railway network running above and below ground – has been the backbone of Stuttgart's local transport system for decades. In 2026, the city will take delivery of its fourth generation of light rail vehicles which, while paying homage to the visual legacy of their predecessors, will feature a distinct, modern aesthetic. For example, the front section of the vehicle with the ergonomically optimised driver's desk gains new visual accents. The interior offers even more flexibility, with more space to accommodate wheelchairs, bicycles, walking frames and pushchairs. The spacious layout, high-quality materials and comfortable, indirect lighting not only enhance the quality of the interior but also foster a heightened sense of security for all users. Repairability and longevity were key considerations during the design phase.

FRANK SCHUSTER **VORSTAND, TRICON AG**

»Neue Fahrzeuge dürfen ihre Vorgängerbahnen nicht alt aussehen lassen.«

»New vehicles shouldn't make their predecessors look outdated.«

FRANK SCHUSTER — BOARD MEMBER, TRICON AG

Die neue Stadtbahn-Generation soll an die Vorgängerbahnen anschließen. Was bedeutet das für Sie als Gestalter?

Die Forderung war klar definiert: Die neuen Fahrzeuge müssen zukunftsorientiert sein, dürfen ihre Vorgänger aber nicht alt aussehen lassen. Das ist nicht ganz einfach, denn die jüngste Variante, DT 8-12 genannt, stammt aus dem Jahr 2012. In dieser Zeit hat sich einiges getan, selbst in der Bahnbranche. Kurz gesagt: Die neue Bahn sollte klar als Mitglied der großen Stadtbahn-Familie erkennbar sein. Wir haben aber kein Re-Design erstellt, sondern ein komplett neues Fahrzeug.

Die Gestaltung von Zügen ist eine komplexe Sache. An welcher Stelle beginnt man da?

Wir beginnen mit dem Exterieurdesign, um genau zu sein, mit der Fahrzeugfront. Die ist aus zweierlei Hinsicht sehr wichtig. Erstens bestimmt die Front, wie mir eine Bahn begegnet. Zweitens tragen Bahnen im urbanen Raum auch zum Gesicht einer Stadt bei. Daher ist der Kopf von Straßenbahnen fast immer individuell gestaltet.

Bezogen auf Stuttgart heißt das?

Stuttgart befindet sich schon immer in einem Spannungsfeld aus Tradition und Moderne. Wir haben versucht, dieses Charakteristikum über die typische Nutzungszeit einer Stadtbahn fortzuschreiben und dabei den künftigen urbanen Kontext mitgedacht. Daraus entstanden verschiedene Konzepte, zunächst für das Exterieur, dann für das Interieur. Der ausgewählte Entwurf lässt sich als geradlinig beschreiben, Kurven kommen nicht vor, Radien sind bewusst reduziert, die Anmutung ist tendenziell architektonischer und technischer als bei den Alternativen. Aber das passt zum Stuttgarter Raum, wo ja viele Tech-Akteure angesiedelt sind. Wir haben kein modisches, sondern ein modernes Design entwickelt, das im ersten Moment irritieren darf und muss. Wir gestalten ja perspektivisch für die Zukunft.

Aber dennoch soll das Design anschlussfähig sein. Ist das kein Widerspruch?

Ich würde das als Herausforderung bezeichnen – und als das, was uns als Designer auszeichnet. Wir entwickeln keine Disruptionen, sondern Perspektiven. Und die greifen das auf, was da ist, um es weiterzuentwickeln. Schließlich geht es ja auch um Akzeptanz bei den Zielgruppen, also um die Menschen, die den Nahverkehr nutzen. Für die gestalten wir, nicht für uns.

The new light rail generation will link up with the previous rail system. What does this mean to you as a designer?

The requirement was clearly specified: the new vehicles must be modern without making their predecessors look outdated. It wasn't an easy task, as the previous variant, known as the DT 8-12, dates back to 2012 and a lot has happened since then, even in the railway industry. In short: the new tram should be clearly recognisable as a member of the larger light rail family. However, we didn't simply redesign; we created a brand-new vehicle.

Designing trains is a complex task. Where do you start?

We start with the exterior design, with the front of the vehicle in fact. This is very important for two reasons. First, the train's frontal aesthetics shape your perception of the railway. Secondly, city railways are key contributors to a city's character. That's why individualised fronts are a common feature of trams.

How does this apply to Stuttgart?

Stuttgart has always been torn between the allure of its heritage and the pull of progress. We have sought to maintain this characteristic during the typical lifetime of a light railway, while also considering the future urban environment. This approach generated a variety of ideas, first for the exterior and then for the interior. You could describe the chosen design as "linear", in that there are no curves, radii are deliberately minimised, and the overall look veers more towards architectural and technical than the other ideas we came up with. But that is appropriate for the Stuttgart region, which is home to many tech companies. We haven't developed a fashionable design, but a modern one that can, indeed must, be unsettling at first glance. After all, we are designing for the future.

But the design has to be compatible with previous ones. Isn't that a contradiction?

I would describe it as a challenge – and that's what characterises us as designers. We don't disrupt; we deliver insights. We pick up on what is already there in order to develop and enhance it. It's also about appealing to our target groups: the people who use local transport. We design for them, not for ourselves.

FRANK SCHUSTER

VORSTAND, TRICON AG

Sie haben dafür extra Nutzende befragt und Zielgruppen neu definiert.
Ja, das war sehr hilfreich für die Innenraum-Konzepte. Wir konnten so fünf Nutzergruppen identifizieren, von denen drei besonders interessant sind, weil deren Erwartungen und Bedürfnisse bisher nicht optimal abgebildet waren. Die erste Gruppe nennen wir die „Mercedes-Fahrenden", die aus ihrem geschützten, komfortablen Auto in die Stadtbahn einsteigen sollen. Die möchten natürlich ein hochwertiges, sauberes und zuverlässiges Fahrzeug. Die zweite Gruppe sind all jene, die etwas mit sich führen, also einen Kinderwagen, einen Rollator, ein Fahrrad oder einen Rollstuhl. Für diese Gruppe haben wir große Mehrzweckbereiche geschaffen, die einfach zu erreichen sind. Und dann waren da noch junge Frauen, denen es in erster Linie um Sicherheit und Distanz geht. Ihnen ist der Blick durch das Fahrzeug wichtig und sichere Sitz- oder Stehplätze.

Apropos Stehplätze, Sie halten von Vollbestuhlungen wenig.
Richtig. Wir haben bei der neuen Stadtbahn sogar mehr Stehplätze vorgesehen. Nicht aus Kapazitätsgründen, sondern um die Gesamtzufriedenheit zu steigern. Das hört sich seltsam an, ich weiß. Aber spätestens, wenn die Sitzplätze belegt sind, muss man stehen. Oder man setzt sich bewusst nicht, weil die Fahrt nur ein, zwei Haltestellen dauert. Stehplätze sind heute Notplätze, ohne Komfort, ohne definierten Ort, blockieren den Raum und fühlen sich unsicher an. Mit Lösungen, die Komfort und Raumstruktur schaffen, wird also der Wert von Stehplätzen erhöht – und damit auch die Zufriedenheit aller Fahrgäste.

Spätestens, wenn es um Stoffe oder Farben geht, werden Entscheidungsfindungen oft komplex. Wie gehen Sie damit um?
Aus diesem Grund haben wir unseren Interieur-Entwurf zuerst ganz ohne Farbe präsentiert. Wir wollten den Blick auf die grundlegende Struktur des Raumes und die Aufteilungen lenken. Farbe lenkt da eher ab und fordert emotional heraus. Daher lassen wir Farbe erst später einfließen, was nicht heißt, dass wir schon früh exakte Vorstellungen haben. Auch mit den textilen Bezügen verfahren wir so. Tatsächlich hat die Stoffentwicklung samt der Detailabstimmung der Blaunuance eine lange Phase in Anspruch genommen.

Einen wichtigen Aspekt haben wir bislang ausgespart: den Arbeitsplatz. Lag dessen Gestaltung auch in Ihrer Hand?
Wir haben sogar ein Arbeitsmodell des Cockpits in Originalgröße aufgebaut. Sowohl, um Sichtwinkel zu prüfen, als auch die ergonomischen Faktoren oder die Platzierung der Außenkamera-Displays. Dieses Mock-Up war, wie auch das des Fahrgastraumes, Grundlage für Zwischendiskussionen mit dem Kunden und für die finale Design-Entscheidung. Letztlich sollen sich die Fahrerinnen und Fahrer am Arbeitsplatz wohlfühlen – und im besten Fall sogar etwas stolz darauf sein.

Komplex bedeutet eine lange Entwicklungszeit, oder?
2020 haben wir erstmals unsere Ideen präsentiert, 2024 dann wurde das Design mit dem Kunden gefixt. Jetzt arbeiten wir mit dem Hersteller an der Umsetzung weiter. 2025 sollen die ersten Exemplare auf die Schiene gehen. Das ist recht schnell, manches Medizinprodukt dauert da länger.

Kunde und Hersteller sind also nicht identisch?
Nein, früher war das so, aber heute werden wir meist von den späteren Betreibern der Bahn beauftragt. So können wir viel besser die Perspektiven der Nutzenden einbringen und für mehr Qualität sorgen.

Tricon wurde 1995 gegründet und firmiert seit 2001 als AG. Die Designagentur mit Sitz in Kirchentellinsfurt ist spezialisiert auf internationale Bahnprojekte, die sowohl den Fern-, den Regional- als auch den Nahverkehr einschließen. Daneben ist das Team im Medical- wie auch Industriedesign aktiv.

www.tricon-design.de

FRANK SCHUSTER   **BOARD MEMBER, TRICON AG**

You conducted user interviews and redefined your target groups.
Yes, that was very helpful for the interior design concepts. We were able to identify five user groups, three of which are especially interesting because their expectations and needs hadn't previously been fully understood. We call the first group the "Mercedes drivers", who leave the comfort and protection of their cars to travel on the light rail network. Not surprisingly, they expect a clean, high-quality, reliable vehicle. The second group are those carrying something with them – a pushchair, a rollator, a bicycle or a wheelchair, for example. For this particular group, we created large multi-purpose areas that are easy to access. And then there was the group of young women who are primarily concerned with safety and space. Having a clear view through the vehicle and safe seating or standing areas are important to them.

Speaking of standing room, you don't seem to think much of full seating.
Indeed so. And we've provided even more standing room in the new light rail vehicles. Not for capacity reasons, but to improve passenger satisfaction. I appreciate that might sound strange, but you will eventually have to stand as a passenger – at the latest when the seats are full. Or when you decide not to sit down because you are only travelling one or two stops. Today's standing areas are uncomfortable, temporary emergency spaces. They obstruct pathways and create a sense of insecurity. However, solutions that create space and enhance comfort can elevate the perceived value of standing areas, thereby increasing overall passenger satisfaction.

Decision-making can become complex when you start dealing with materials and colour. How do you handle this?
This is why we didn't use any colour at all when we presented our first interior design. We wanted to emphasise the basic layout and space allocation. Colour tends to be distracting and emotionally charged, which is why we didn't introduce colour until later. That doesn't mean we hadn't already developed a colour concept, of course. We adopt the same approach with textiles. It actually took a long time to create the fabric, including carefully matching the unique shade of blue.

We've left out one important aspect so far: the driver's workplace. Did you also design that?
We even built a full-scale replica of a working cockpit to optimise driver sightlines, ergonomics and the placement of external camera displays. The mock-ups of both the cockpit and passenger compartment facilitated iterative discussions with the customer and informed the final design. Drivers deserve a comfortable workspace and, ideally, one they can also be proud of.

Complex means a long development time, right?
We first presented our ideas in 2020 and finalised the design with the customer in 2024. We're now working with the manufacturer to realise the design. The first units should be operational in 2025. That's fairly quick; some medical products take longer.

So, your customer isn't the manufacturer?
No, that used to be the case, but today our customers are normally the railway operating companies themselves. This allows us to involve the users directly and to deliver superior products.

Tricon was founded in 1995 and has operated as a public limited company since 2001. The design agency based in Kirchentellinsfurt specialises in international rail projects, including long-distance, regional and local commuter trains. The team's expertise also extends to medical and industrial design.

www.tricon-design.de

SILVER TL3Z PRO BIKE-RÜCKLICHT
→ SEITE/PAGE BIKE TAIL LIGHT
166

SPECIAL MENTION   APZ 1003   KOMMUNALE GERÄTETRÄGERSERIE
                             MUNICIPAL EQUIPMENT CARRIER

→ SEITE/PAGE 167

SILVER TL3Z PRO BIKE-RÜCKLICHT / BIKE TAIL LIGHT

JURY STATEMENT

Design und Funktionalität kommen hier trefflich zusammen. Die Integration des üblicherweise additiven Reflektors ist bestens gelungen und trotz der grazilen Auslegung ist die Lichtstärke hervorragend. Für E-Biker und -Bikerinnen erhöht sich damit die Sicherheit – auch dank der automatischen Bremsanzeige.

A flawless fusion of design and functionality. The seamless integration of the reflector has been a great success and, despite the slim form factor, the light intensity is outstanding. This, together with the automatic brake light function, promises greater safety for e-bikers.

HERSTELLER/MANUFACTURER
Supernova Design GmbH
Gundelfingen

DESIGN
Inhouse/In-house

Dieses Rücklicht wurde speziell für puristisch gestaltete E-Bikes konzipiert, integriert zusätzlich ein StVZO-konformes, automatisches Bremslicht und rahmt den vorgeschriebenen Heckreflektor. In den schlanken, homogen leuchtenden Lichtlinien arbeiten 32 Mikro-LEDs, welche ein Beschleunigungssensor beim Bremsen verzögerungsfrei noch heller schaltet – oder Notbremsungen durch schnelles Blinken anzeigt. Intelligente Algorithmen im Sensor verhindern, dass beispielsweise Schlaglöcher das Bremslicht auslösen.

Das Multifunktions-Rücklicht gibt es für Fahrradhersteller als Komplett-Einheit mitsamt Schutzblech – und als universellen Nachrüstsatz für ältere E-Bikes.

Designed for minimalist e-bikes, this tail light also features an automatic, StVZO-compliant brake light and integrates the legally required rear reflector within the illuminating area. The slim unit is uniformly illuminated by 32 micro-LEDs. An acceleration sensor ensures that they brighten instantly when braking and flash rapidly when making an emergency stop. Intelligent algorithms in the sensor prevent potholes or similar hazards from triggering the brake light.

The multifunctional tail light is available to bicycle manufacturers as a complete unit including mudguard or as a universal retrofit kit for existing e-bikes.

SPECIAL MENTION — APZ 1003 — KOMMUNALE GERÄTETRÄGERSERIE / MUNICIPAL EQUIPMENT CARRIER

JURY STATEMENT

Ein sehr überzeugendes, detailliert durchdachtes Konzept, das nahezu alle Einsatzszenarien abdeckt. Dank der Modularität ist die variantenreiche Produktion für das mittelständische Unternehmen überhaupt erst machbar.

A versatile, well-conceived design that caters to a broad spectrum of uses. By leveraging a modular concept, the medium-sized company is able to deliver a highly customisable product with a wide range of production variants.

HERSTELLER/MANUFACTURER
HANSA – Maschinenbau
Vertriebs- und Fertigungs GmbH
Selsingen

DESIGN
Lumod GmbH
München

Das Einsatzspektrum kommunaler Nutzfahrzeuge ist erstaunlich breit – und damit auch die Anforderungen an deren Konfiguration sowie Produktion. Die neu entwickelte Serie ist daher modular aufgebaut und ermöglicht so unterschiedliche Fahrzeugbreiten, Kabinenhöhen sowie Aufbauten. Mit diesem Konzept lassen sich auch individuelle Einzelfahrzeuge wirtschaftlich herstellen.

Die geräumig ausgelegte Kabine bietet beste Sicht und Ergonomie – ihre Front visualisiert das neu entwickelte, horizontal angelegte Markengesicht. Details wie auf die Reifenbreite anpassbare Kotflügel, in den A-Säulen platzierte Scheibenwischer sowie die funktionale Zusammenführung bislang getrennter Elemente verbessern sowohl die Nutzung als auch die Wartung. Aus der Einfachheit macht das Design eine Tugend: Die Rahmenkonstruktion bleibt unverkleidet und wird zu einer visuellen Klammer, die Eigenständigkeit signalisiert und die wesentlichen Merkmale der Fahrzeuge hervorhebt.

Because municipal commercial vehicles are used for a surprisingly wide range of tasks, they need to be produced in a wide variety of configurations. This newly developed range of vehicles therefore boasts a modular design that accommodates different vehicle widths, cab heights and body options. The concept means that vehicles can be tailored to meet individual requirements at an affordable price.

The spacious cab delivers excellent visibility and ergonomics and features a front end that embodies the brand's new, horizontal design language. Details such as mudguards that can be adjusted to the width of the tyres, A-pillar-integrated wipers and the consolidation of previously separate components all contribute to an enhanced user experience and simplified maintenance. The design celebrates simplicity: its exposed frame acts as a visual accent, emphasising the vehicle's uniqueness and core functionality.

1   → SEITE/PAGE
     170, 174

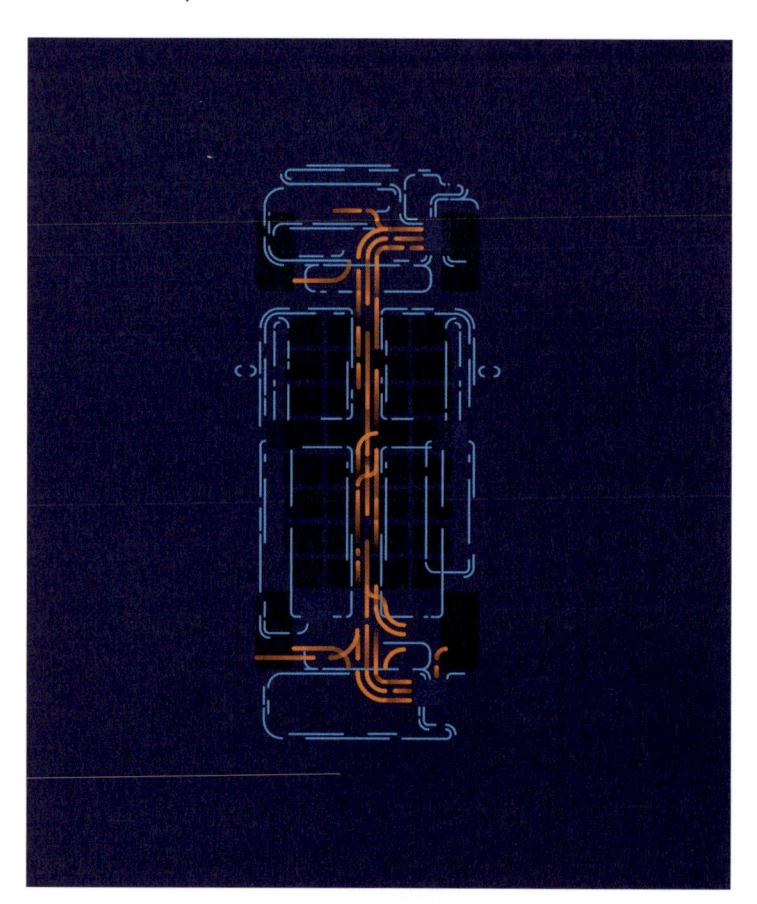

2   → SEITE/PAGE
     171, 175

3   → SEITE/PAGE
     172, 176

KOMMUNIKATIONSDESIGN
COMMUNICATION DESIGN

SILVER:
1 **ARBEIT IM WANDEL**
  Bundesagentur für Arbeit
  Nürnberg/Nuremberg

2 **100**
  Fraport AG
  Frankfurt

SPECIAL MENTION:
3 **LEONI**
  LEONI AG
  Nürnberg/Nuremberg

Marken wollen kommuniziert sein – über Publikationen, digitale Formate, Abbildungen oder Events. Differenzierung und Positionierung gehen Hand in Hand mit Informationsaufbereitung, emotionaler Ansprache sowie einzigartigen Elementen mit visueller oder haptischer Qualität.

Brands strive to establish a strong presence across various channels, from traditional publications to digital platforms, images and live events. Effective differentiation and positioning require a strategic blend of informative content, emotionally resonant messaging and visually engaging or tactile elements.

14

SILVER   ARBEIT IM WANDEL   AUSSTELLUNGSKONZEPTION
         → SEITE/PAGE   EXHIBITION CONCEPT
         174

SILVER	100	JUBILÄUMSBUCH ANNIVERSARY BOOK
→ SEITE/PAGE 175		

SPECIAL MENTION	LEONI BRAND DESIGN	BRAND DESIGN
	→ SEITE/PAGE 176	BRAND DESIGN

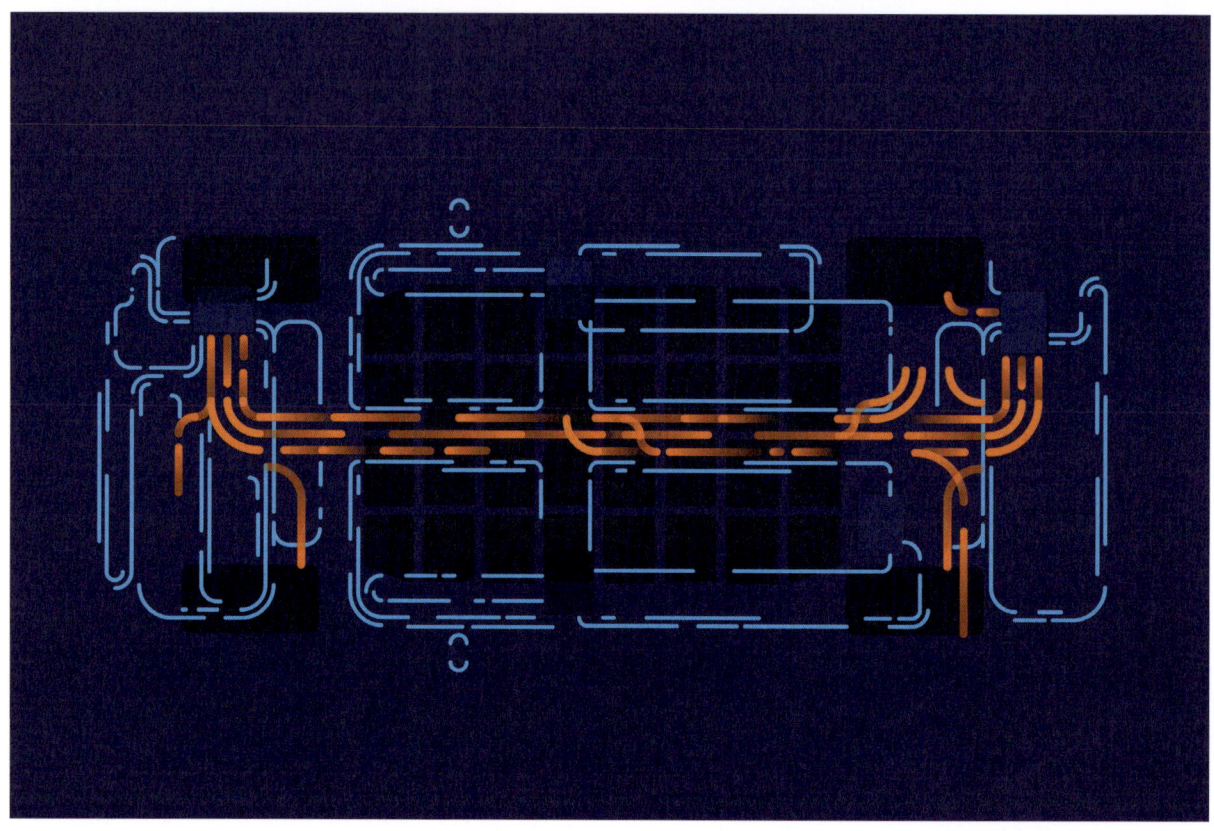

172
173

SILVER

ARBEIT IM WANDEL

**AUSSTELLUNGSKONZEPTION
EXHIBITION CONCEPT**

> **JURY STATEMENT**
>
> Die Ausstellung ist nicht nur technisch auf dem aktuellsten Stand, sondern überzeugt auch mit ihrer konsequenten Bildsprache. Ästhetik und Interaktionen passen exakt zur jungen Zielgruppe und natürlich zum Thema. Behörde und aktuelle Konzepte schließen sich also doch nicht aus.
>
> The exhibition is not only technologically cutting-edge but also boasts a compelling and cohesive visual identity. The aesthetics and interactions are perfectly suited to both the young target group and the topic. Contrary to popular belief, government departments and modern creative concepts are not necessarily mutually exclusive.

HERSTELLER/MANUFACTURER
Bundesagentur für Arbeit
Nürnberg/Nuremberg

DESIGN
Echo & Flut GmbH
Stuttgart
Christian Hammer
Marzell Ruepp
Michael Wiedemann

Berufe verändern sich permanent: Sie verlieren an Relevanz, sterben aus, neue kommen hinzu. Dies veranschaulicht die Wanderausstellung der Agentur für Arbeit, allerdings mit Blick in die Zukunft. Sie zeigt also neue Chancen und motiviert, das Neue anzupacken. Bis 2025 ist die Schau in den Berufsinformationszentren zu sehen, inklusive aufwendiger Interaktionen, darunter eine VR-Zeitreise, ein Arbeitsplatz-Konfigurator sowie ein Exoskelett zum Testen. Die sechs Themeninseln wurden gemeinsam mit einem Expertenteam des Fraunhofer-Institutes IAO entwickelt.

Parallel dazu lässt sich die Schau auch online als 3D-Anwendung besuchen. Alle Inhalte sind dort hinterlegt, teils auch interaktiv spielbar.

Occupations are constantly changing: some are declining, others are disappearing, while new ones are emerging. This is the theme of the Federal Employment Agency's travelling exhibition, which offers a glimpse into the future of work, highlights new opportunities and inspires visitors to embrace change. The exhibition, which includes elaborate interactions such as a VR journey through time, a workplace configurator and a hands-on "exoskeleton", will visit career information centres until 2025. The six themed islands were developed together with a team of specialists from the Fraunhofer Institute IAO.

An online 3D version of the exhibition is also available, featuring all the content, including interactive elements.

JURY STATEMENT

Ein sehr gelungenes Beispiel dafür, wie man ein komplexes Unternehmen und dessen vielschichtige Geschichte darstellen kann. Sehr hochwertig, solide und filigran zugleich, voller Infografiken und Abbildungen. Letztere sind trotz unterschiedlicher Entstehungszeit stimmig zusammengeführt.

A truly successful demonstration of how to present the intricate history of a large and complex organisation. Of exceptional quality, the book is meticulously constructed and detailed, and replete with infographics and illustrations. Despite spanning various historical periods, the visual elements are harmoniously integrated.

HERSTELLER/MANUFACTURER
Fraport AG
Frankfurt

DESIGN
Cicero Kommunikation GmbH
Wiesbaden
Stefanie Laib
Dr. Dirk Michael Becker

Zum 100-jährigen Jubiläum ließ sich der Flughafen Frankfurt, genauer, die Fraport AG, ein Jubiläumsbuch erstellen. Das zeigt in 12 Kapiteln und auf 248 Seiten nahezu alle Aspekte, die mit dem Flugverkehr vor Ort zu tun hatten und haben. Druck- und gestaltungstechnisch bietet es so manche Raffinesse, beginnend bei der goldenen „100" auf dem Cover über Sonderfarben im Inneren bis hin zu einem wiederkehrenden Muster, das sich aus der Rollfeld-Draufsicht ableitet. Auf 1500 gedruckte Exemplare limitiert, lassen sich die Inhalte auch in einer frei zugänglichen Online-Variante mit identischen Gestaltungsmerkmalen aufrufen.

Frankfurt Airport, officially known as Fraport AG, has published an anniversary book to commemorate its centenary. In 12 chapters and 248 pages, the book offers a detailed exploration of the airport's rich history of air traffic. The book boasts numerous design refinements within its pages, from the golden "100" on the cover to the use of special colours and a recurring tarmac-inspired pattern within its pages. Limited to a print run of 1500 copies, the book is also available in a freely accessible online version with an identical design.

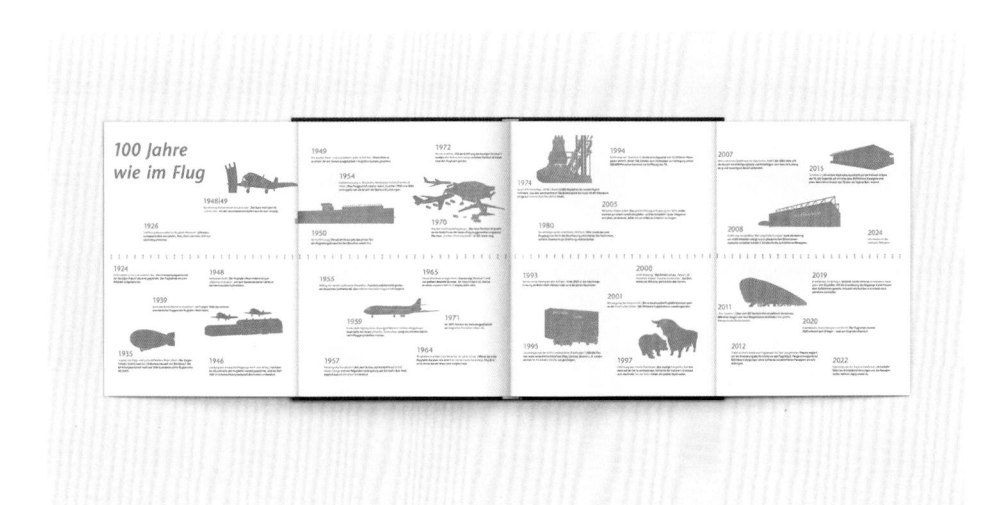

SPECIAL MENTION   **LEONI**   **BRAND DESIGN**
BRAND DESIGN

> **JURY STATEMENT**
>
> Das neue Brand Design wirkt sehr modern, aber keinesfalls modisch. Die sehr komplexe Aufgabe des medienübergreifend wirksamen Re-Branding wurde bestens gelöst. Und das mit einfachen Mitteln.
>
> The new brand design is very modern without being trendy. The complex challenge of cross-media rebranding has been elegantly solved with a simple yet effective solution.

HERSTELLER/MANUFACTURER
LEONI AG
Nürnberg/Nuremberg

DESIGN
design hoch drei GmbH & Co. KG
Stuttgart

Wenn sich Unternehmen neu aufstellen, kann es zu Dissonanzen mit dem Corporate Design kommen. So transformiert sich derzeit das Unternehmen Leoni vom reinen Kabelhersteller zum Entwickler von Fahrzeug-Bordnetzen. Mit einem neuen Brand Design soll nun diese Positionierung und Strategie zum Ausdruck kommen – und zugleich eine Differenzierung im Wettbewerb gelingen.

    Das Brand Design nutzt Linien und Punkte als zentrale Elemente und bezieht sich damit auf die Struktur von Bordnetzen: Die Linie steht für das Kabel, der Punkt für den Hub im Netz. Einfache Designprinzipien also, die sowohl funktional als auch modern wirken und konsistent über alle Medien anwendbar sind.

Structural changes within a company can often lead to inconsistencies in its established corporate design. Leoni, for example, is currently evolving from a cable manufacturer to a developer of vehicle wiring systems. The new brand design is intended to effectively convey the company's strategic direction and establish a clear market differentiation.

    The brand design is built upon lines and dots, reflecting the structure of wiring systems: cables as lines, hubs as dots. This simple yet modern approach lends itself to all media platforms.

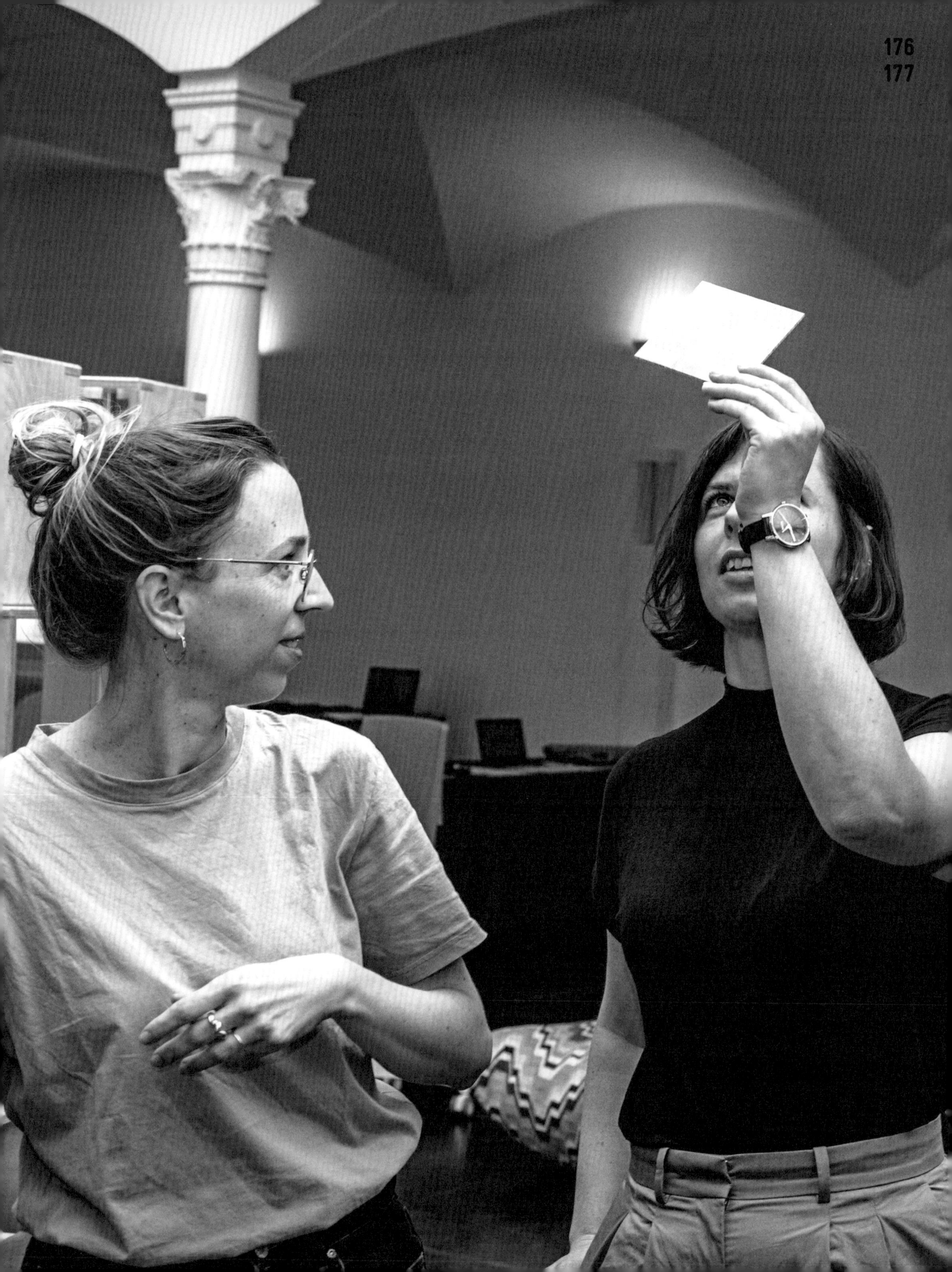

1 → SEITE/PAGE
180–181

MATERIALS & SURFACES
MATERIALS & SURFACES

SILVER:
1 **KARUUN®**
karuun GmbH
Kißlegg

Technik beeinflusst das Design, auch Werkstoffe tun dies mehr denn je. Materialien mit innovativen Eigenschaften eröffnen Nutzungsszenarien, die zu mehr Nachhaltigkeit, geringerem Ressourcenverbrauch oder optimierter Funktionsintegration leiten. Die Grundlage dafür schafft die multidisziplinäre Kooperation von Forschung, Engineering und Design.

Technology has always influenced design, and materials are having a greater impact than ever before. Materials with innovative properties can enable more sustainable practices, reduce resource consumption and optimise functional integration. The foundation for this is established through multidisciplinary collaboration by specialists from research, engineering, and design.

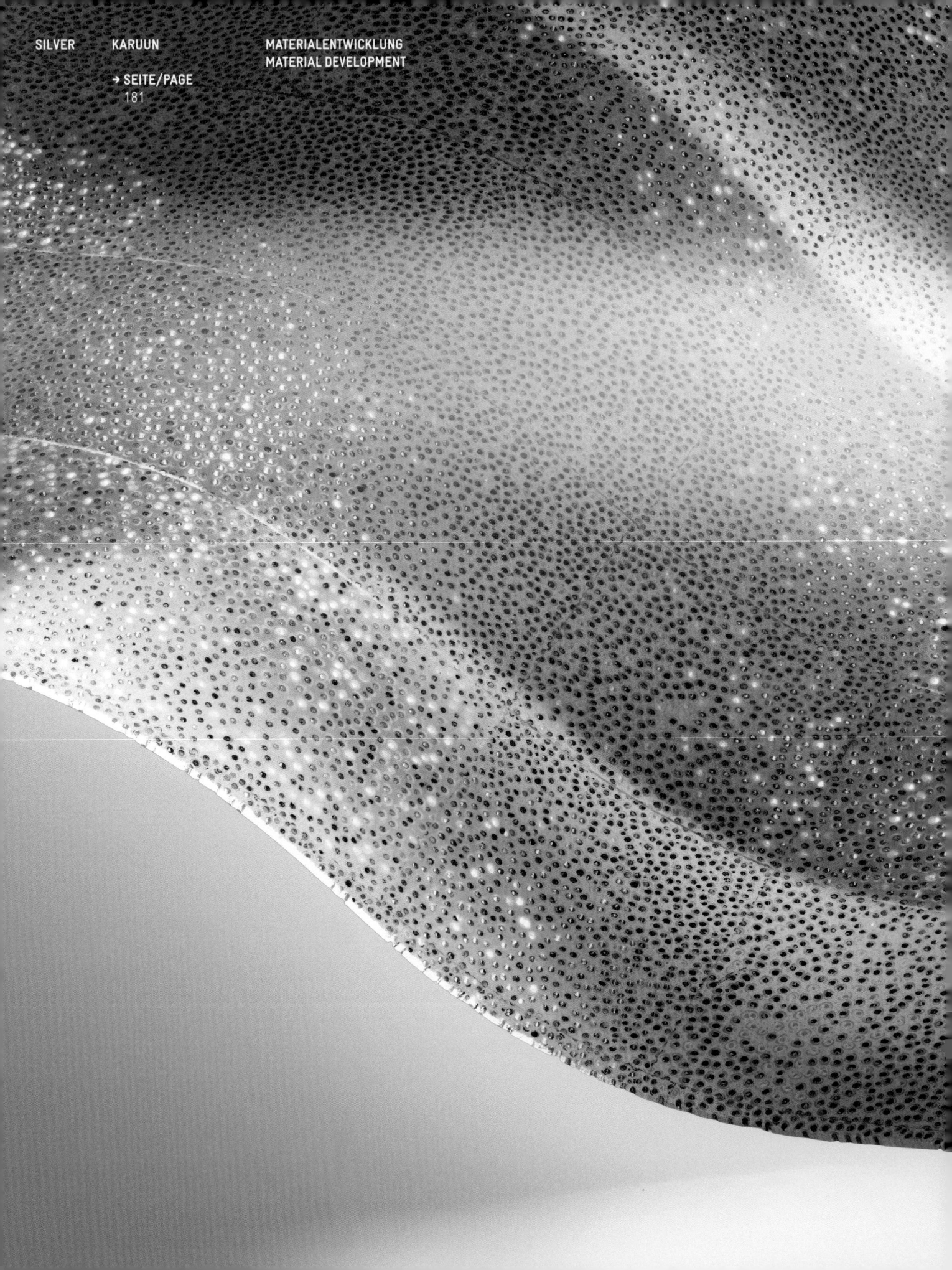

SILVER KARUUN MATERIALENTWICKLUNG
MATERIAL DEVELOPMENT
→ SEITE/PAGE
181

SILVER — KARUUN® — MATERIALENTWICKLUNG / MATERIAL DEVELOPMENT

JURY STATEMENT

Naturbasierte Materialien können eine ganz eigene, faszinierende Ästhetik entfalten – das beweist das Karuun®-Konzept trefflich. Zudem werden dank der sonstigen Eigenschaften neue Anwendungen möglich. Ein tolles Beispiel für die aktuell entstehende Generation von Werkstoffen auf biogener Basis.

The Karuun® concept perfectly illustrates the potential of natural materials to exhibit a distinctive and fascinating aesthetic. Thanks to its other properties, new applications are also possible. This is a great example of the current generation of biogenic-based materials.

HERSTELLER/MANUFACTURER
karuun GmbH
Kißlegg

DESIGN
Inhouse/In-house

Rattan ist eigentlich kein neues Material, es wird schon lange in traditioneller, handwerklicher Arbeit verwendet. Mit Karuun liegt nun ein auf Rattan basierender, industriell verwendbarer Werkstoff vor, der sich die typische Kapillarstruktur für visuelle und funktionale Zwecke zu eigen macht. Die patentierte Verarbeitung nutzt nicht nur den gesamten Querschnitt der Stangen, sie erlaubt auch, diese in furnierähnliche Platten oder große Blöcke zu pressen, die im Automotive- oder Baubereich als Halbzeug Anwendungen finden können. In die Kapillaren werden dabei UV-stabile Pigmente eingebracht, was die Struktur betont und Karuun eine ganz besondere Ästhetik verleiht. Sprich: Karuun ist farbig, kann massiv oder lichtdurchlässig sein – je nach Konfektionierung. Zudem wird es von Partnern in Indonesien produziert, stärkt also die dortige Rattan-Tradition.

Rattan is not actually a new material; it has a long association with traditional crafts. Karuun is a novel industrial material derived from rattan, which capitalises on its natural capillary structure for both visual appeal and practical applications. Through a patented process, the entire cross-section of the rods is used to create veneer-like panels or large blocks, providing semi-finished components for the automotive and construction sectors. The UV-stable pigments introduced into the capillaries emphasise the structure and lend Karuun a very special aesthetic. In other words, Karuun is coloured – solid or translucent depending on the process used. It is produced by partners in Indonesia, thus strengthening the local rattan tradition.

CAROLIN SCHMITT **PHOENIX DESIGN GMBH + CO. KG, STUTTGART**

»Intelligentes Design kann nachhaltiges Verhalten positiv verstärken, wenn wir Zusammenhänge aufzeigen und bei der Systemgestaltung ansetzen.«

»By understanding system interactions and using this knowledge to design systems more intelligently, we can positively reinforce sustainable behaviours.«

Carolin Schmitt ist seit 2016 als Principal Design Researcher bei Phoenix Design tätig. Als studierte Informationsdesignerin mit Schwerpunkt UX-Design leitet sie Research und Strategie in Innovationsprojekten für Kunden aus verschiedenen Branchen. Sie ist zudem Dozentin für Service Design an der Hochschule der Medien in Stuttgart und arbeitet als Systemische Coachin für Entwicklung von Teams und Organisationen.

www.phoenixdesign.com

Carolin Schmitt has been a principal design researcher at Phoenix Design since 2016. After graduating as an information designer with a specialisation in UX design, she now leads research and strategy for innovation projects across a range of industries. She also lectures in service design at Stuttgart Media University and works as a systemic coach for team and organisational development.

www.phoenixdesign.com

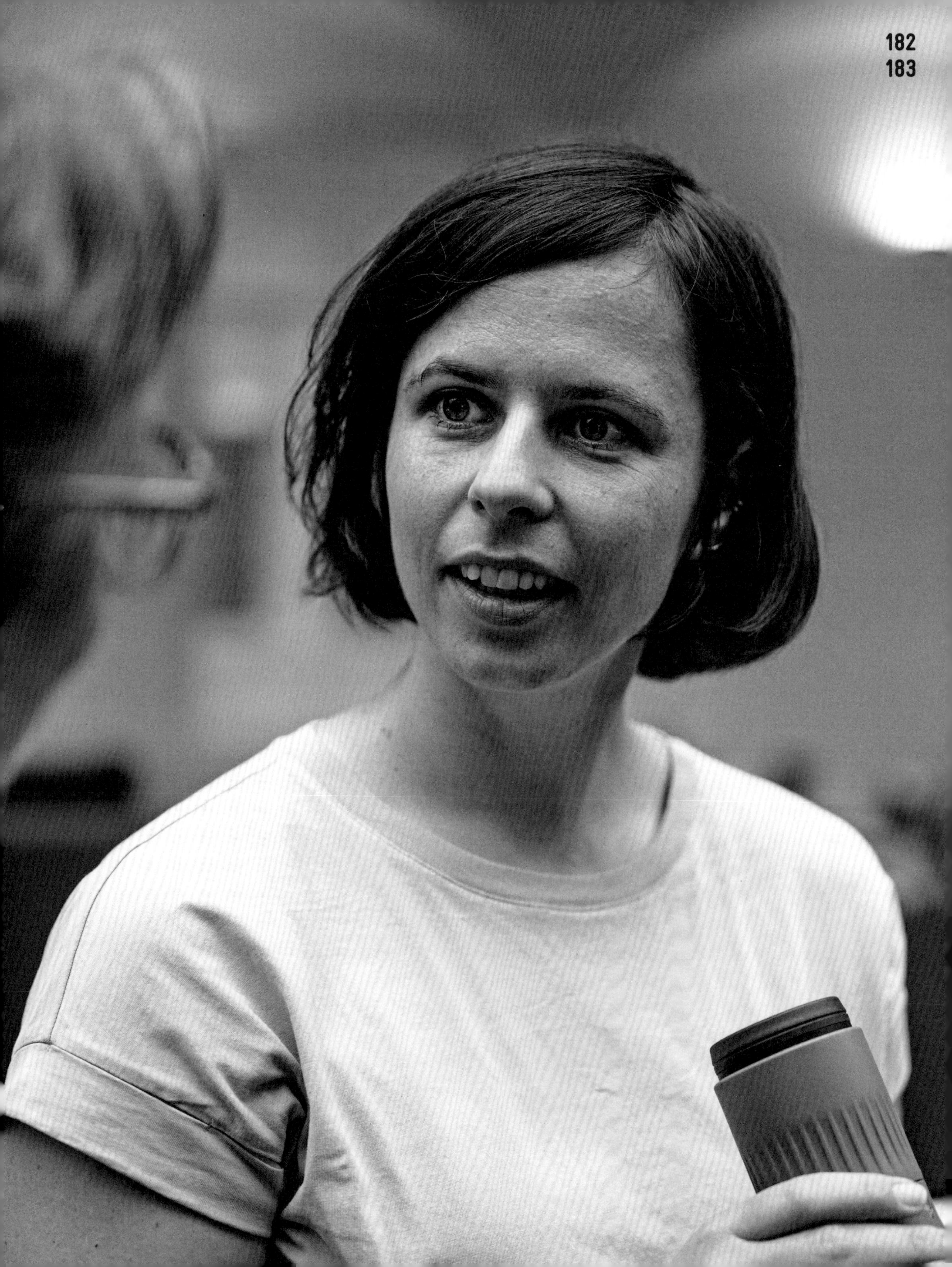

MIA SEEGER PREIS 2024

MIA SEEGER PREIS 2024

Jährlicher Wettbewerb der Mia Seeger Stiftung
für junge Designerinnen und Designer
mit freundlicher Unterstützung vieler Förderer

The Mia Seeger Foundation's annual
competition for young designers is supported
by the generosity of its many sponsors.

MIA SEEGER PREIS 2024
MIA SEEGER PRIZE 2024

DIE JURY
THE JURY

❶ BARBARA LERSCH
Kulturmanagerin,
Hans Sauer Stiftung, München
→ Cultural manager,
Hans Sauer Foundation, Munich

❷ STEFAN LIPPERT
Designer, UP Designstudio, Stuttgart;
Mia Seeger Preisträger 1993 und
Stipendiat 1993/94
→ Designer, UP Designstudio, Stuttgart;
Mia Seeger prize winner 1993
and scholarship winner 1993/94

❸ MONA MITJTHAB
Sozialunternehmerin und
Designerin, Mosan Sanitation Solution,
Zürich/Guatemala
→ Social entrepreneur and
designer, Mosan Sanitation Solution,
Zurich/Guatemala

❹ DANIEL RAUH
Designer, Shift GmbH, Falkenberg (Wabern)
→ Designer, Shift GmbH, Falkenberg
(Wabern)

❺ OLIVER STOTZ
Industriedesigner, Wuppertal;
Mia Seeger Preisträger 1992
→ Industrial designer, Wuppertal;
Mia Seeger prize winner 1992
stotz-design.com

❻ JULIA VOIGTLÄNDER
Industriedesignerin und Grafikdesignerin,
Rat für Formgebung, Frankfurt
→ Industrial designer and
graphic designer, German Design Council,
Frankfurt

MIA SEEGER PREIS 2024 / MIA SEEGER PRIZE 2024
10.000 EURO FÜR JUNGE DESIGNERINNEN UND DESIGNER / 10,000 EUROS FOR YOUNG DESIGNERS

Zum 33. Mal konnte die Mia Seeger Stiftung den Mia Seeger Preis über insgesamt 10.000 Euro an junge Designerinnen und Designer vergeben. Stolze 128 Einreichungen von 38 Hochschulen zeigen sehr deutlich, wie nachhaltig das Motto der Stifterin Mia Seeger „was mehr als einem nützt" ist und dass sich immer mehr Studierende und Lehrende mit dem Thema Social Design beschäftigen.

Die Jurierung der eingereichten Projekte fand am 3. Juni 2024 statt. Die 6 Jurorinnen und Juroren nahmen in Präsenz und auf digitalem Wege an der Jurysitzung teil. Die Einreichungen erfolgten wieder rein digital, keine Modelle, keine postalischen Einreichungen. Nach einer ersten Vorrunde wurden 55 Arbeiten der engeren Wahl intensiv begutachtet und diskutiert. Im Mittelpunkt der Bewertung stand neben der Qualität der Gestaltung auch die gesellschaftliche Relevanz der Konzepte und deren Impact für die Gemeinschaft. Geprüft wurde, ob es den Zielen der United Nations Sustainable Development Goals (UN SDGs) entspricht und ob es bereits vergleichbare Ansätze, Produkte oder Ideen gibt, die in der Recherche offengelegt sind. Als Ergebnis der Jurierung wurde eine Shortlist mit 6 Nominierungen für Preise und Auszeichnungen – noch ohne Rangfolge – veröffentlicht.

Ein besonderer Dank richtet sich an die finanziellen Unterstützer für den Preis 2024 Rat für Formgebung, Hans Schwörer Stiftung, Recaro, Hans Sauer Stiftung und Baden-Württembergische Bank. Großer Dank gilt ebenfalls den langfristigen Partnern Design Center Baden-Württemberg, Rat für Formgebung und UP Designstudio.

For the 33rd time, the Mia Seeger Foundation is delighted to award the Mia Seeger Prize worth a total of 10,000 euros to young designers. An impressive 128 submissions from 38 universities reflects the growing interest in social design among students and teachers and echoes the enduring value of the motto of the foundation's founder, Mia Seeger – "for the benefit of everyone".

On 3 May 2024, the judging panel convened at the premises of UP Designstudio in Stuttgart to evaluate the submitted projects. Six jurors participated in the judging session in person and virtually. Once again, all entries were submitted digitally, with no physical samples or mailed submissions accepted. After narrowing the field down to 55 projects, the jury proceeded to review and discuss their selections in more detail, considering not just the quality of the designs but also their social relevance and how they might impact the community. They also investigated how closely the entries were aligned with the United Nations Sustainable Development Goals (UN SDGs) and whether there were other similar approaches, products or ideas in existence. Finally, the jury issued a shortlist containing six nominations for prizes and awards, not yet ranked in any particular order.

Special thanks go to the German Design Council, the Johannes Schwörer Foundation, Recaro, Defortec, the Hans Sauer Foundation and the Baden-Württembergische Bank for their financial support for the 2024 Award. We would also like to thank our long-term partners Design Center Baden-Württemberg, the German Design Council and UP Designstudio.

MIA SEEGER PREIS 2024
MIA SEEGER PRIZE 2024

ORMO – ORAL MOTOR SKILLS

JURY STATEMENT

Ohne das Vermögen, klare und präzise Worte zu formulieren, werden Betroffene oft von der Teilhabe am gemeinschaftlichen Leben ausgeschlossen. Mit ihrem Masterprojekt ORMO – oral motor skills schafft Meret Oppermann eine ebenso spielerische wie auch ernsthaft durchdachte Methode zur Unterstützung der gezielten Sprachtherapie. Ihre Ausarbeitung, vom Storyboard über ergonomische Studien, bis hin zur Patentprüfung dokumentiert die gewissenhafte Bearbeitungstiefe. ORMO setzt im positiven Sinne einer „Gamification" Anreize zur kontinuierlichen Verbesserung der Fähigkeiten und sorgt für Kontinuität in der Anwendung. Das ausgezeichnete Projekt nützt mehr als Einem, indem es hilft Schwellen abzubauen und miteinander ins Gespräch zu kommen. Es ist eine innovative, zeitgemäße Lösung, die durch technische, aber auch soziale Überlegungen die Jury begeistert hat.

ENTWURF/DEVELOPER
Meret Oppermann

STUDIUM/DEGREE COURSE
Muthesius Kunsthochschule, Kiel
Medical Design

BETREUUNG/SUPERVISORS
Prof. Detlef Rhein
Prof.in Dr. habil. Christiane Kruse

Die Mundmuskulatur spielt eine zentrale Rolle beim Sprechen. Die Kontrolle dieser Muskeln hilft dabei, die Intonation und Betonung von Wörtern und Lauten zu steuern sowie die Artikulation und den Gesichtsausdruck zu koordinieren. Eine geschwächte oder gestörte Mundmuskulatur kann das tägliche Leben stark beeinträchtigen.

Meret Oppermann hat in ihrer Masterthesis an der Muthesius Kunsthochschule in Kiel eine Methode entwickelt, um die Mundmotorik spielerisch zu trainieren. Sprachlich beeinträchtigte Kinder und Erwachsene werden dabei unterstützt, ihre Sprach- und Schluckdefizite auszugleichen. ORMO ist ein „Joystick" für die Zunge mit dem man, begleitend zu einer Sprachtherapie, die Mund- und insbesondere die Lippen- und Zungenmuskulatur stärkt. Ein Controller im Mundraum steuert durch Zungenbewegungen und Erzeugung eines Unterdrucks das digitale Spiel. Drucksensoren erweitern die Funktionalität, um die Lippenmuskulatur zu aktivieren. Die Beißschiene passt sich durch das elastische Silikon unterschiedlichen Kieferformen an und verteilt die Kraft gleichmäßig auf die Zahnreihe. Die eingebaute Technik ist herausnehmbar, damit unterschiedliche Silikonaufsätze genutzt werden können. Fortschritte und Messungen werden über eine App aufgerufen und können als Daten in der logopädischen Behandlung verwendet werden. Spaß beim Üben und Lernen ist eine wichtige Voraussetzung, um die Motivation über einen längeren Zeitraum zu behalten und das Gelernte zu verinnerlichen.

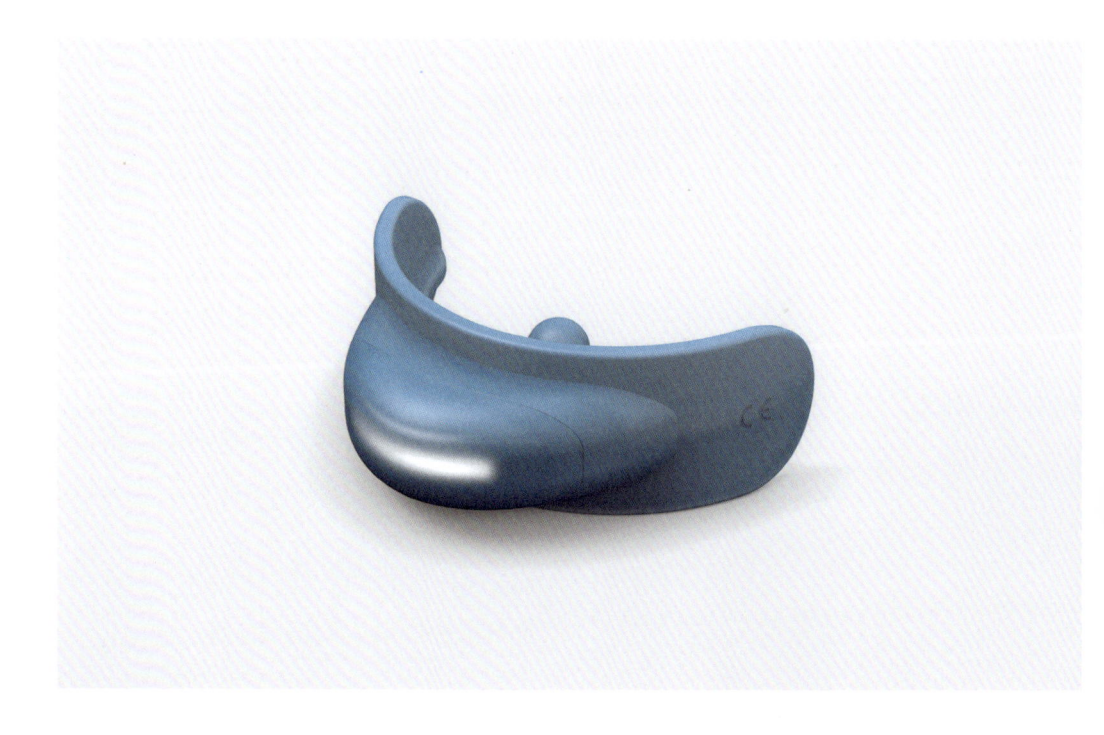

ORMO – ORAL MOTOR SKILLS

JURY STATEMENT

People who cannot speak clearly and accurately are often excluded from participating in community life. In her master's project ORMO – oral motor skills – Meret Oppermann developed a thoughtfully designed, game-play approach to supporting targeted speech therapy. Her study paper, from storyboard to ergonomic studies to patent examination, is a testament to the conscientiousness and thoroughness of her work. In the positive spirit of "gamification", ORMO incentivises continuous skill improvement by maintaining the interest of the user. This award-winning project benefits everyone by helping users break down barriers and engage in dialogue. It is an innovative and timely solution that impressed the jury by addressing both technical challenges and social needs.

The muscles of the mouth play a crucial role in speech. They allow for nuanced control over intonation and emphasis, while also coordinating articulation and facial expressions. Weak or malfunctioning mouth muscles can significantly impact essential daily activities.

In her master's thesis at the Muthesius Academy of Fine Arts and Design in Kiel, Meret Oppermann developed a play-based method of training oral motor skills that helps children and adults with speech impairments communicate more effectively and manage swallowing problems. ORMO is an "in-mouth joystick" that can be used alongside speech therapy to strengthen oral muscles, particularly those in the lips and tongue. It uses tongue movements and suction to interact with a sensor that allows the user to control a digital game on a screen. Pressure sensors extend the functionality by activating the lip muscles. Made from flexible silicone, the mouthpiece comfortably conforms to different jaw shapes and ensures even pressure distribution across the teeth. The built-in technology is removable and can be transferred to different silicone attachments. An app is available to track progress and provide data to support speech therapy treatment. Enjoying the practice and learning process is essential for maintaining long-term motivation and internalising what you have learned.

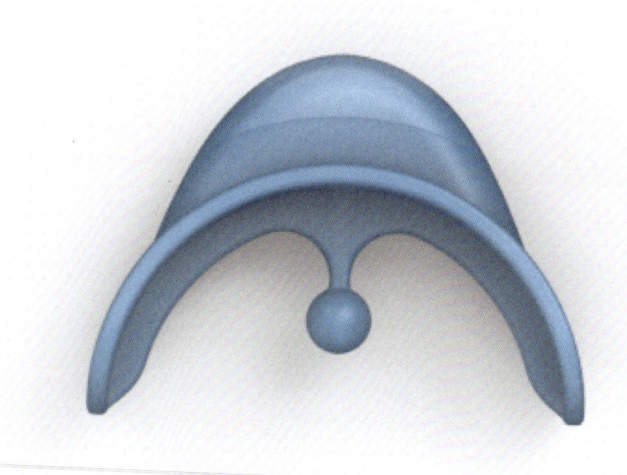

MIA SEEGER PREIS 2024
MIA SEEGER PRIZE 2024

ORMO – ORAL MOTOR SKILLS

ENTWURF/DEVELOPER
Meret Oppermann

STUDIUM/DEGREE COURSE
Muthesius Kunsthochschule, Kiel
Medical Design

BETREUUNG/SUPERVISORS
Prof. Detlef Rhein
Prof.in Dr. habil. Christiane Kruse

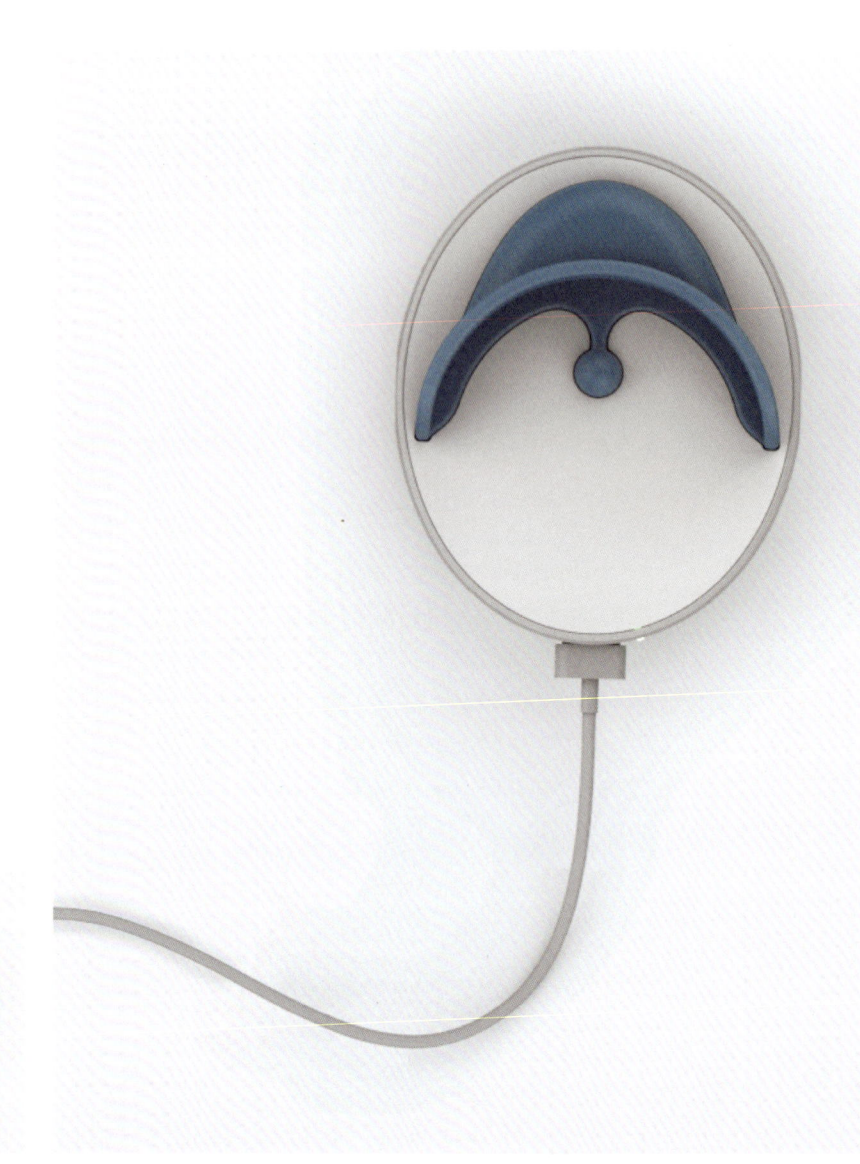

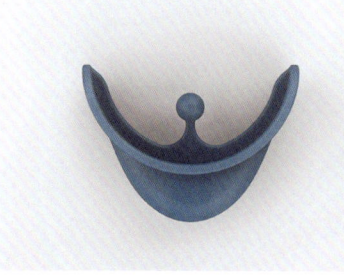

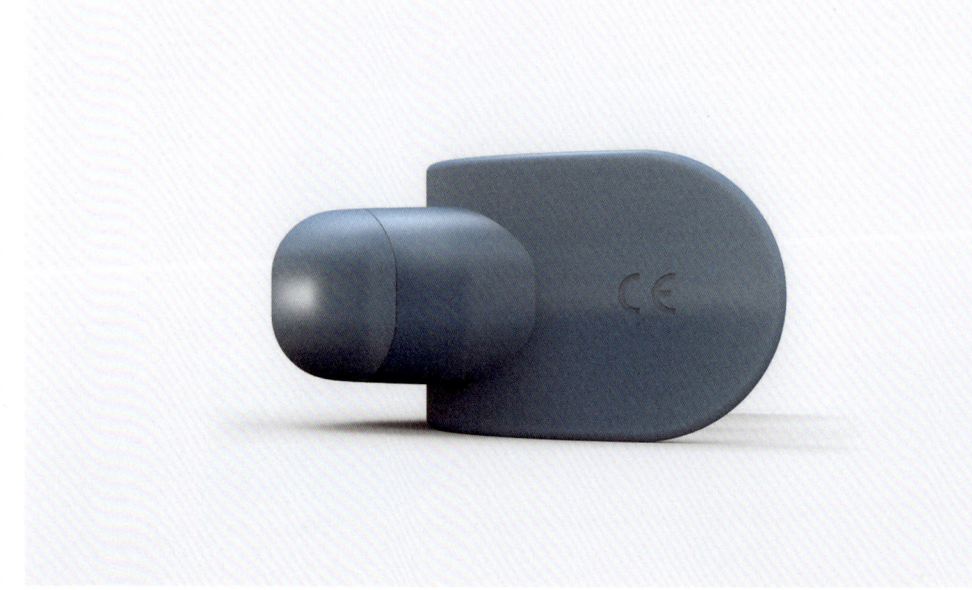

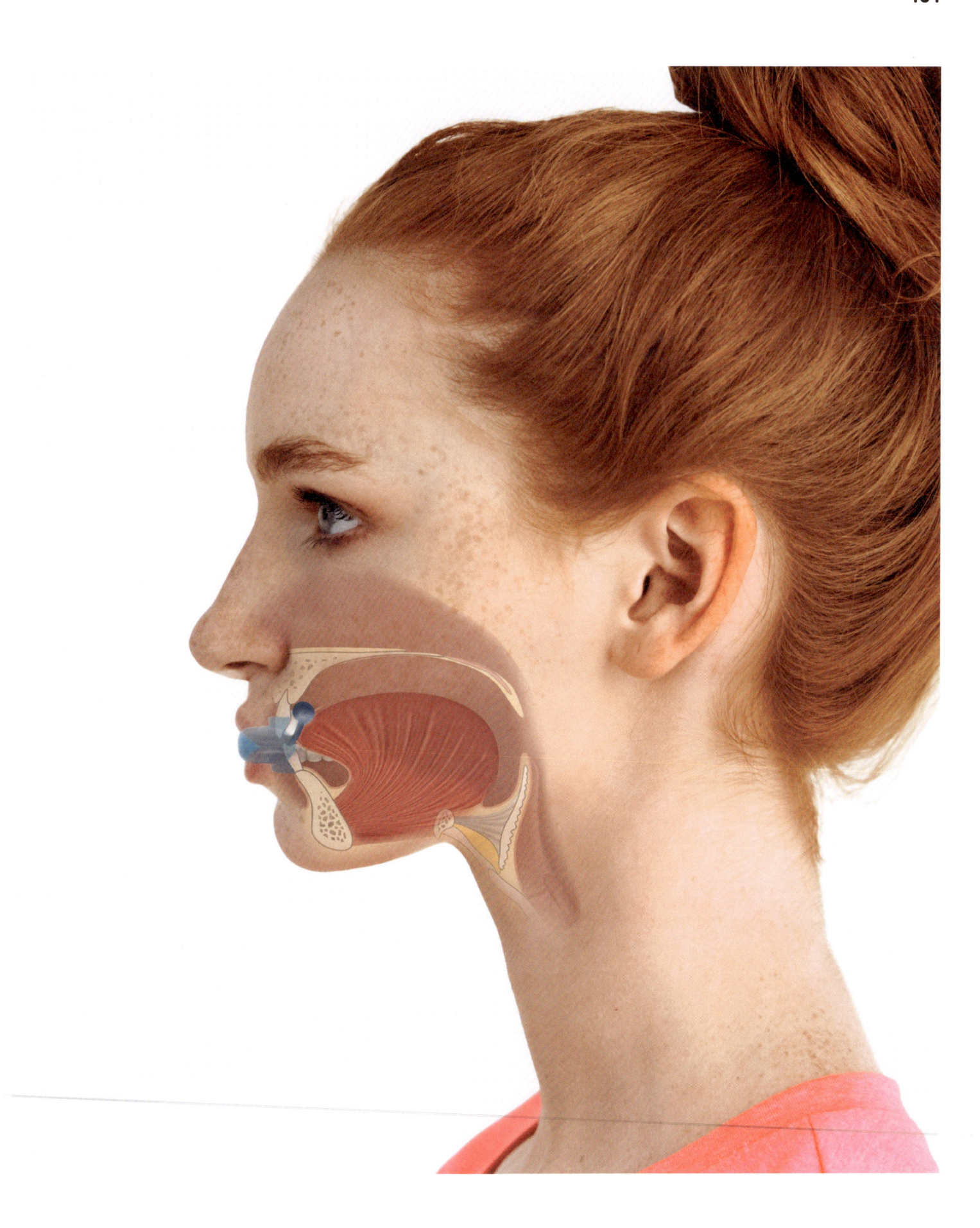

ORMO – ORAL MOTOR SKILLS

MIA SEEGER PREIS 2024
MIA SEEGER PRIZE 2024

MONO WOOL – REGENERATIVE SOFTNESS
MONO WOOL – REGENERATIVE SOFTNESS

JURY STATEMENT

Die immer noch viel zu großen Mengen von Produkten aus schlecht rezyklierbaren Verbundwerkstoffen stehen dem zirkulären Wirtschaften entgegen. Die umfassende und genaue Recherche von Michelle Müller unter dem Aspekt „Regenerative Weichheit" mündet in einem maximal reduzierten Lösungsvorschlag. Mono Wool überzeugt die Jury durch die Konzentration auf nur ein Material, das ebenso intelligent, wie maschinengerecht zu einem homogenen Produkt verarbeitet wird. Was dem Einzelnen mehr Sitzkomfort bietet, dient der Gesellschaft, indem es vorhandene Ressourcen nutzt.

The flood of products made from hard-to-recycle composite materials is hampering the circular economy. Michelle Müller's comprehensive and meticulous research into "regenerative softness" has yielded an elegantly simple solution. Mono Wool convinced the jury by focusing on a single material, intelligently processed into a uniform and machine-friendly product. This design maximises user comfort while utilising existing resources to minimise environmental footprint.

ENTWURF/DEVELOPER
Michelle Müller

STUDIUM/DEGREE COURSE
Kunsthochschule Berlin Weißensee
Produktdesign

BETREUUNG/SUPERVISORS
Prof. Barbara Schmidt
Prof. Dr. Lucy Norris

Nicht das fertige Möbelstück, sondern der Polsteranteil, also das Textil und die Auswahl der darin enthaltenen Materialien stehen im Fokus von Mono Wool.

In Deutschland werden jährlich rund 2,4 Mio. Tonnen Sperrmüll entsorgt. 22% davon sind Polster und Verbundmöbel, die nur für die thermische Verwertung als brauchbar eingestuft werden. Kurz gesagt: sie werden verbrannt. Im Rahmen ihrer Masterthesis hat Michelle Müller nach Alternativen zu Polstern aus ölbasierten Schaumstoffen gesucht. Mono Wool geht den Weg einer radikalen Minimierung. Mit der Verwendung von Rohwolle ergibt sich das Potenzial, ein Polster aus nur einem einzigen Material herzustellen. Der Bezug wird mit Hohlräumen gestrickt, gefüllt und durch einen Klapp-Mechanismus zu einer Sitzschale geformt. Durch die 3D-Stricktechnologie kann der Bezugsstoff ohne viel Handarbeit, als fertiges Teil aus der Maschine gelassen werden. Mono Wool ist ein Polster aus 100% Wolle, das lokal, kreislauffähig und sozial verträglich gedacht ist.

The focus of Mono Wool is not on the finished item of furniture, but rather on its upholstery components, i.e. the textiles and the selection of materials used.

Around 2.4 million tonnes of bulk waste are discarded in Germany every year. 22% of this is upholstery and composite furniture, which is categorised as suitable for thermal recycling only. In other words: it is burned. As part of her master's thesis, Michelle Müller looked for alternatives to upholstery made from oil-based foams. Mono Wool embraces the philosophy of radical minimisation. Raw wool offers the possibility of single-material upholstery. The cover is knitted with hollow spaces, which are filled and formed into a seat shell using a folding mechanism. The 3D knitting technology delivers finished items while eliminating the need for extensive manual labour. Mono Wool is 100% wool upholstery designed to be local, circular and socially responsible.

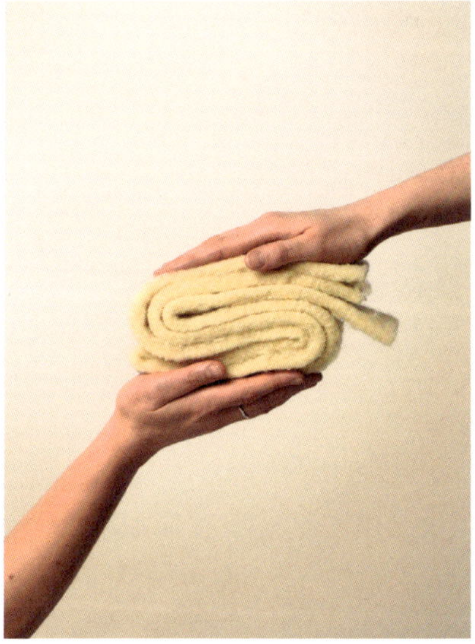

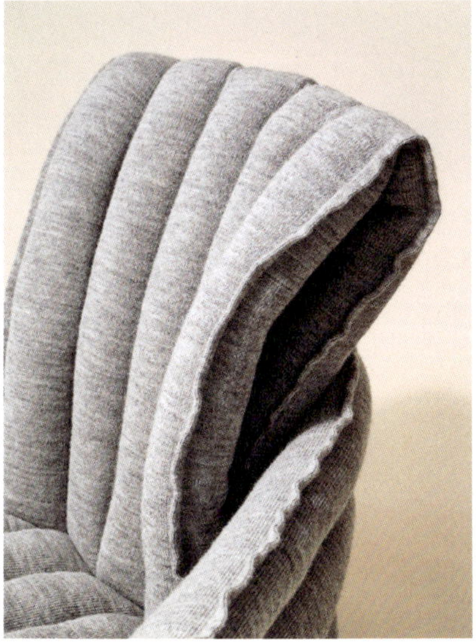

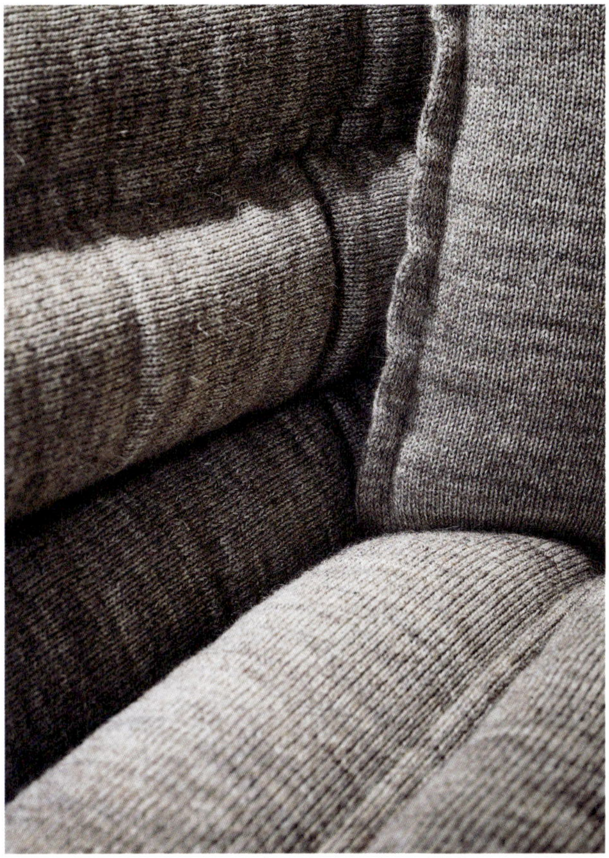

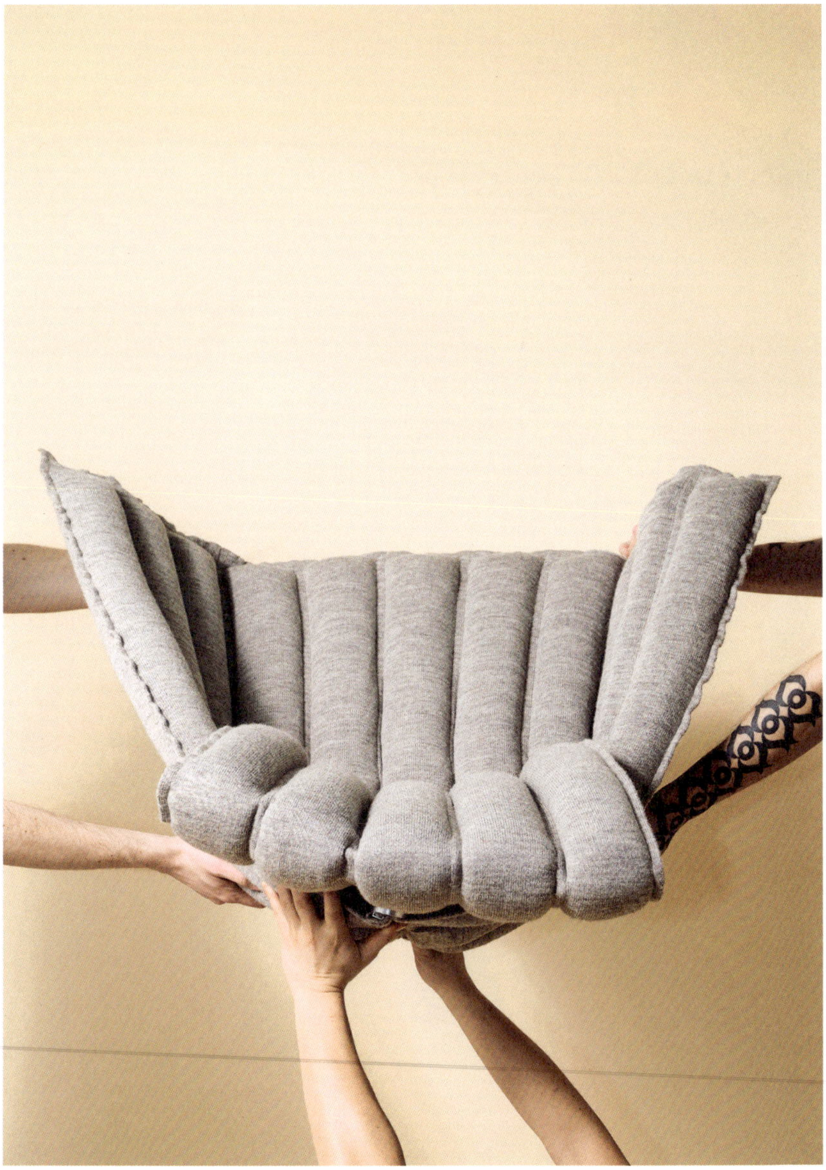

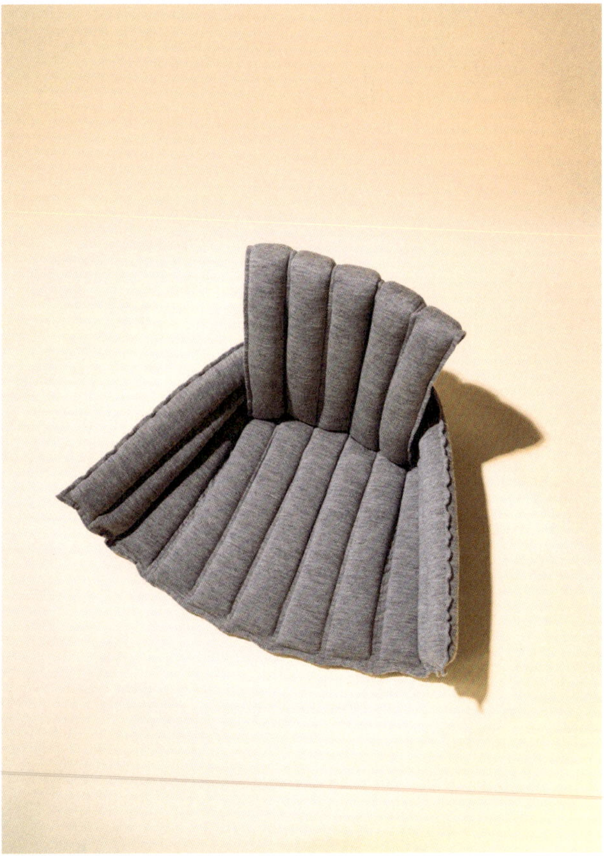

MIA SEEGER PREIS 2024
MIA SEEGER PRIZE 2024

PROPAGANDA NUTZEN
USING PROPAGANDA

JURY STATEMENT

Der erste Blick in das Handbuch „Propaganda nutzen!" von Yannik Schäfer irritiert die Leserschaft. Porträts von unliebsamen Gestalten der Zeitgeschichte springen ins Auge. Eine Anleitung zu Agitation und Polemik für Anfänger im Taschenbuchformat? Braucht das die Welt und nützt es mehr als Einem? Diese Frage beantwortet die Jury mit einem klaren Ja! Die Art und Weise, in der aktuell politische Diskussionen geführt werden, macht diese satirische Offenlegung notwendig. Die herausragend gestaltete Arbeit immunisiert und weckt das Interesse für mehr Engagement, nicht nur in der lokalen Politik.

Some readers of Yannik Schäfer's book "Propaganda nutzen!" (Using Propaganda!) may initially be taken aback, as it contains portraits of unpopular figures from contemporary political life. Is this a beginners' guide to agitation and polemics in paperback form? Is this really what the world needs and is it even of general interest? The jury answered both of these questions with a resounding yes! The current state of political discourse makes this satirical exposé essential reading. This exceptionally well-crafted work not only serves to inoculate the reader against political manipulation but also ignites a passion for deeper political involvement at all levels.

ENTWURF/DEVELOPER
Yannik Schäfer

STUDIUM/DEGREE COURSE
Duale Hochschule, Ravensburg
Medien/Mediendesign

BETREUUNG/SUPERVISORS
Prof. Herbert Moser,
Prof. Dr. Holger Lund,
Florian Tscharf

Medien waren schon immer ein Mittel von Diktaturen, um ihre eigenen Meinungen und Ziele durchzusetzen. Doch was früher analog funktionierte, geschieht heute digital.

Die altbekannten Techniken der politischen Agitation sind für einen Großteil der Bevölkerung nicht greifbar. Yannik Schäfer bringt diese Rhetorik in die deutsche Kommunalpolitik und zeigt anhand einer fiktiven Bürgermeisterwahl, wie Propagandatechniken funktionieren und wie man sie anwenden kann. Ein Handbuch für den Aktenkoffer und das begleitende digitale Coaching vermitteln Propagandatechniken, um erfolgreich gewählt zu werden. Im digitalen Coaching werden diese aufgegriffen und anhand praktischer Beispiele vertieft. Das Projekt bewegt sich auf einem schmalen Grat zwischen Ironie und bitterem Ernst, indem es die Leserschaft anleitet, selbst im Sinne der Propaganda aktiv zu werden. Das Verstehen der zugrundeliegenden Methoden soll sensibilisieren, um entsprechende Manipulationen im Alltag zu entlarven.

The media has always served as a tool for dictatorships to promote their agendas and manipulate public opinion. Although the analogue systems upon which the media once relied have now gone digital, the familiar techniques of political agitation are still not obvious to most people.

To illustrate the manipulative power of propaganda techniques, Yannik Schäfer illuminates the inner workings of German local politics by constructing a fictitious mayoral campaign. This manual for the briefcase teaches the propaganda techniques that help candidates get elected. It is supplemented by online coaching based on practical examples. The project traces a fine line between irony and bitter seriousness by showing readers how to become effective propagandists. The manual aims to expose the everyday manipulations we face by helping us to understand the underlying methodologies employed.

Propaganda
nutzen!

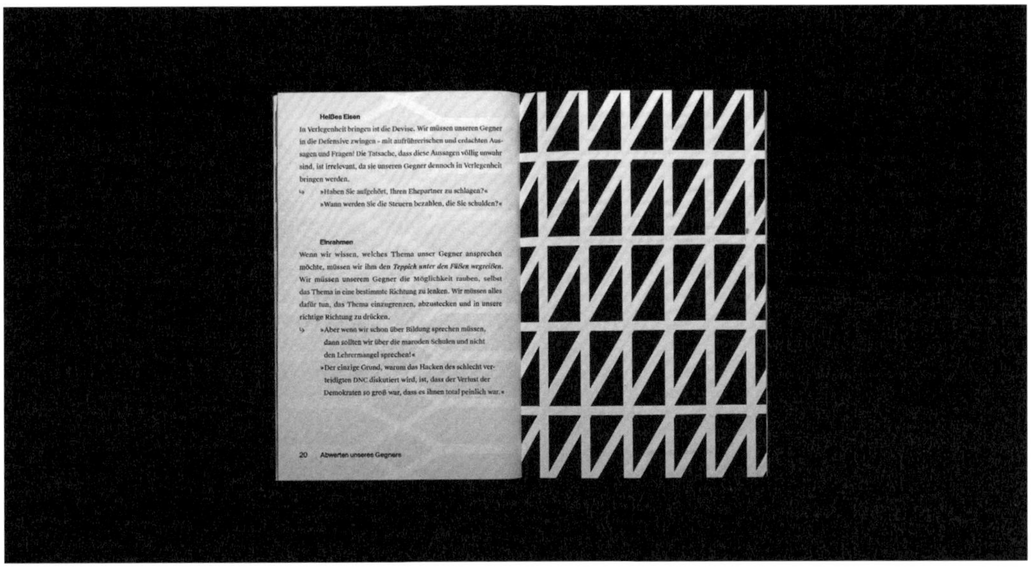
Heißes Eisen
In Verlegenheit bringen ist die Devise. Wir müssen unseren Gegner in die Defensive zwingen - mit aufrührerischen und erdachten Aussagen und Fragen! Die Tatsache, dass diese Aussagen völlig unwahr sind, ist irrelevant, da sie unseren Gegner dennoch in Verlegenheit bringen werden.
»Haben Sie aufgehört, Ihren Ehepartner zu schlagen?«
»Wann werden Sie die Steuern bezahlen, die Sie schulden?«
Einrahmen
Wenn wir wissen, welches Thema unser Gegner ansprechen möchte, müssen wir ihm den Teppich unter den Füßen wegreißen. Wir müssen unserem Gegner die Möglichkeit rauben, selbst das Thema in eine bestimmte Richtung zu lenken. Wir müssen alles dafür tun, das Thema einzugrenzen, abzustecken und in unsere richtige Richtung zu drücken.
»Aber wenn wir schon über Bildung sprechen müssen, dann sollten wir über die maroden Schulen und nicht den Lehrermangel sprechen!«
»Der einzige Grund, warum das Hacken des schlecht verteidigten DNC diskutiert wird, ist, dass der Verlust der Demokraten so groß war, dass es ihnen total peinlich war.«
20 Abwerten unseres Gegners

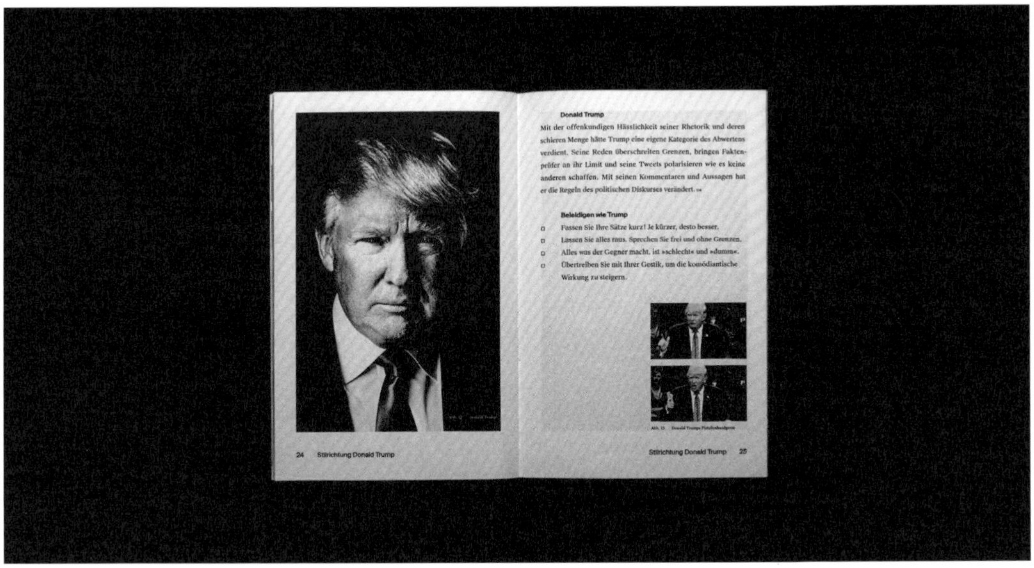
Donald Trump
Mit der offenkundigen Hässlichkeit seiner Rhetorik und deren schieren Menge hätte Trump eine eigene Kategorie des Abwertens verdient. Seine Reden überschreiten Grenzen, bringen Faktenprüfer an ihr Limit und seine Tweets polarisieren wie es keine anderen schaffen. Mit seinen Kommentaren und Aussagen hat er die Regeln des politischen Diskurses verändert.
Beleidigen wie Trump
Fassen Sie Ihre Sätze kurz! Je kürzer, desto besser.
Lassen Sie alles raus. Sprechen Sie frei und ohne Grenzen.
Alles was der Gegner macht, ist »schlecht« und »dumm«.
Übertreiben Sie mit Ihrer Gestik, um die komödiantische Wirkung zu steigern.
24 Stilrichtung Donald Trump
Stilrichtung Donald Trump 25

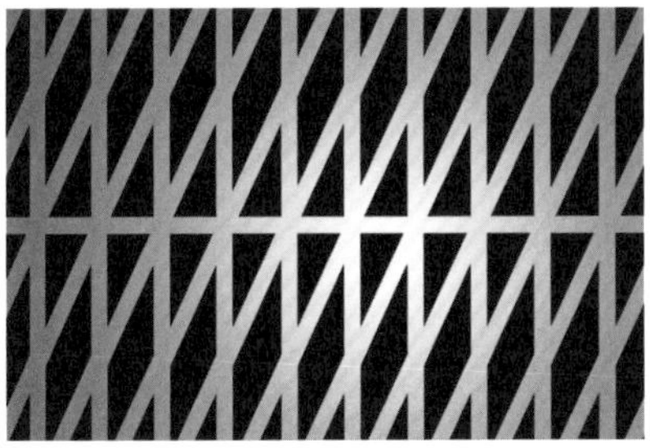

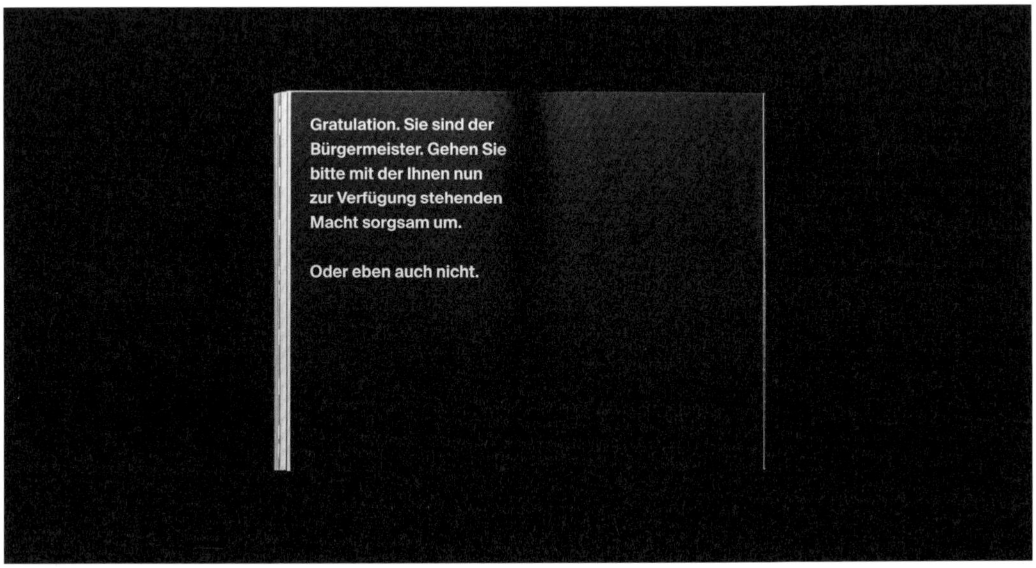
Gratulation. Sie sind der Bürgermeister. Gehen Sie bitte mit der Ihnen nun zur Verfügung stehenden Macht sorgsam um.
Oder eben auch nicht.

MIA SEEGER PREIS 2024
MIA SEEGER PRIZE 2024

DER MIA SEEGER STIFTUNG
PRESENTED BY THE MIA SEEGER FOUNDATION

WAS MEHR ALS EINEM NÜTZT

Auch in diesem Jahr wurden wieder Konzepte und Produkte ausgezeichnet, die sich mit wichtigen Aspekten unseres Lebens und Zusammenlebens befassen und hierfür neuartige, sinnvolle Lösungen vorschlagen. Dabei soll der Art, wie Menschen – beruflich oder privat, alt oder jung, gesund oder krank – untereinander kommunizieren und miteinander umgehen, besonderes Augenmerk gelten.

FOR THE BENEFIT OF MANY

Once again this year, we celebrate ideas and products that offer innovative and meaningful solutions to the challenges of daily life and our shared world. We have paid particular attention to the way in which people communicate and interact, considering factors like workplace, home environment, age group, and health status.

ANERKENNUNG
HIGHLY COMMENDED

PROBESITZEN
TRIAL SEATING

JURY STATEMENT

Mit großem Engagement, kleinem Budget und einem spannenden Prozess haben die 5 Gestalterinnen mit prototypischen Sitzmöbeln auf die unbefriedigende Situation am Hansaplatz aufmerksam gemacht. Wo bisher das Verweilen bewusst unterbunden wurde, ist für kurze Zeit eine einladende Infrastruktur ohne Konsumzwang entstanden. Ein bemerkenswerter Ansatz zum Nachdenken über den Wert von menschenfreundlichen Freiräumen in der Stadt. Auch gute Prozesse nutzen mehr als einem – die Jury freut sich über prozessorientierte Einreichungen, die relevante gesellschaftliche Fragen behandeln.

Despite their limited budget, the five enthusiastic designers developed an exciting campaign using prototypical seating furniture to draw attention to the unsatisfactory situation on Hansaplatz. They created a pleasant, temporary, free-to-use infrastructure in a place where people had previously been encouraged to move on. The campaign sparked a thoughtful conversation about the importance of having people-centred open spaces in the city. Because good processes benefit everyone, the jury welcomes process-orientated entries that address pressing social issues.

Die Probesitzen-Aktionen für mehr Teilhabe an der Gestaltung des Hansaplatzes sollen den Diskurs anregen und die Wünsche nach Veränderung der Nachbarschaft sichtbarer machen.

Mit ihren gestalterischen Interventionen haben die Designerinnen von der HFBK Hamburg auf den Missstand der fehlenden unkommerziellen Sitzmöglichkeiten im öffentlichen Raum aufmerksam gemacht. Aus einem Workshop entstand die Frage: Was passiert, wenn Wohnzimmer, Arbeitsplatz und Balkon im öffentlichen Raum stehen? Das Ziel der nächsten Probesitzen-Aktion war es, eine Infrastruktur mit zwölf Sitzmöglichkeiten für selbstorganisierte Nachbarschaftstreffen zu schaffen.

The aim of the "trial seating" campaigns for greater involvement in the design of Hansaplatz in Hamburg is to stimulate discussion and highlight the neighbourhood's desire for change.

The creative interventions by designers from the HFBK University of Fine Arts Hamburg have drawn attention to the lack of non-commercial seating in public spaces. The question was first posed in a workshop: what happens when living rooms, workplaces and balconies are set up in public spaces? The "trial seating" campaign constructed a temporary seating arrangement with twelve seats that could be used for neighbourhood social gatherings.

ENTWURF/DEVELOPERS
Irini Schwab mit
Anna Ulmer
Tina Henkel
Maren Hinze
Tatjana Schwab

STUDIUM/DEGREE COURSE
Hochschule für bildende Künste Hamburg
Bildende Künste – Design

BETREUUNG/SUPERVISOR
Prof. Dr. Jesko Fezer

ANERKENNUNG
HIGHLY COMMENDED

SNAB – RETTET LEBEN
SNAB – SAVES LIVES

JURY STATEMENT

Spätestens, wenn hektisch nach dem rettenden Adrenalin-Injektor gesucht wird, sei es unterwegs im Rucksack oder daheim in sämtlichen Schubladen, wird klar: am besten ist es, das Gerät immer dabei zu haben. Um dies zu ermöglichen, hat Julian Oberenzer eine innovative und besonders flache Anordnung der Komponenten gefunden. Unauffällig am Oberschenkel getragen, sorgt Snab beispielsweise beim Sport für ein sicheres Gefühl des Einzelnen und entlastet seine Mitmenschen, die oft hilflos neben dem Geschehen stehen. Ein bekanntes Problem, in der Form neu gedacht, überraschend einfach gelöst und individuell gestaltbar!

In a moment of crisis – whether you're frantically digging through your backpack or searching drawers at home – the value of having immediate access to an adrenaline injector becomes undeniably clear. To make this possible, Julian Oberenzer has developed an innovative, slim version of this life-saving device. Discreetly carried on the thigh, Snab offers peace of mind during activities such as sports and takes the pressure off bystanders who don't know how to help. A familiar problem, tackled in a fresh way, surprisingly easy to solve, and completely customisable!

Ein anaphylaktischer Schock kann im schlimmsten Fall zum Tod führen, weshalb die schnelle Verabreichung von Adrenalin lebensrettend ist. Adrenalin-Injektoren, die mitgeführt und selbst angewendet werden können, haben viele Betroffene aber nicht immer bei sich.

Julian Oberenzer hat einen Injektor gestaltet, der dauerhaft mitgeführt wird und zum Injizieren nicht abgenommen werden muss. Alle Komponenten mit Details wie Sicherungen, Nadellängen und die Tankgröße wurden neu überdacht und angeordnet. Befestigt wird Snab mittels eines rutschsicheren Neopren-Bandes mit Magnetverschluss am Oberschenkel.

An anaphylactic shock can be fatal if not treated promptly. This is why the rapid administration of adrenaline is lifesaving. Unfortunately, many of those affected do not carry an adrenaline injector for self-administration.

Julian Oberenzer has developed an injector you can carry with you at all times and that operates without having to be removed first. The entire design – including the smallest details such as the safety caps, length of the needles and capacity of the carrier tube – has been re-engineered. Snab attaches to the thigh with a non-slip neoprene strap and a magnetic fastener.

ENTWURF/DEVELOPER
Julian Oberenzer

STUDIUM/DEGREE COURSE
Hochschule für Gestaltung
Schwäbisch Gmünd
Produktgestaltung

BETREUUNG/SUPERVISOR
Prof. Gerhard Reichert

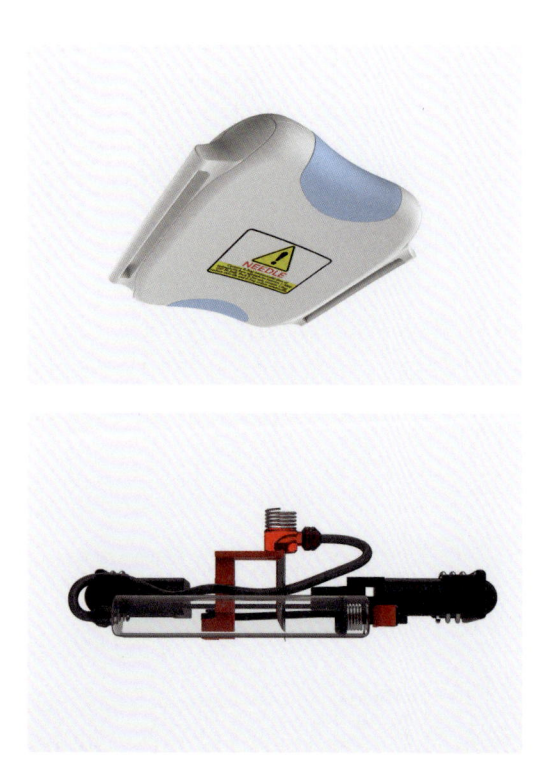

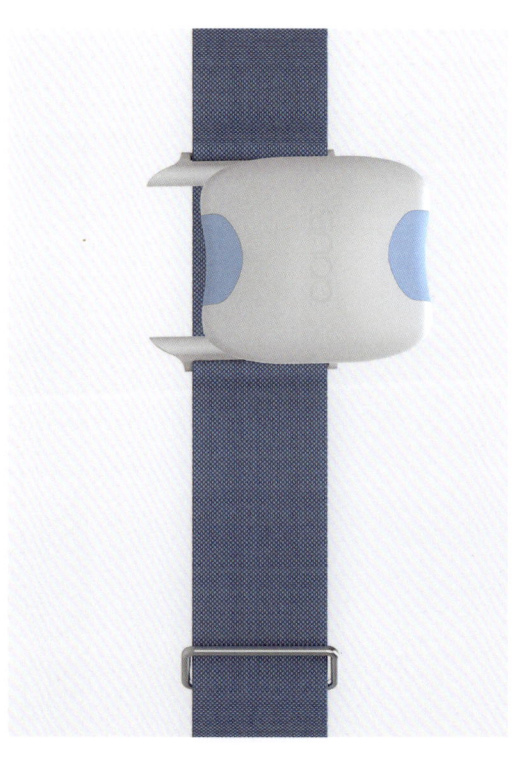

ANERKENNUNG
HIGHLY COMMENDED

VELOCITY
VELOCITY

198
199

JURY STATEMENT

Im täglichen Pendlerverkehr bietet die Kombination von individuellen und öffentlichen Transportmitteln ein großes Potential zur Entzerrung der Verkehrsströme. Dass auf diesem Wege oft Engpässe zu überwinden sind, hat jeder Pendelnde schon erlebt. Felix Stockhausen hat eine dieser räumlichen Schnittstellen lokalisiert und sorgt im Fahrradabteil für Abhilfe. Die weichen Trenn- und Fixierungselemente sorgen für mehr Orientierung, Sicherheit und Komfort. Die Jury hat darüber diskutiert, ob diese Lösung auch mit nachhaltigem Material funktioniert und würde eine Iteration in diese Richtung begrüßen.

The integration of individual and public transport has the potential to balance traffic flow during peak commuting hours. Every commuter has already experienced the bottlenecks that currently exist. Felix Stockhausen has localised one of these spatial interfaces and provides an effective solution for the bicycle compartment. The padded dividers that separate and secure the bicycles maintain a neat, safe environment that enhances user convenience. The jury wondered whether this solution would also work with sustainable materials and would welcome a reappraisal in this direction.

ENTWURF/DEVELOPER
Felix Stockhausen

STUDIUM/DEGREE COURSE
Bauhaus-Universität Weimar
Produktdesign

BETREUUNG/SUPERVISORS
Prof. Andreas Mühlenberend
Dr. Andreas Karguth

Um das Zusammenspiel aus Fahrrad und Bahn zu einer flächendeckenden Alternative zum Auto werden zu lassen, ist es notwendig die Mitnahmemöglichkeiten von Fahrrädern attraktiver zu gestalten.

Mit seinem Projekt Velocity – Optimierung der Fahrradmitnahme im S-Bahn-Verkehr, adressiert Felix Stockhausen die besonderen Herausforderungen, wie die schnelle Taktung, kurze Haltezeiten und ein hohes Aufkommen an Fahrradmitnahmen zu Hauptverkehrszeiten. Das Herzstück ist eine flexible Funktionswand aus weichen Elementen, die ein geordnetes Rangieren und Parkieren der Fahrräder ermöglicht. Durch ihre konische Form bieten die Elemente einen stabilen Halt.

To make bicycles and trains a truly competitive alternative to cars, we need to make the process of bringing bikes on trains more attractive.

Felix Stockhausen's Velocity project – Optimisation of Bicycle Transport on Suburban Trains – tackles the specific challenges posed by the trains' tight schedules and short stopping times – and the high volume of bicycles at rush hours. The concept utilises flexible, padded walls that allow bicycles to be manoeuvred and parked in an orderly fashion. The conical shape of the wall elements provides stable support.

MIA SEEGER STIFTUNG

THE MIA SEEGER FOUNDATION

IMPRESSUM/PUBLISHING DETAILS

HERAUSGEBER/PUBLISHED BY
Mia Seeger Stiftung

REDAKTION/EDITOR
Dr. Jons Messedat, Stuttgart/Lindau

ÜBERSETZUNG/TRANSLATION
Stephen McLuckie, Dorchester GB

GRAFIKDESIGN/GRAPHIC DESIGN
stapelberg & fritz, Stuttgart

AUSSTELLUNGSGESTALTUNG/ EXHIBITION DESIGN
Thomas Simianer, Stuttgart

KOORDINATION MIT FOCUS OPEN/ COORDINATION WITH FOCUS OPEN
Birgit Herzberg-Jochum
Renate Seeger

JURYVORBEREITUNG/ JUDGING ORGANISED BY
Team UP Designstudio

DIGITALE TECHNIK, VIDEO-KONFERENZEN/ DIGITAL TECHNOLOGY, VIDEO CONFERENCES
Stefan Lippert, UP Designstudio

Mia Seeger Stiftung
c/o Design Center
Baden-Württemberg
im Haus der Wirtschaft
Willi-Bleicher-Straße 19
D-70174 Stuttgart
T +49 711 123 2781
F +49 711 123 2771

E-Mail: design@rps.bwl.de
www.mia-seeger.de
instagram.com/miaseeger

Abbildung rechts: Mia Seeger in der Zentrale des Deutschen Werkbundes in Berlin, 1928; Foto: Cami Stone, Stadtarchiv Stuttgart aus dem Nachlass Mia Seeger/ Right: Mia Seeger at the headquarters of the Deutscher Werkbund in Berlin, 1928; photo: Cami Stone, from the Mia Seeger papers held by Stuttgart City Archives

Mia Seeger war die »Grande Dame« des Design. Mit der Weißenhofsiedlung 1927 in Stuttgart begann ihre Laufbahn. Bald war sie an weiteren Ausstellungen des Deutschen Werkbundes beteiligt.

Die Bundesrepublik hat sie vielfach als Kommissarin zu Triennalen in Mailand entsandt und zur ersten Leiterin des Rat für Formgebung berufen, den sie zwölf Jahre lang führte. Sie war selbst keine Designerin, sondern Design-Vermittlerin und -Beraterin. 1986 rief sie die nach ihr benannte Stiftung ins Leben, deren Zweck die Bildung junger Gestalterinnen und Gestalter ist. Mit der Absicht, besonders den Nachwuchs im Design zu fördern und ihn dabei zur Auseinandersetzung mit sozialen Fragen aufzufordern, schreibt die Stiftung jährlich den Mia Seeger Preis unter dem Motto „Was mehr als einem nützt!" aus.

Die kontinuierliche Ausschreibung des Mia Seeger Preises ist nur durch die großzügige Unterstützung von drei langfristigen Kooperationspartnern möglich:

Die Stiftung dankt dem Design Center Baden-Württemberg sehr herzlich dafür, dass die Preisverleihung im Rahmen der jährlichen Preisverleihung und Ausstellung „FOCUS OPEN – Internationaler Designpreis Baden-Württemberg" erfolgen kann und für die Unterstützung bei der Vorbereitung und Organisation, der Ausstellung und des Presserundgangs.

Außerdem bedankt sich die Stiftung ganz besonders für die dauerhafte finanzielle und personelle Unterstützung bei der Stiftung Rat für Formgebung.

Des Weiteren dankt die Stiftung dem UP Designstudio für die Übernahme der Geschäftsführung mit allen anfallenden Verwaltungstätigkeiten, Bearbeitung der Bewerbungen sowie die Zusammenstellung, Vorbereitung und Durchführung der Jury.

Über ihre Arbeit informiert die Stiftung auf ihrer Internetseite: www.mia-seeger.de Darüber hinaus gibt es News und Posts rund um Design mit sozialem Anspruch auf: instagram.com/miaseeger

Mia Seeger was the "grande dame" of design. Her career began with the Weissenhof Estate in Stuttgart in 1927. She was soon involved with further exhibitions by the Deutscher Werkbund.

The Federal Republic of Germany frequently sent her to the Triennial exhibitions in Milan as its commissioner and appointed her the first director of the German Design Council, which she headed for 12 years. She herself was not a designer but a design mediator and adviser. In 1986, she established the foundation that bears her name, which is dedicated to the education of aspiring designers. In order to nurture young talent and challenge them to tackle social issues, the foundation invites entries for the annual Mia Seeger Prize under the motto "for the benefit of many".

The continued presentation of the Mia Seeger Award is only possible thanks to the generous support of three long-term partner organisations.

The Foundation would therefore like to thank the Design Center Baden-Württemberg for allowing the award ceremony to take place during the annual award ceremony and exhibition "FOCUS OPEN – International Design Award Baden-Württemberg" and for its support in preparing and organising the exhibition and press tour.

The Foundation also wishes to thank the German Design Council Foundation for its ongoing financial and personnel support.

Finally, the Foundation would like to extend its appreciation to UP Designstudio for managing the project, including all the administrative tasks, application processing, and the recruitment, preparation and direction of the jury.

The Foundation describes its work in detail at www.mia-seeger.de and publishes news and posts about design with a social slant on Instagram at www.instagram.com/miaseeger.

MIA SEEGER PREIS
2024

MIA SEEGER PRIZE
2024

APPENDIX
A–Z

ADRESSEN/ ADDRESSES

A

Galerie Sammlung Amann
Schwabstr. 69/1
70197 Stuttgart
T +49 711 3968 5457
www.galerie.sammlungamann.com
S/P 151

B

Braake Design
Turnierstr. 3
70599 Stuttgart
T +49 711 4599 9890
www.braake.com
S/P 30

Bundesagentur für Arbeit
Regensburger Str. 104
90478 Nürnberg
T +49 911 179 2123
www.arbeitsagentur.de
S/P 174

Busch-Jaeger Elektro GmbH
Freisenbergstr. 2
58513 Lüdenscheid
T +49 2351 956 1600
www.busch-jaeger.de
S/P 130, 131

C

Cicero Kommunikation GmbH
Taunusstr. 52
65183 Wiesbaden
T +49 611 949 155 40
www.cicero-kommunikation.de
S/P 175

CityCaddy UG (haftungsbeschränkt)
Stresemannstr. 90
22769 Hamburg
T +49 176 3248 5338
www.citycaddy.de
S/P 64

corporate friends® GmbH
Pulsnitzer Str. 46
01917 Kamenz
+49 3578 7043 0550
www.corporatefriends.de
S/P 102

D

dBcover Solutions® S.L.
Avenida Benelux, 91
03600 Elda
+34 6623 543 42
Spanien/Spain
www.harmonium.es
S/P 80

defortec GmbH
Breitwasenring 15
72135 Dettenhausen
T +49 7157 72118 20
www.defortec.de
S/P 65

design hoch drei GmbH & Co. KG
Glockenstr. 36
70376 Stuttgart
T +49 711 55 03 77 30
www.design-hoch-drei.de
S/P 176

dreiform GmbH
Kalscheurener Str. 19
50354 Hürth
T +49 221 987423 0
www.dreiform.de
S/P 150

E

Echo & Flut GmbH
Adlerstr. 41
70199 Stuttgart
T +49 711 9689 3582
www.echoundflut.com
S/P 174

Entwurfreich GmbH
Fleher Str. 32
40223 Düsseldorf
T +49 211 1596 4350
www.entwurfreich.com
S/P 130

F

Förderverein Obstbaumuseum Glems e.V.
Eberbergstr. 24
72555 Metzingen-Glems
T +49 7123 87623
www.obstbaumuseum-glems.de
S/P 139

formquadrat GmbH
Brucknerstr. 3-5
4020 Linz
Österreich/Austria
T +43 7327 77244
www.formquadrat.com
S/P 27, 112

Fraport AG
Gebäude 178
60547 Frankfurt
T +49 69 6900
www.fraport.com
S/P 175

G

Gardin Ltd.
99 Park Drive Milton Park
OX14 4RY Abingdon
Großbritannien/United Kingdom
T +44 7748 7666 20
www.gardin.ag
S/P 31

Grohe AG
Feldmühleplatz 15
50545 Düsseldorf
T +49 211 9130 3000
www.grohe.de
S/P 71

H

HANSA – Maschinenbau Vertriebs- und Fertigungs GmbH
Raiffeisenstr. 1
27446 Selsingen
T +49 4284 9315 0
www.hansa-maschinenbau.de
S/P 167

höfats GmbH
Albert-Einstein-Str. 6
87437 Kempten
T +49 831 98 90 94 60
www.hofats.com
S/P 113

Hohenloher Schuleinrichtungen GmbH & Co. KG
Brechdarrweg 22
74613 Öhringen
T +49 696 0
www.hohenloher.de
S/P 121

J

Elke Jensen
Stresemannstr. 90
22769 Hamburg
T +49 176 3248 5338
www.citycaddy.de
S/P 64

K

karuun GmbH
Jägerstr. 23
88353 Kißlegg
T +49 7563 913 8401
www.karuun.com
S/P 181

KASCHKASCH GbR
Gutenbergstr. 33
50823 Köln
T +49 221 169 23 895
www.kaschkasch.com
S/P 81

**Klaiber + Oettle
Architekten und Ingenieure GbR**
Kornhausstr. 14
73525 Schwäbisch Gmünd
+49 7171 997 9220
www.klaiberundoettle.de
S/P 152

Martin Kreis
In den Strutäckern 22
73527 Schwäbisch Gmünd
+49 176 239 78 567
S/P 152

L

LEONI AG
Marienstr. 7
90402 Nürnberg
T +49 911 2023 0
www.leoni.com
S/P 176

LIXIL Global Design
Feldmühleplatz 15
50545 Düsseldorf
T +49 211 9130 3000
www.lixil.com
S/P 71

Lukuli Design GmbH
Bergstr. 74
73733 Esslingen
+49 179 6344 7966 2
www.lukuli-design.de
S/P 103

Lumod GmbH
Machtlfinger Str. 21
81379 München
T +49 89 7105 1828
www.lumod.com
S/P 167

M

Magnosco GmbH
Justus-von-Liebig-Str. 2
12489 Berlin
T +49 30 9120 75357
www.magnoso.com
S/P 39

MOJA Design GmbH
Römerstr. 32
70180 Stuttgart
+49 711 219 505 71
www.moja-design.de
S/P 80

N

**NO W HERE | Architekten Designer
Volpp Amann GbR**
Schwabstr. 69/1
70197 Stuttgart
T +49 711 1691 6662
www.nowherearchitekten.de
S/P 151

O

Okuvision GmbH
Aspenhaustr. 25
72770 Reutlingen
T +49 7121 159 350
www.okuvision.de
S/P 65

P

PARO DESIGN®
Quellenstr. 7
70376 Stuttgart
+49 1733236344
www.parodesign.de
S/P 82

R

Wilhelm Renz GmbH + Co. KG
Hans-Klemm-Str. 35
71034 Böblingen
T +49 7031 2188 0
www.renz.de
S/P 81

Rosenbauer International AG
Paschinger Str. 90
4060 Leonding
Österreich/Austria
T +43 7326 7940
www.rosenbauer.com
S/P 27

S

Georg Schlegel® GmbH & Co. KG
Kapellenweg 4
88525 Dürmentingen
T +49 7371 502 0
www.schlegel.biz
S/P 29

Schleich GmbH
Am Limes 69
73527 Schwäbisch Gmünd
+49 7171 8001 22
www.schleich-s.com
S/P 114

serien Raumleuchten GmbH
Hainhäuser Str. 3-7
63110 Rodgau
+49 6106 6909 0
www.serien.com
S/P 91

**Sprimag Spritzmaschinenbau
GmbH & Co. KG**
Henriettenstr. 90
73230 Kirchheim/Teck
T +49 7021 579 153
www.sprimag.com
S/P 30

Stadler Deutschland GmbH
Heinz-Brandt-Str. 6
13158 Berlin
T +49 30 91911616
www.stadlerrail.com
S/P 159

**StarMed GmbH –
medical rescue systems**
Hauptstr. 8
88719 Stetten am Bodensee
T +49 7532 4459 900
www.starmed.eu
S/P 49, 57

ANDREAS STIHL AG & Co. KG
Badstr. 115
71336 Waiblingen
T +49 7151 26 0
www.stihl.de
S/P 150

Stuttgarter Straßenbahnen AG
Schockenriedstr. 50
70565 Stuttgart
T +49 711 7885 0
www.ssb-ag.de
S/P 159

Syntegon Technology GmbH
Stuttgarter Str. 130
71332 Waiblingen
T +49 7151 14 0
www.syntegon.com
S/P 26

Supernova Design GmbH
Industriestr. 26
79194 Gundelfingen
+49 761 600 629 0
www.supernova-lights.com
S/P 166

SWAROVSKI OPTIK AG & Co. KG
Daniel-Swarovski-Str. 70
6067 Absam
Österreich/Austria
T +43 5223 5110
www.swarovskioptik.com
S/P 112

T

Thinkable Studio GmbH
Freiburger Str. 8
77652 Offenburg
T +49 781 9675 9279
www.thinkablestudio.com
S/P 31

TRICON AG
Bahnhofstr. 26
72138 Kirchentellinsfurt
T +49 7121-680870
www.tricon-design.de
S/P 159

U

UnternehmenForm GmbH & Co. KG
Nesenbachstr. 48
70178 Stuttgart
+49 711 9988 780
www.unternehmenform.de
S/P 83

UP Designstudio GmbH
Löffelstr. 40
70597 Stuttgart
T +49 711 32654 60
www.updesignstudio.de
S/P 121

V

VISUELL – Studio für Kommunikation GmbH
Tübinger Str. 97a
70178 Stuttgart
T +49 711 64868 0
www.visuell.de
S/P 139

W

WE-EF LEUCHTEN GmbH
Töpingerstr. 16
29646 Bispingen
T +49 5194 909 0
www.we-ef.com
S/P 104

Wiha Werkzeuge GmbH
Obertalstr. 3-7
78136 Schonach
T +49 7722 9590
www.wiha.com
S/P 28

whiteID GmbH & Co. KG
Nicolaus-Otto-Str. 8
73614 Schorndorf
T +49 7181 991198 0
www.white-id.com
S/P 26, 114

WILDDESIGN GmbH
Munscheidstr. 14
45886 Gelsenkirchen
T: +49 209 702 642 00
www.wilddesign.de
S/P 39

NAMENSREGISTER/ INDEX OF NAMES

A

Galerie Sammlung Amann
S/P 151

B

Braake Design
S/P 30
Bundesagentur für Arbeit
S/P 174
Busch-Jaeger Elektro GmbH
S/P 130,131

C

Cicero Kommunikation GmbH
S/P 175
CityCaddy UG (haftungsbeschränkt)
S/P 64
corporate friends® GmbH
S/P 102

D

dBcover Solutions® S.L.
S/P 80
defortec GmbH
S/P 65
design hoch drei GmbH & Co. KG
S/P 176
dreiform GmbH
S/P 150

E

Echo & Flut GmbH
S/P 174
Entwurfreich GmbH
S/P 130

F

Förderverein Obstbaumuseum Glems e.V.
S/P 139
formquadrat GmbH
S/P 27, 112
Fraport AG
S/P 175

G

Gardin Ltd.
S/P 31
Grohe AG
S/P 71

H

HANSA – Maschinenbau Vertriebs- und Fertigungs GmbH
S/P 167
höfats GmbH
S/P 113
Hohenloher Schuleinrichtungen GmbH & Co. KG
S/P 121

J

Elke Jensen
S/P 64

K

karuun GmbH
S/P 181
KASCHKASCH GbR
S/P 81
Klaiber + Oettle Architekten und Ingenieure GbR
S/P 152
Martin Kreis
S/P 152

L

LEONI AG
S/P 176
LIXIL Global Design
S/P 71
Lukuli Design GmbH
S/P 103
Lumod GmbH
S/P 167

M

Magnosco GmbH
S/P 39
MOJA Design GmbH
S/P 80

N

NO W HERE | Architekten Designer Volpp Amann GbR
S/P 151

O

Okuvision GmbH
S/P 65

P

PARO DESIGN®
S/P 82

R

Wilhelm Renz GmbH + Co. KG
S/P 81
Rosenbauer International AG
S/P 27

S

Georg Schlegel® GmbH & Co. KG
S/P 29
Schleich GmbH
S/P 114
serien Raumleuchten GmbH
S/P 91
Sprimag Spritzmaschinenbau
GmbH & Co. KG
S/P 30
Stadler Deutschland GmbH
S/P 159
StarMed GmbH –
medical rescue systems
S/P 49, 57
ANDREAS STIHL AG & Co. KG
S/P 150
Stuttgarter Straßenbahnen AG
S/P 159
Syntegon Technology GmbH
S/P 26
Supernova Design GmbH
S/P 166
SWAROVSKI OPTIK AG & Co. KG
S/P 112

T

Thinkable Studio GmbH
S/P 31
TRICON AG
S/P 159

U

UnternehmenForm GmbH & Co. KG
S/P 83
UP Designstudio GmbH
S/P 121

V

VISUELL – Studio für
Kommunikation GmbH
S/P 139

W

WE-EF LEUCHTEN GmbH
S/P 104
Wiha Werkzeuge GmbH
S/P 28
whiteID GmbH & Co. KG
S/P 26, 114
WILDDESIGN GmbH
S/P 39

FOCUS OPEN
2024

VOM MUSTER-LAGER ZUM DESIGN-BOOSTER

Der Focus Open 2024 präsentiert auch in diesem Jahr wieder höchst aktuelle Design-Innovationen, die eine unabhängige Fachjury aus einem großen Paket unterschiedlichster Einreichungen auswählte. Ausgelobt vom Design Center Baden-Württemberg, ist dieser Designaward ein wesentlicher Teil der Wirtschaftsförderung des Landes Baden-Württemberg – und das seit langer Zeit.

AUFBRUCH 1848
In diesem historischen Jahr scheitert zwar die Badische Revolution, dafür gründet der württembergische König Wilhelm I. in Stuttgart die „Königliche Centralstelle für Gewerbe und Handel". Die Zeiten sind turbulent, sowohl in politischer als auch in wirtschaftlicher Hinsicht, denn die Industrialisierung kommt mit voller Wucht nun auch im bislang eher landwirtschaftlich geprägten Württemberg an. Die „Centralstelle" vermittelt den Betrieben im Land den Stand der Technik, aber auch den Stand der Gestaltung. Im O-Ton von damals klingt die Aufgabe so: „Erwerb von vorzüglichen Mustern, Werkzeugen und Verfahrensarten – und die entsprechende Verwendung derselben für den vaterländischen Gewerbestand". 1848 ist somit die Geburtsstunde einer innovationsgeprägten, mittelständisch-industriellen Wirtschaft, eines Erfolgsmodells, das bis heute wirkt.

Zwei Jahre später nimmt die „Centralstelle" konkrete Formen an: Ferdinand von Steinbeis wird Technischer Rat und richtet das „Musterlager" ein. Das wiederum versammelt ganz konkrete Beispiele von Produkten aus aller Herren Länder, soll inspirieren, informieren, Benchmarks zeigen und „die Geschmacksbildung fördern". Die Sammlung wächst rasant, Ende des 19. Jahrhunderts kommt sie auf einen Bestand von rund 70.000 Exponaten, die 1896 einen eigenen Ort bekommen: ein repräsentatives Gebäude im Herzen Stuttgarts, zugleich ein Statement für das neue ökonomische Selbstbewusstsein des Landes. Es ist die erste Institution dieser Art weltweit.

DIE MODERNE KOMMT AN

Die württembergische Wirtschaft hat die Steinbeis'schen Impulse aufgegriffen und setzt die neuen Erkenntnisse immer erfolgreicher um. Folglich verliert die Mustersammlung an Relevanz, andere Formen der Förderung werden wichtiger. Aus der „Centralstelle" wird 1921 das „Landesgewerbeamt" – bis heute als LGA bekannt – das über Jahrzehnte ein Synonym für gelungene Mittelstandsförderung bleibt. Jetzt kommt die Moderne auch im Volksstaat Württemberg an, 1927 zeigt der Deutsche Werkbund mit der legendären Weißenhofsiedlung, wie moderner Wohnungsbau aussehen kann. Die begleitende Ausstellung findet selbstverständlich im LGA statt.

GESTALTUNG WIRD DESIGN

Von Design ist noch keine Rede, selbst 1949 noch nicht, als Wilhelm Wagenfeld im Landesgewerbeamt seine Arbeit als Referent für Industrielle Formgebung aufnimmt. Ab 1952 werden Baden und Württemberg vereinigt: Ein neues, großes und wirtschaftlich potentes Bundesland entsteht. Im gleichen Jahr startet in Ulm die Hochschule für Gestaltung (HfG), die sich als Bauhaus-Nachfolgerin versteht. 1959 dann gründet sich in Stuttgart der VDID, der Verband Deutscher Industriedesigner. Spätestens jetzt ist Design als Disziplin präsent. Dennoch tut man sich mit dem Begriff offensichtlich noch schwer: Das ab 1962 im Landesgewerbeamt angesiedelte „LGA-Zentrum Form" lässt den neuen Begriff zwar noch vermissen, aber das formulierte Ziel wird deutlich: „Design in Baden-Württemberg sichtbar machen und auf die wirtschaftliche Bedeutung der Arbeit des Designers aufmerksam machen." An dieser Mission hat sich bis heute im Grunde nichts geändert.

1969 ist die Design-Scheu dann endgültig überwunden – das „LGA-Zentrum Form" wird zum „Design Center Stuttgart", der Standort im Landesgewerbeamt bleibt.

DYNAMIK UND HIGHLIGHTS

In den folgenden Jahrzehnten entwickelt sich das Design Center Stuttgart zu einem Hotspot des Designs. Es geht nun nicht mehr allein um die wirtschaftliche Relevanz des Designs, sondern auch um seine gesellschaftliche, kulturelle, ja völkerverbindende Rolle. Dafür sorgen vor allem temporäre Ausstellungen, die weit über Stadt und Land begeistern, nicht nur in der Design-Community. So schweift mitten im Kalten Krieg der Blick über den Eisernen Vorhang und zeigt, dass auch in der UdSSR oder in der DDR die Formgestaltung gepflegt wird. 1986 findet mit „Erkundungen" ein grandioser Designkongress statt, 1989 widerlegt eine Ausstellung, dass Design eine rein männliche Angelegenheit ist: „Frauen im Design" bringt eine Diskussion in Gang, die bis heute nachhallt.

DER AWARD IM WANDEL

Designförderung lebt von der Präsentation gelungener Beispiele – Best Practice eben. Das leistet der jährliche Designaward, den die heute als Design Center Baden-Württemberg positionierte Institution auslobt. Der schon immer nichtkommerzielle Preis ist eine Ausnahme in der internationalen Award-Landschaft. Er lief lange als „Deutsche Auswahl", um dann zum „Internationalen Designpreis des Landes Baden-Württemberg" weiterentwickelt zu werden. Seit 2009 firmiert er unter dem Label „Focus Open Internationaler Designpreis Baden-Württemberg". Dieser Staatspreis ist so etwas wie ein Anker, der alle Aktivitäten des Design Center Baden-Württemberg verbindet. Dazu gehören beispielsweise Erstberatungen in Sachen Design-Implementierung oder für Design-Newcomer, Ausstellungen über zeitrelevante Themen für Professionals, Workshops, Kooperationen und natürlich der Blick nach vorne. Denn Design ist eine Disziplin, die Innovationen vorantreibt, nutzbar macht und ein besseres Morgen im Blick hat. Design ist interdisziplinär, visionär, dynamisch und wandelt sich permanent. Und mit ihm auch das Design Center Baden-Württemberg.

FOCUS OPEN
2024

FROM SAMPLE STORE TO HUB FOR INNOVATIVE DESIGN

This year's Focus Open 2024 once again features a collection of innovative designs, carefully chosen from a wide range of submissions by an independent jury of experts. Sponsored by the Design Center Baden-Württemberg, this design award is an important and well-established part of the State of Baden-Württemberg's business development support programme.

1848 – A NEW BEGINNING

King Wilhelm I of Württemberg established the Royal Central Office for Trade and Commerce in Stuttgart in the same pivotal year in which the failed Baden Revolution occurred. These were turbulent times politically as well as economically, as the state grappled with its transition from an agrarian to an industrial society. The Central Office was established to encourage businesses in the state to make the most of the latest technologies and design concepts. The Office declared its purpose to be the "procurement and judicious application of exemplary models, implements and methods for the advancement of the state's commercial enterprises." 1848 thus marked the birth of an innovation-orientated, mid-sized industrial economy – a successful model that continues to this day.

Two years later, the Central Office assumed a more tangible form when Ferdinand von Steinbeis, as technical advisor, created a "sample warehouse". The warehouse gathered together a carefully selected assortment of products from all over the world, intended to inspire, inform, provide benchmarks and "encourage good taste". The collection grew rapidly, amassing around 70,000 exhibits by the end of the 19th century. This rapid expansion necessitated a dedicated space and, in 1896, it found a new home in a prestigious building in Stuttgart's city centre, a powerful testament to the country's growing economic influence. It was the first institution of its kind in the world.

THE MODERN AGE ARRIVES

Thanks to the practical implementation of Steinberg's initiatives, Württemberg's economy experienced growing success. As a result, the need for the collection of samples decreased while other support measures assumed greater significance. In 1921, the Central Office became the Landesbewerbeamt (State Trade Office) and the LGA has remained a model for the successful promotion of small and medium-sized enterprises ever since. In what many believe heralded the modern age in the state of Württemberg, the legendary Weissenhof Estate, built in 1927 by the Deutscher Werkbund design movement, highlighted the potential of modern housing. The accompanying exhibition was, of course, held at the LGA.

STRUCTURE BECOMES DESIGN

Few people were talking about design in 1949 when Wilhelm Wagenfeld took up his position as consultant for industrial design at the LGA. In 1952, Baden and Württemberg were merged, creating a new, large and economically powerful federal state. In the same year, the Ulm School of Design (HfG), seen as the successor to Bauhaus, came into being. In 1959, the VDID, the Association of German Industrial Designers, was founded in Stuttgart. Although design had become established as a discipline by this time, the term remained open to interpretation. While the LGA-Zentrum Form, which was established within the LGA in 1962, hadn't included the term in its name, its mission remained clear: "to draw attention to design in Baden-Württemberg and to the economic value of the work of designers." This mission has not changed to this day.

By 1969, the reluctance to appreciate the value of design had finally dissipated. The LGA-Zentrum Form became the Design Center Stuttgart and continued to operate from the LGA building.

DYNAMICS AND HIGHLIGHTS

In the decades that followed, the Design Center Stuttgart became a hotspot for design. Today, it has broadened its focus beyond the economic significance of design to include its social, cultural and unifying impact on society. Temporary exhibitions form an important part of its programme, inspiring audiences far beyond the city and country, and not just within the design world. Even at the height of the Cold War, the Design Center extended its reach beyond the Iron Curtain to show that design was also alive and well in the USSR and GDR. In 1986, a grand design congress and exhibition entitled "Explorations" was held in Stuttgart, while in 1989, the "Women in Design" exhibition showed that design was not a purely male affair, setting in motion a discussion that still resonates today.

THE AWARD IN TRANSITION

Effective design promotion hinges on the compelling presentation of successful examples, or best practices. The annual Design Award, presented by the institution now known as the Design Center Baden-Württemberg, sets out to do this. Proudly non-commercial, the award stands apart from the commercialised landscape of international awards. It was known for a long time as the Deutsche Auswahl (German Selection) before being renamed the International Design Award of the State of Baden-Württemberg. It has operated under the name of Focus Open International Design Award Baden-Württemberg since 2009. This state-sponsored award is the unifying element that links all the activities of the Design Center Baden-Württemberg. These include, for example, initial consultations on design implementation, advice for newcomers to design, exhibitions on current topics for professionals, workshops, collaborations and, of course, forecasts for the future of the industry.

Design is a creative process that drives innovation, prioritises usability and aims to build a better world. It is interdisciplinary, visionary, dynamic and constantly changing. As is the Design Center Baden-Württemberg.

LET'S THANK ...

**GRAFIKDESIGN
GRAPHIC DESIGN**
stapelberg&fritz
Daniel Fritz

**TEXT & REDAKTION
TEXT & EDITORIAL SUPERVISION**
Armin Scharf
Gabriele Betz

JURY
Prof. Tulga Beyerle
Andreas Brunkhorst
Henning Rieseler
Mirjam Rombach
Alexander Schlag
Carolin Schmitt

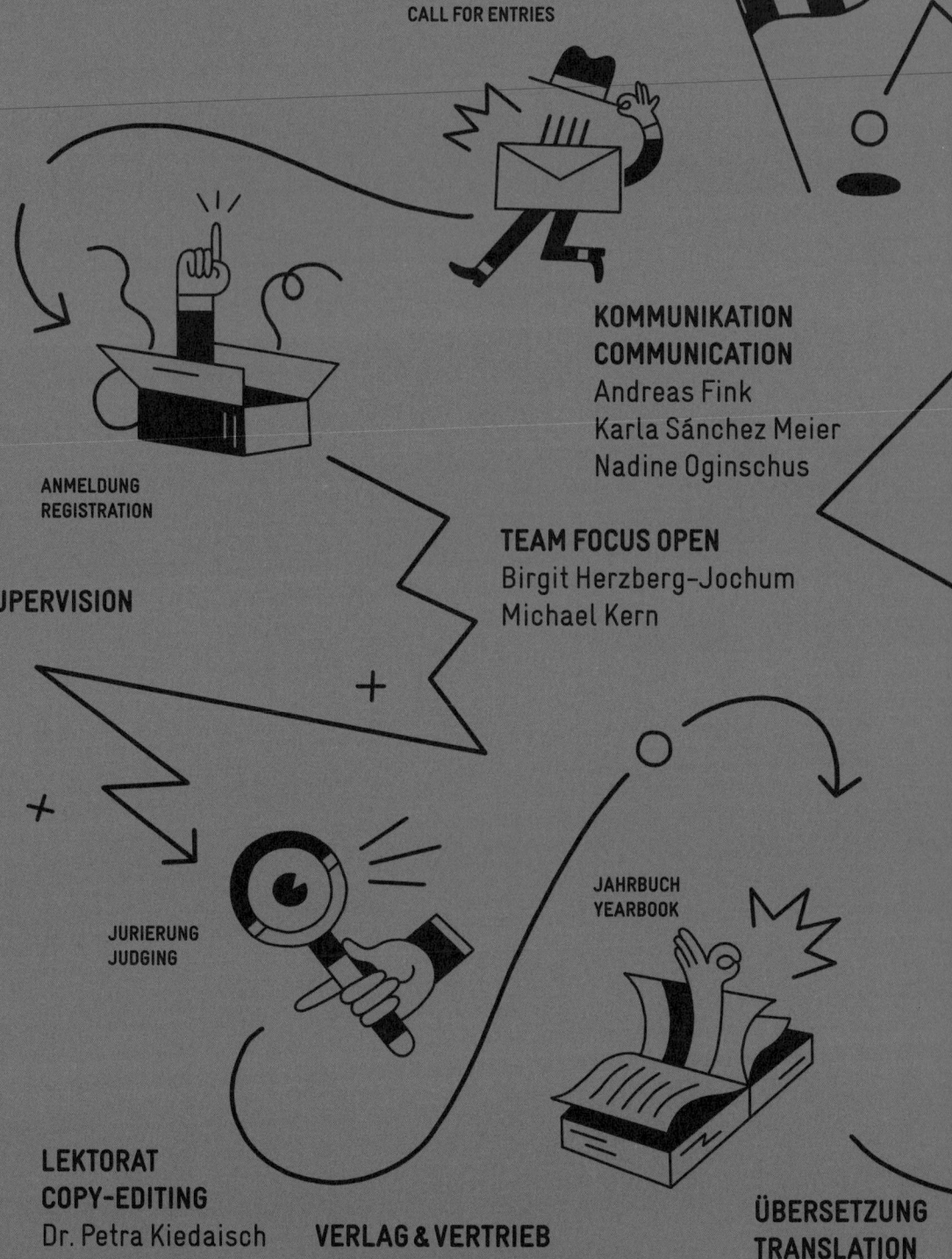

**LEKTORAT
COPY-EDITING**
Dr. Petra Kiedaisch
Gabriele Betz

AUSSCHREIBUNG
CALL FOR ENTRIES

ANMELDUNG
REGISTRATION

**KOMMUNIKATION
COMMUNICATION**
Andreas Fink
Karla Sánchez Meier
Nadine Oginschus

TEAM FOCUS OPEN
Birgit Herzberg-Jochum
Michael Kern

JURIERUNG
JUDGING

JAHRBUCH
YEARBOOK

**VERLAG & VERTRIEB
PUBLISHING & DISTRIBUTION**
avedition
Dr. Petra Kiedaisch

**ÜBERSETZUNG
TRANSLATION**
Stephen McLucki

FILME
FILMS
Moritz Schmieg

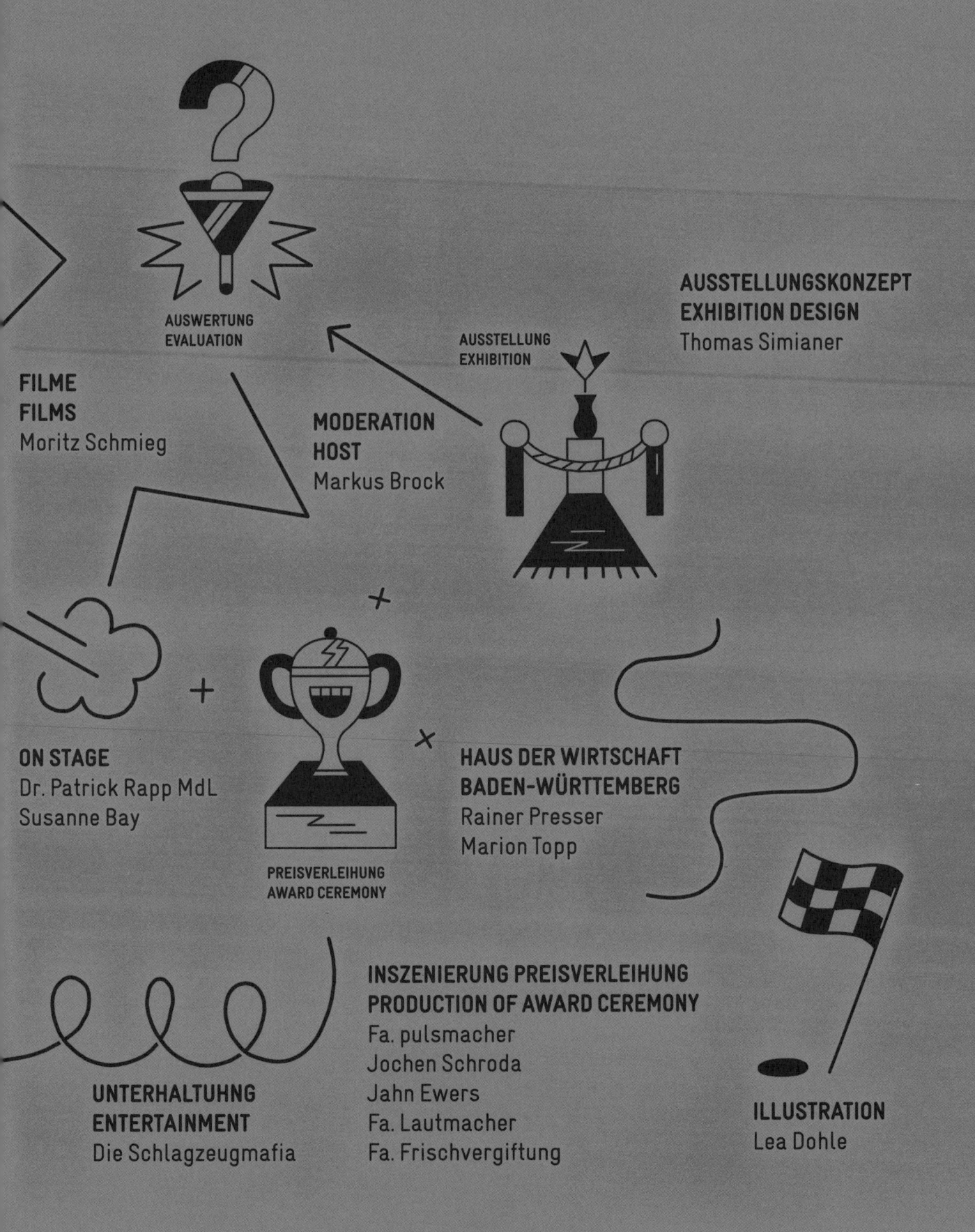

AUSWERTUNG
EVALUATION

AUSSTELLUNG
EXHIBITION

AUSSTELLUNGSKONZEPT
EXHIBITION DESIGN
Thomas Simianer

MODERATION
HOST
Markus Brock

ON STAGE
Dr. Patrick Rapp MdL
Susanne Bay

PREISVERLEIHUNG
AWARD CEREMONY

HAUS DER WIRTSCHAFT
BADEN-WÜRTTEMBERG
Rainer Presser
Marion Topp

UNTERHALTUHNG
ENTERTAINMENT
Die Schlagzeugmafia

INSZENIERUNG PREISVERLEIHUNG
PRODUCTION OF AWARD CEREMONY
Fa. pulsmacher
Jochen Schroda
Jahn Ewers
Fa. Lautmacher
Fa. Frischvergiftung

ILLUSTRATION
Lea Dohle

DESIGN IM DIALOG

Beratung, Fortbildung, Information und Präsentationen – das Design Center Baden-Württemberg ist eine nicht-kommerzielle Plattform für Design-Profis, Einsteiger und Unternehmer zugleich

DESIGN LESE
Vorträge, Medienpräsentationen und Diskussionsrunden zu aktuellen Themenbereichen aus Industrie, Design, Technik, Forschung und Wirtschaft.

DESIGN LESE LECTURES
Lectures, media presentations and panel discussions on up-to-the-minute topics from industry, design, technology, research and business.

EINSICHTEN
Austauschplattform für Industrie, Designwirtschaft, Forschung und Ausbildung. Unternehmen, Designagenturen und auch Design-Ausbildungsstätten erhalten die Möglichkeit, sich im Haus der Wirtschaft in Stuttgart detailliert zu präsentieren.

EINSICHTEN PRESENTATION PLATFORM
A platform for industry, the design sector, research and education where companies, design agencies and design schools are given the opportunity to stage detailed presentations at the Haus der Wirtschaft in Stuttgart.

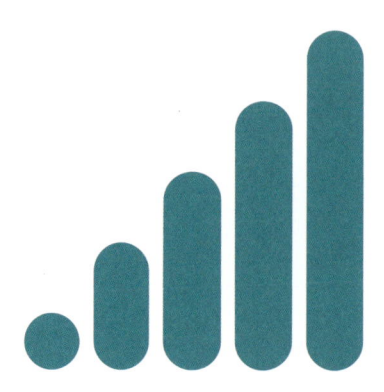

DESIGN1ST BERATUNG
Im Rahmen unserer kostenfreien Design1st Beratung erhalten Unternehmer*innen Auskunft zu allen Fragen rund um Designleistungen und zu direkten Kooperationsmöglichkeiten mit der Designwirtschaft.

DESIGN1ST ADVISORY SERVICE
Our free Design1st advisory service provides entrepreneurs with information about anything to do with design services and advises them on the possibilities for direct cooperation with the design sector.

FIT FOR MARKET
Der richtige Schutz innovativer Produkte, die Anmeldung von Marken, die Honorierung kreativer Leistung oder die Vertragsgestaltung mit Designer*innen sind Themenfelder dieser Veranstaltungsreihe.

FIT FOR MARKET
This series of events covers topics like the right protection for innovative products, registering trademarks, appropriate payment for creative services and contractual arrangements with designers.

DESIGN IN DIALOGUE

Advice, training, information and presentations – the Design Center Baden-Württemberg is a non-commercial platform aimed not just at design professionals but at newcomers and entrepreneurs too.

214 215

DESIGN CENTER ROADSHOW
Veranstaltungen mit und bei unterschiedlichsten externen Kooperationspartnern, als Foren des Austauschs zwischen Industrie und Designwirtschaft.

DESIGN CENTER ROADSHOW
Events hosted by a wide range of external cooperation partners as forums where industry and the design sector can swap ideas and views.

DESIGN BIBLIOTHEK
Präsenzbibliothek für Designprofis und Designinteressierte, mit Online-Katalog und einem spezialisierten Publikationsbestand von rund 10.000 Büchern rund um das Thema Gestaltung.

DESIGN LIBRARY
A bricks-and-mortar library for design professionals and anyone interested in design, with an online catalogue and a specialised collection of around 10,000 publications on all aspects of design.

RETHINK:DESIGN KLIMARELEVANZ
Unser Format mit dem besonderen Augenmerk auf klimagerechte und zukunftsfähige Konzepte, Gestaltungslösungen und Forschungsansätze. In Interviews, Vorträgen und Ausstellungen präsentieren wir die Vielschichtigkeit der Nachhaltigkeit und des Klimaschutzes.

RETHINK:DESIGN CLIMATE RELEVANCE
Our format with a special focus on climate-friendly and sustainable concepts, design solutions and research approaches. We present the complexity of sustainability and climate protection in interviews, lectures and exhibitions.

KONGRESSE & WORKSHOPS
Veranstaltungen zur Vermittlung von Know-how aus den unterschiedlichsten designrelevanten Disziplinen und Forschungsbereichen, aber auch aus dem weiten Feld des Marketings.

CONGRESSES & WORKSHOPS
Events that share know-how from all sorts of design-relevant disciplines and research areas, as well as from the broad field of marketing.

IMPRESSUM/ PUBLISHING DETAILS

HERAUSGEBER/PUBLISHER
Design Center Baden-Württemberg
Regierungspräsidium Stuttgart
Willi-Bleicher-Straße 19
70174 Stuttgart
T +49 711 123 26 84
design@rps.bwl.de
www.design-center.de

**TEXT UND REDAKTION/
TEXT AND EDITORIAL SUPERVISION**
Armin Scharf
Tübingen
www.bueroscharf.de
Gabriele Betz
Tübingen

LEKTORAT/COPY-EDITING
Petra Kiedaisch
Gabriele Betz
Tübingen
www.gabriele-betz.de

ÜBERSETZUNG/TRANSLATION
Stephen McLuckie
Dorchester
www.dorchestertranslations.co.uk

GRAFIKDESIGN/GRAPHIC DESIGN
stapelberg&fritz GmbH
Stuttgart
www.stapelbergundfritz.com

**FOTOS DER JURY/
PHOTOS OF THE JURY**
Moritz Schmieg
Thomas Simianer

ILLUSTRATIONEN/ILLUSTRATIONS
Lea Dohle Illustration Stuttgart
www.leadohle.de

LITHOGRAFIE/LITHOGRAPHY
Corinna Rieber Prepress
www.rieber-prepress.de

DRUCK/PRINTING
Offizin Scheufele GmbH & Co. KG
Stuttgart
www.scheufele.de

PAPIER/PAPER
Juwel Offset,
PEFC-zertifiziert/
PEFC certified

**VERLAG UND VERTRIEB/
PUBLISHING AND DISTRIBUTION**
av edition GmbH
Senefelderstraße 109
70176 Stuttgart
T +49 711/2202279-0
kontakt@avedition.de
www.avedition.de

© 2024
av edition GmbH,
Design Center Baden-Württemberg
und die Autoren/and the authors

Alle Rechte vorbehalten./
All rights reserved.

ISBN 978-3-89986-418-2
Printed in Germany

Publikation anlässlich
der Ausstellung
»FOCUS OPEN 2024
Internationaler Designpreis
Baden-Württemberg
und Mia Seeger Preis 2024«

8. November 2024 bis
24. Januar 2025

Publication on the occasion
of the exhibition
»FOCUS OPEN 2024
Baden-Württemberg International
Design Award and
Mia Seeger Prize 2024«

8 November 2024 to
24 Januar 2025

VERANSTALTER/ORGANISER
Design Center Baden-Württemberg
Regierungspräsidium Stuttgart
Willi-Bleicher-Straße 19
70174 Stuttgart
T +49 711 123 26 84

**VERANTWORTUNG UND KONZEPTION/
RESPONSIBILITY AND CONCEPT**
Christiane Nicolaus

**PROJEKTLEITUNG/
PROJECT MANAGER**
Birgit Herzberg-Jochum

ORGANISATION/ADMINISTRATION
Michael Kern

**AUSSTELLUNGSKONZEPT/
EXHIBITION DESIGN**
Thomas Simianer

**INSZENIERUNG PREISVERLEIHUNG/
PRODUCTION OF AWARD CEREMONY**
pulsmacher GmbH
Ludwigsburg
www.pulsmacher.de

Lautmacher GmbH
www.lautmacher.com

Frischvergiftung
Maximilian Pfisterer &
Willy Löbl GbR
www.frischvergiftung.de

FOTONACHWEIS/PHOTOCREDITS:
S/P 34, 62, 64: Enver Hirsch
S/P 74, 78, 82: Heiko Pothoff
S/P 91: Christoph Lison
S/P 134, 147, 151: Sue Barr